IMPERIUM EUROPA

ARISTOCRATIC MANIFESTO

FOR

IMPERIVM
EVROPA

NORMAN LOWELL

ARKTOS
LONDON 2019

| **ISBN** | 978-1-912975-19-8 (Softcover) |
| | 978-1-912975-20-4 (Ebook) |

| **EDITING, COVER** | |
| **AND LAYOUT** | John Bruce Leonard |

 Arktos.com   fb.com/Arktos    @arktosmedia   arktosmedia

Dedicated to those
brave Men and Women
fighting for our
Race and Civilisation and
our Sacred Island of Melita
'The strong are strongest when alone'

TABLE of CONTENTS

ACKNOWLEDGEMENTS

To the late Padre Milne (Church of Scotland) who gave me an education.

To the late SED Brown (Editor SA Observer) who opened my eyes.

To *Ch'uan Shu* (Martial Art) that gave me tenacity and fighting spirit.

My appreciation to all Imperium Europa and Viva Malta adherents — who stood by me in moments of trial and tribulation: who were spied upon, arrested on suspicion of criminal acts they never committed.

My loyalty and camaraderie to the *core* group who works so hard every-day for our complete and total victory. I am with you until the end.

And finally, to those erudite Pan-Europeanists: Dr. Tomislav Sunic and David Stennett and that firebrand, Constantin von Hoffmeister, who graced this book with their wisdom.

NORMAN LOWELL

2012

ANNO ZERO!

EDITOR'S COMMENTARY

What a man does for pay is of little significance. What he is, as a sensitive instrument responsive to the world's beauty, is everything!
— H.P. LOVECRAFT

ON MARCH 27TH, 2008, NORMAN Lowell was convicted on three counts of 'inciting racial hatred' and one count of 'insulting the President' — convictions that together brought a two-year prison sentence suspended for four years, and more importantly, the inability to run in the 2009 elections for the European Parliament. Subsequently, the initial appeal to these charges was found to be 'null' on October 15th, 2008 (with the judge upholding the previous court's ruling based, not on any legal construct, but on a mere legal technicality). These nefarious charges were brought to bear on Norman for a written piece he posted on the internet almost half a decade ago, and for two speeches he gave in Malta at two separate indoor meetings in April/May 2006.

Of course, Maltese authorities could not show, let alone prove, that Norman had 'incited racial hatred'; after all, there would have to be at least one criminal act committed on Norman's behest. No crime of 'incitement' has ever taken place in Malta. It has always been obvious that Norman's real 'crime' was simply defending his beloved Malta and the rest of Europe against a tidal onslaught of economic refugees from the Dark Continent. A long, drawn-out assault that will make, in time, the Norman invasion of Britain pale in comparison. The added conviction for 'insulting the President,' whom Norman called a 'good gardener, but a lousy President', almost isn't worth mentioning, except for the fact that it's an actual law in a so-called modern European country, and people are selectively being persecuted with it.

Before this great mockery of Western jurisprudence began, I had the honour and pleasure of first meeting Norman Lowell on the beautiful island of Malta during his initial run for the European Parliament in 2004. I was invited to come meet 'Norman and friends' and get acquainted with Norman's movement. I knew nothing about Malta, except for its location (and even that I had to double-check). After almost a week on the island, I had a whole new life-changing perspective. The island is truly a gem in the Mediterranean: well-preserved fortresses and barracks from the days of the great Knights of St. John, the Neolithic solar stone monuments such as the Hypogeum; a hearty people who are simple yet patriotic, kind and curious about the world — and what splendid nature near the Victoria Lines at the 'sacred spot'! It is truly a sacred island, a treasure out at sea. However, there was a darker side (literally!) to the island; I could see the devastating effects of over-development (empty concrete skeletons dotting the roadsides), trash spread around the streets due to an obviously selfish man-centred creed. And of course, how could I forget: hordes of out-of-place blacks and Arabs who motored across the Mediterranean Sea on their invasion path to ancient European homelands.

As I walked around town with Norman, getting a local's tour, I was both amazed at his popularity (honks, waves, and shouts of support were plenty), and shocked at the number of people who said they agreed with him entirely and would vote for him with their second or third preference vote. Second or third! When I asked some young patriotic Maltese why not first, they replied, 'My family would kill me. We must vote for the MLP with our firsts.' Here it was, Malta's entire future at stake — in the hands of voters who agreed, but were too cowardly to vote because sour family tradition dictated that voting for back-stabbing criminals and traitors came first. After all, one couldn't have the back-stabbing criminals and traitors in the 'other party' getting into power!

Despite these setbacks, there was also hope. The people surrounding Norman are some of the finest people I've ever met. Intelligent, beautiful, dedicated men and women who really care about their island country, Europe, and the entire Europid race. Even after election defeat, their heads always stayed high, and they vowed to continue their fight. Wavering has never been an option, not with what is at stake. With people like that in the fight, victory is only a matter of *time*. Their love and determination is exemplified by the fact that this little island is the focal point of Norman's big *IDEA*.

New Right purists promote pan-European cooperation (coalition of countries; Europe of one hundred flags), and Eurasianists promote a 'Moscow-Berlin-Paris' axis (these three capitals being their respective leading lights for Europe); it is somewhat unfortunate, however, that these two schools are still stuck in the destructive, 19th-century orientated idea of Nationalism which has led to disastrous consequences for the Europid race (with World War II being the final stanza of death). Only an emerging few are now promoting the progressive, race-saving ideology of pan-Europeanism. 'Aryan Futurism', as one of Europe's mightiest sons, the late Alisdair Clarke, called it: Norman Lowell gives it the name Imperium Europa.

What then is this idea of Imperium Europa? This book among other things will answer that very question, and the subsidiary questions it inevitably carries with it. How this vast Empire, in which primacy of the Europid race and its survival takes all precedent, will function. What role economics, art and morality will play in daily life. How an anything-goes attitude will be encouraged in order to spur the development of individuality, creativity and innovation. How, as in ancient Sparta, the martial spirit of vitality and life-affirmation will rule. How reaching for the stars will no longer be a catchy maxim, but a life philosophy drilled into the young from an early age.

This book is Norman's view on all the above and more. The reader will also be treated to two very different kinds of prefaces. One by the respected Croatian author Dr. Tomislav Sunic, a former university professor of political studies and diplomacy and reigning Croatian diplomat; the other, by controversial German essayist and poet, Constantin von Hoffmeister, whose incendiary writings and provocative thoughts have enraged thinkers and activists on the left, right, middle, and everywhere in between on the political spectrum.

Finally, it is my hope that the readers will set aside their personal and political biases when reading *Imperium Europa*, and on occasion, close their eyes and imagine the world of Norman Lowell. It's a beautiful image to behold, and for some, including myself, it's a reality we fight to bring into the world.

MAGNA EUROPA EST PATRIA NOSTRA!
DAVID STENNETT
ARNSTEIN, GERMANY

Illustrations can be found at:
http://www.imperium-europa.org/thebook/
Visit http://www.arktos.com/ to order additional copies.

PREFACE

by Dr. Tomislav Sunic

When writing a preface to the book of a fellow traveller, the writer often falls into the trap of his own bias. He may often be tempted to heap on unwarranted eulogies. In order to skip over the serious flaws that the author's book may present, the preface writer may resort to a myriad of colourful epithets. Much, of course, will depend on the book's subject matter and the display of the author's main thesis. If the book is designed as a pamphlet, then the preface take a certain tone and form; if, by contrast, the subject matter is a scholarly treatise backed up by bibliographic notes, then the preface will take a different turn again. All depends on what kind of readership the book is tailored to, and how the author of the book is trying to spur the reader's interest.

None of this concerns Mr. Norman Lowell's book, which carries the strong and clear title, *Imperium Europa*. The book can be depicted as a combination of sociological treatise, pamphlet, and credo — briefly, a handbook for a white European revolutionary trying to turn back the clock of history. There is no question that the title of the book alone may be reason enough to encourage those unfamiliar with the name of the author to glance at its content. And what will this putative buyer, be he a reader or even a critic, discover? He will discover the island. Yes, the island — both in its real and its figurative sense. The sacred European island of Melita, now known as Malta, is the starting point of Lowell's book.

One might recall that the imagery of the island has quite often been in usage as a metaphor for either a utopian or a dystopian narrative, as is the case of the respective novels of Aldous Huxley, Thomas Moore, R. L. Stevenson, or Jack London. The plot surrounding a distant island, located

in the far away antipodes, has always offered authors of different temperament a treasure trove of unimaginable discoveries. The island may contain hidden gold, or better yet exhibit naked women of stunning physical
beauty. But the island may also turn out to be a barren landscape of harsh
climatic conditions ideal for testing the valour and virility of a stranded
would-be hero.

The sacred European island of Melita, alias Malta, is a very real island,
not far from Africa and not far from Europe. The insular Malta best encapsulates the neurotic mindset of Europeans, which Lowell now wishes
to regenerate as a symbol for a new European identity. Lowell's book is
not a surreal fantasy, but a deadly-serious synopsis of a survival manual
for the European race. The author carefully examines the whole gamut
of subjects in his book — each of which, to be sure, would necessitate a
separate volume: from the history of Malta, to the present days of modern
democracy — all the way down to how Europeans must exit the cycles of
the dark ages. One notices immediately that the author possesses a solid
knowledge of Traditional thinkers, such as Julius Evola or René Guénon
and hundreds of others who were equally concerned about the pending
catastrophe of Europe. Lowell deserves praise for providing us with a concise, down-to-earth *vademecum* that goes beyond metaphysical speculations and that can serve as an excellent introduction for a neophyte in
search of his stolen racial, geographic and linguistic roots. It takes a great
deal of verbal alacrity and brilliant handling of the English language to
provide a diversified readership with such a concise description of the
current ills facing Europe. In his endeavour Lowell does the job masterfully, notably by combing elliptic sentences, often spiced up with sarcasm,
with lengthy scholarly rhetoric that could easily put to shame postmodern
'experts' on nationalism and the European race. Thus, even an uninitiated
or lazy reader will grasp at once the main theme of the book, and will not
hesitate to consider using some of Lowell's suggestions.

Why Malta, and what is the significance of this tiny speck on the world
map? The author points out that the troubled waters of Malta represent a
symbol of rough seas surrounding the European continent. Malta is the

epitome of Europeans' future identity, a continent historically torn between Asiatic-Semitic influences on the one hand, and European Nordic influence on the other. Lowell, however, avoids bleating in self-serving refrains about the imminent collapse of the European civilisation — a theme so dear to cultural pessimists and other self-proclaimed 'cultural conservatives.' Instead, he promptly utters the truth many Europeans know, but are afraid of saying aloud, namely that the ongoing onslaught of foreign races onto the European shores will necessitate this time around a far more radical response. Short of some rude reawakening, and barring appropriate political tools, the future of Malta and its larger European appendix looks not just bleak but outright horrid. The modern democratic system in Europe and the United States, fraught with the ideology of racial bastardisation and spearheaded by plutocratic elites, has now entered its finale. This travesty of liberal democracy is not only visible in the ruling and corrupted class of Malta, but surfaces daily in the acts and words of venal white politicians all over the Western hemisphere. Lowell realises very well that the disastrous consequences of the democratic experiment in Malta and in Europe will present the most daunting task for new European rulers. In the years to come the global aftershocks of so-called multicultural democracy will be almost impossible to cure. 'From the peak of power and prestige, in just one hundred years democracy dragged the white race into a minority species facing extinction.'

The senseless drive for global utopia is bringing about a system hostile to the very biological survival of European peoples. From Malta to Massachusetts, in order to enforce intellectual conformism, the modern democratic system uses perverse mind control — all in the name of 'human rights' and 'tolerance.' Numerous racially aware and highly educated Europeans, including Lowell himself, are facing social ostracism and harassment, even imprisonment, by the thought police. Thought crime is no longer a literary metaphor, but has become a foundation of the judicial dogma of modern democracy. The new trademark of this multicultural democracy is the invention of the lurid newspeak, such as 'hate crimes', 'hate speech', 'multi-ethnic sensitivity training', all of whose implacable usage against free spirits results in consequences far more insidious than those brought by the former communist system.

The pleasure of reading Lowell consists in the fact that, before making a suggestion as to how to arrest the drowning of Malta, alias Europe, he deciphers the root causes of the problem. Before recommending the choice of his heavy artillery for the future regeneration of Europeans, such as shipping criminals and aliens into outer space, or sending them back into the exotic countries of their origin, Lowell urges Europeans to clearly define their main enemy. Alas, the answer is unexpected, yet predictable: the main enemy of Europe are Europeans themselves! Therefore, and contrary to many European nationalists, the author rejects petty European nationalism, as he considers it the main motor behind Europe's decline.

Lowell is objective to such a point that before rejecting the Other, he exhorts intelligent Europeans to re-examine their troubled Same.

The retrieval of European Sameness, be it of Maltese, Croatian, English or German provenance, means first and foremost shedding and shredding vestiges of their non-European mindset, along with discarding their self-inflicted modern ideological transplants — such as have been formulated throughout centuries by early Bedouin prophets and their Semitic secular successors. In one of his paragraphs, which probably best captures Lowell's criticism of Europe's divisiveness, one must single out an important sentence: 'Nation versus nation, state against state, sub-nation opposed to sub-nation and other configurations of all these; a tragedy for the White race.' Only by transcending parochial tribalism and by projecting themselves on their own planetary and later on the cosmic level, will Europeans be able to find their lost Aryan-Greco-Roman-Indo-European-Promethean identity — and yes, start trekking to new solar galaxies.

Malta, given its formidable history, should serve as a new custodian of Europe's cultural memory; it should become a new *genius loci* destined for educating a new cadre for a new European spiritual aristocracy. After all, who has benefited most, asks Lowell rhetorically, from the eternal divisions among Europeans and their fratricidal wars? Lowell sagely poses this rhetorical question, a question which should become a prerequisite for modern scholars and future European leaders: *Cui bono?* Who benefits from intra-European squabbling? Clearly not Europeans, but rather a host of non-European enemies whose main goal, ever since the birth of the Levantine Jesus Christ, has been to turn Europe into a multiracial dumping ground for the *odium generis humani.* We have seen over and over again, in a period spanning two thousand years, where Oriental dogmas of egalitarianism and multiracialism have taken Europe: to the Catholic inquisition, the communist gulags and the liberal 'warm death'.

Many other themes which Lowell diligently discusses in detail in his book should be singled out. It is an ideal reader for younger Europeans, who have been victims of the incessant 'dumbing down' process — courtesy of the modern democratic system and its hagiographers. Lowell also shows good knowledge of sociobiology and its important scientific breakthrough in the research of the human genome — a field of study which has yielded empirical data on racial differences and differences in IQ — yet also a field prudently avoided by the modern democratic thought police. *Mens sana in corpore sano!* (Healthy mind in a healthy body!) was an old adage of the old Latins, an adage which more and more whites are becoming aware of and which will be desperately needed for breeding future European leaders. And why deny the age-old fact that every biped instinctively looks at the face of his mate or his interlocutor before making the first pass or the first move? Yes, we must concur with Lowell that a person's character is best seen in his facial and racial traits or as the old Latins used to say *In facie legitur homo!* Without becoming conscious of their genealogy and without safeguarding their gene pool, Europeans will degenerate into grotesque colourful zombies and perishable commodities whose production was well pre-planned by the alien ideologues of panmixia, be they of the Judeo-Christian, Liberal or Communistic brand.

There is nothing esoteric or secretive in Lowell's prose. For that matter, we may add, there is nothing new in the subject matter he discusses either. Similar dilemmas facing the European man were discussed by great thinkers of Antiquity, such as the Stoic Seneca or Tacitus, who were well aware of the morbidity of imported Oriental tales. So why then do not we study history and look for inspiration among the Ancients? The answer to that lies in the postmodern religion of economics, i.e. the dictatorship of well-being, which is crippling the mind and soul of young Europeans faster and more insidiously than the landscape of the former communist Kolyma. 'Warm death', as the great anthropologist Konrad Lorenz once wrote, is a logical offshoot of the modern fun society in which we all live; it is an ultimate stage of the system that has enslaved the masses without leaving traces of blood. Alas, rivers of blood will soon flow regardless!

Accordingly, Europe now requires a big shock to wake it up from its torpor. Most likely this shock will soon originate within the very foundations of the democratic system itself, which has kept Europe enslaved for such a long period of time. At least one could say that the myths of eternal progress and the mendacity of democracy can no longer sustain themselves. There are cracks appearing everywhere. However, it is a sad fact that Europeans will again lose tens of millions of their best men before achieving victory. Why wait for vicious prodding from the Other, before realising that Europe's destiny lies above economics and material success? Why must the European wait for the repulsive Other, before discovering his beautiful European Self? Modern capitalism and its embodiment in American and European democracy are scheduled very soon to face unforeseen tremors before Europeans realise that a new chapter of the white man's history has begun. 'Communism and Capitalism, two sides of the same coin, joining hands against patriots, nationalist, racialist forces all over the world', as Lowell aptly puts it. After the breakdown of communism, it is now the turn of its twin brother America to face the same fate, albeit in a far gorier fashion, which will finally make the clean slate for a new Renaissance.

The most important remark by the author of the book concerns the role of politics in the *Imperium*. Politics must always lie ahead of economics; it must be the true vector of Europe's destiny. The reign of petty speculators, the terror of fun society guided by *Homo oeconomicus*, must be replaced by highly trained spirited and spiritual statesmen whose sole interests must focus on the betterment of the common good, i.e. the Imperium. But above all, cultural achievements must thrive as the true spiritual realm of European mankind. The Imperium must excel in architectural endeavours and encourage the proliferation of plastic arts. Malta again must serve as a model, as her walled-off nature is best suited for the future architectural plans in Europe. The invisible high-tech wall will be erected in order to separate Europeans from aliens for aeons, and assure the future of European progeny. The Imperium must lay its first foundation stone before 2012, as by then, multifaceted tectonic shocks and the speed of history will become unstoppable — and unforgivable.

DR. TOMISLAV SUNIC
ZAGREB, CROATIA,
NOVEMBER 26, 2007

OUR MOTHERLAND:
IMPERIUM EUROPA

BY *CONSTANTIN VON HOFFMEISTER*

The nations are dead, for Europe is born.
— FRANCIS PARKER YOCKEY

NORMAN LOWELL HAS A VISION. A vision of what Europe will become. Not what Europe should become, but what Europe *will* become. According to Lowell, the year 2012 will be the year 0. Time will start afresh for our race. A new beginning, a new dawn — a new aeon approaches. While ancient traditions will be upheld and cherished, modern technology will be implemented to both boldly innovate new paths and persistently perpetuate former greatness. Lowell wants Aryan heroes of yore, like the ancient Spartan warrior Leonidas, to be cloned, thus ensuring that the new genetically enhanced generation of natural leaders will be supported by proven leaders from our glorious past. A new species of Aryan supermen will once again rule the planet and — at last! — the cosmos beyond.

Lowell is right when he stresses the importance of the unity of *all* Europeans. Only as a unified bloc will the White race be able to overcome the anti-Occidental forces which have as their ultimate goal the total destruction of Magna Europa (Europe and its daughters AmeriKa, Canada, Chile, Argentina and Australasia) and the complete annihilation of all Europids on the planet. Alas, a White racial bloc (composed of Anglo-Saxons, Teutons, Slavs and Latins) that asserts itself as such will be able once and for all to overcome internal divisions only if it ruthlessly crushes all signs of resurging petty nationalisms. There is no place for separatist tendencies in the *Imperium Europa*. A fragmented Europe, as the past has proven beyond a shadow of a doubt, is a weak Europe. The need for a Europe that is truly *one* is a pressing need indeed: a Europe 'from sea to shining to sea', from Dublin to Vladivostok is the *only* Europe that has any chance of survival in the cataclysmic events that lie ahead. Like Friedrich Nietzsche, one has to learn to become 'a good European' instead of a good German, a good Russian, a good Englishman, etc.

Our true motherland is the *Imperium Europa*. We must forge a new identity! We must create the new European man! Nations are concepts that betray the imperial destiny of the worker as the creator of a new cosmos. The economy, as well as society at large, must be centralised. This is why we need an *Imperium Europa*. While each nation has the right to retain its cultural and ethnic autonomy, chauvinist nationalisms must be crushed. We must oppose petty nationalism as a provincial dead-end form of worship. The only nation that must be worshipped is Holy Europe. The mixing of different European nationalities should therefore be encouraged. We must support judicious sexual unions between Russian women and German men, Spanish men and Swedish women. Only by radically breaking down the artificial barriers dividing Europe can we create the new breed of man — a breed that has *one* allegiance only, allegiance to the *Imperium Europa*!

Imperial capitalism, as opposed to international capitalism, is the best economic system for the future empire. There will be no need for an influx of cheap labour in the form of racially alien immigrants or 'guest workers' if all citizens of the empire can freely trade within the empire's borders, without the pressure that the current global financial system imposes upon Europe by flooding its gates with inferior goods, services and people. Europe simply cannot compete with the incredibly low standards of the Third World. Hence, Europe must force itself to rigidly adhere to its own standards, which should be nothing less than excellent. In opposition to Lowell, I would dare argue that some form of social commitment from the side of the state is necessary to ensure that the weaker elements of the population are properly taken care of. After all, the elite exists to serve the masses and not the other way around. Hence, free-market socialism seems to be the appropriate model for implementing both the necessary competition to guarantee progress and the vital security net that the state must provide for its citizens in need. Socialism denotes the ineludible bond of common ancestry.

Lowell is correct when he argues that all life on Earth might be extinguished at any moment by a meteorite. This is why, according to Lowell, our race must get off this planet and start colonising space. While avoiding danger might be one of the reasons for racial expansion in deep space, another — and more natural! — incentive is the mere existence of the Promethean aspect of our race soul, an existence that can never be denied and never be suppressed. Self-sufficiency is the key. However, it is imperative that we do not limit our scope to this planet only. We must ever strive to become the Faustian beasts that we were always meant to be. The sun must circle around us! Domination of our own by ourselves is a necessary prerequisite, in order to establish the Imperium of the End, ruled by the dictatorship of the class that creates. There is no Aryan nation. There is only an Aryan class. Programs to colonise and eventually terraform new planets need to be established (after all, the threat of meteorites threatening our race on Earth is a very real one). NOVA EVROPA will be the first Aryan settlement on Mars

The Prolet-Aryan is the creator and sustainer who destroys the old order, paving the way for the new and improved. He lends a guiding hand to the lesser races, elevating them with his own ascent to godhood. The red flag of socialism is the flag of blood, the blood that flows in the veins of the Aryan worker-soldiers of the coming empire of war, struggle and conquest. Like the socialist flag, Mars is red. Mars is not only a planet but also the god of war. Hence, war must be declared in the name of blood and the red planet colonised in the name of socialism. Yuri Gagarin showed us the way. We must follow!

Because of its non-universal nature and ethnic character, Paganism (in all its incarnations, be they Odinism or Mithraism) is Europe's only legitimate religion. Christianity is indeed, as Norman Lowell calls it, 'an abject religion fit for children and slaves.' The main and most glaring problem that Europe has with Christianity is that this religion is not European, either in nature or origin. No matter how much of Christianity has been Paganised (or Europeanised), in its essence it remains a Semitic cult from the desert of the Middle East. Anti-Semitic European Christians are the epitome of hypocrisy as they worship a dead Jew on a piece of wood (which, to make it even clearer, had 'I.N.R.I.' — 'Jesus of Nazareth, King of the Jews' — written on it) while at the same time denigrating all Jews (even European ones) collectively as enemies of the West. Lowell has good reasons to attack the Church. The Church, being the official representative of an alien creed, has made its anti-European intentions known. The Jesuits in Malta ('refuse collectors' as Lowell correctly calls them) and their Catholic brothers elsewhere in Europe favour unrestricted immigration, based on the insane Christian belief that your enemy should be loved and not fought. The times of the Crusades, when the Church actually favoured the defence of Europe against her enemies from the desert, are gone. The current behaviour of the Church merely proves that Europe flourished not because of but in spite of Christianity. As self-aware and confident Europeans, we must praise Dr. Faustus the Aryan, not Jesus the Semite!

Influenced by the Belgian geopolitician Jean Thiriart, Lowell shows himself to be a true libertarian when he argues that, while the future empire should be strictly guarded against external threats, inside the empire complete freedom for the individual should reign (e.g. legalisation of drugs, freedom of speech, etc.). To put it another way: it should not matter what one does in private when one is a loyal citizen of the empire in public. In the future European empire, the private and public spheres of life will be strictly separate. Or as Thiriart argued, the Imperium (concerned with imperial decisions) is distinct and not necessarily a reflection of the Dominium (concerned with personal decisions). If one wants to hire a hooker and shoot up heroin, one should be free do so. We do not need moralising pundits in the empire. The empire will not be a nanny state, composed of repressed individuals and zealous Puritans. In short, the future European empire will not become a for Whites only carbon copy of the contemporary US of A!

Lowell astutely points out a fact that many White nationalists (especially the chauvinist European variety) like to forget: AmeriKa is an integral part of Magna Europa. Contemporary White Americans (AKA the only true Americans) are not nearly as emasculated as contemporary Europeans. (White) Americans still have an essentially healthy imperial vision. It is thus a shame that AmeriKa's vigorous, and basically Faustian, drive for world domination is not based on a race-affirming ideology (as it was in the glory days of Teddy Roosevelt). From a Machiavellian point of view, there is nothing wrong with AmeriKa's subjugation of the Middle East. However, this endeavour would only be noble if it served an Aryan objective. Vinland awake! It is not too late. If AmeriKa once again realised its holy mission to assert European might (as opposed to abstract and false values, such as 'universal' [no such thing] democracy) across the globe, it would be able to safeguard European man's iron grip of dominance. Invading countries like Iraq and Iran would be noble pursuits if it were done to exploit these countries (for the benefit of the White race only) instead of 'liberating' them (for the benefit of a multiracial and bastardised elite). Lowell's message must be heeded by Washington: AmeriKa must come home into the future *Imperium Europa*. A bridge across the Bering Strait!

Lowell prophesies that in the future Imperium, all citizens will be 'proud to belong to that Biological Aristocracy that is the Europid Race.' That is what I call Gene Pool Romanticism, the mystical glorification of blood and the rational exaltation of the whole (as opposed to the individual parts that make up the whole). While individuals are many, the Race is one. Through generations and through aeons, in links unbroken, from Christopher Columbus to Neil Armstrong, individuals of the Race have conquered new ground for the Race as a whole. As the late John Tyndall said, Armstrong's was 'a giant leap for White mankind!'

time has come
to close the window
shut out the draft
the filthy stench
to breathe the air
of freedom
to rule all
here
and evermore
an empire
to bind
perplexing vision
fit for masters
not sheep
IMPERIUM EUROPA
EST PATRIA NOSTRA!

CONSTANTIN VON HOFFMEISTER
MOSCOW, RUSSIA
OCTOBER 19TH, 2007

IMPERIUM EUROPA

The *IDEA* that Changed the World

A MESSAGE
FOR THE
VERY FEW

I have a message;
To all those solitary seagulls above the clouds;
To all Individualists wherever they may be.
To those solitary souls in today's torture chambers.
To the great despisers and despised.

Never compromise your intellectual integrity.
Uphold your rational, independent mind.
Uphold your truth openly, without fear.
This is the most noble, selfish act.
Be yourself!

Discard the altruistic morality;
It is a code of death.
Disown the life of a sacrificial animal.
Disrobe yourself of your sense of guilt.
You were not born with original sin.

Discover a new sense of life.
Refuse to apologise for your ability.
Refuse to apologise for your virtues.
Refuse to apologise for your success.
Refuse to maim yourself.

Bear out these intellectual dark ages that enshroud you.
Suffer in silence the purgatory you are in.
Resist the onslaught of the many-too-many.
Do not succumb.
Endure.

Learn that happiness is not evil.
Seek your greatest joy, your greatest good.
Realise that heaven is here and now.
It is living time.
Be!

An Idea unexpressed in action is a fraud.
Action without idea is self-destruction.
Be a thought-deed man.
Overcome yourself.
It can be done!

Act alone or with those you trust.
Be a voice of hope for those yearning for one.
Act as a focal point to those without a bearing.
Be thyself.
Be!

Retain your European identity.
Proclaim the sanctity of race.
Believe in the Sacred Gene Pool.
Treasure this noble heritage.
Eternity must be ours!

Never again a fratricidal war.
Never again White Man against White.
Never again cousin killing cousin.
Never again a blood-soaked Europe.
Never again!

Recognise the foe:
that tribe of international rodents.
Corrupters of civilisations; crucifiers.
Creators of communism: carrion of capitalism.
The great masters of the lie.
Defy them!

Visualise a United Europe;
From Vladivostok to the Emerald Isle.
An IMPERIUM EUROPA;
With Latin as its common tongue.
Extend your hand to Europe-Overseas.
Reach for the stars!

Lay the foundations for a New Leadership:
An elite of Supermen.
Genetically, these Gods exist —
somewhere they must be.
Will them, find them, create them!
They must live again.

I am the bearer of a sacred fire.
I must keep the torch aflame.
I am the last in a line.
If I fail — then all else will have failed before me.

CREDO.

1981–1996

2012: Anno Zero!

See Illustration 1 (http://www.imperium-europa.org/thebook)

I

NATIONAL UNITY

MILLIONS OF ORDINARY PEOPLE IN Western countries truly believe that they are living in a democratic system. They vote (when they bother to do so) every few years and then resume their everyday lives, their minds preoccupied with mundane problems that prevent them from thinking and seeing the real picture. The mass media, controlled by the international manipulators, carry on and reinforce this democratic deception. In actual fact, our present system is a charade, a travesty of Democracy.

TRAVESTY OF DEMOCRACY

In England in 1974, the Labour Party under Harold Wilson won the elections with 38 percent of the vote. Labour stood on an anti-Europe platform. Wilson had solemnly proclaimed on TV that, if the British joined Europe, they would lose their English breakfast! On the other hand, the Conservatives and the Liberals were both for Europe and together they garnered 62 percent of the vote. Yet Britain was deprived of another five years of European association, since Wilson, ignoring the wishes of the majority, doggedly kept Britain out.

In India in 1998 the people went to the vote: 420 million of them! The world media proclaimed proudly that *here* was Democracy in action. That this was the largest Democracy, and an example to the rest of the world.

Columnists waxed lyrical about the Indians and their democratic credentials — crooning that we should all learn from them. Eventually the result came out: a dead heat, a hung parliament! With the speaker having the casting vote — and thus total power! A mockery of Democracy.

Italy had its fair share, too. Fifty years of democratic treachery, double-dealing, ministers of musical-chairs, alliances formed and re-formed overnight — in short, the whole, squalid democratic game. Fifty-five governments in fifty years. When Berlusconi finally came to power, in alliance with the Lega Nord, all thought that an era of stability had begun. However, Bossi quit the government and joined the communists and the socialists. Thus, we had millions of votes cast for a certain type of government, suddenly propping up its direct opposite.

President Scalfaro, a squalid socialist and the greatest traitor in the whole of Italian history, did not have the decency to call another election, at least out of respect to the millions of voters betrayed by Bossi. On TV the President pompously proclaimed, with a straight face, that now that parliament had a new majority, things could carry on as normal and that he could not see the need for fresh elections. This is present day Democracy!

Recently in the USA, Boobus Bush II, as he surely will be remembered, the stupidest President in the entire history of the USA, came to power. Out of a voting population of 100 million he won by just 300 votes! In actual fact, Black Americans had mistakenly swapped ballot pages. These had been altered from the previous presidential elections with the parties represented on opposite pages. These illiterate people thought they were voting for the Democrats when in fact, they had voted Republican. This is present day Democracy!

MALTA

In Malta, Democracy has been the integral cause for the present mess we are in. A brief chronology of major events reveals this turgid path, the blunders, the wrong turns of our politics this century.

1950 — A few votes cost us Integration with Britain. Actually the pro-Integration vote was the largest, but failed an outright majority. The second largest vote comprised the abstentions, some 30 percent. And yet, Integration was lost, and with it, Europe. For had Malta joined Britain, we would have been in Europe with Edward Heath, without the huffing and puffing that finally squeezed us into Europe some thirty years later.

1960s — A truly democratic epoch. When elections used to be held under an atmosphere of spiritual terror. When cloistered nuns were bussed to election booths chanting '*Perlini, perlini!*' A puzzled electoral officer, who asked a priest what this meant, received the reply: 'Just to remind them they have to vote for Pellegrini!'

1972 — A handful of votes gave Malta twenty years of squalid social-ism. Just seven votes made the difference between total power and total nothingness, for twenty long dark years.

1998 — Dom Mintoff, *in piena autonomia,* used his democratic right in parliament and voted according to his conscience, bringing down his own socialist government. For once in fifty years, we had one man voting according to what *he* truly believed. He was nearly lynched!

This then is Democracy! A system of government pandering to the greatest number of votes. Politicians always with an eye on the next elec-tion and nothing else. The lowering of standards, the elevation of medioc-rity. In short, the lowest form of government.

We of *Imperium Europa* do not believe in the Aristocracy of Democ-racy. We believe in the Democracy of Aristocracy. A democracy amongst peers — as in the Athens of old, where out of 30,000 Athenians only 10,000 were voters. And the quality of those voters! A study of a few years ago concluded that the average intelligence of the Athenian voter was akin to that of the very best Members of the House of Commons today. In Athens, it was truly a Democracy of Aristocracy.

It is clear that we cannot go on like this. Democracy is in its last throes. It will be remembered as a tragic interlude in the political history of the White Man. An experiment that failed, and badly, and whose consequenc-es will take hundreds of years to heal and correct. From the peak of power and prestige, in just 100 years Democracy dragged the White Race into

a minority species facing extinction. A minority that is shorn of the will
to fight the numerous enemies assailing it. A Biological Aristocracy that
somehow, against all odds, must survive.

Yes, it is time to change course. We must devise new forms of government. We must end this Travesty of Democracy.

NATIONAL UNITY GOVERNMENT

Malta, like every other White nation, is in a mess. Actually the island is
bankrupt. Bankrupt in every sense of the word: spiritually, culturally, politically, environmentally, economically, financially, and socially. A country with no real leadership. We are not even a nation. We have no real European identity, speaking Arabic as we do. We have lost our pre-war spirit.

This is plain to see for anyone with a minimum of intelligence and
common sense. Why is this? Why should an island of such beauty, mys-
tique, with such potential to be a haven of high quality living, find itself in
such a state? What is the cause of all this?

Basically, it is the Maltese's uncanny ability to be like the village festa band:
out of step and out of tune with events. We have missed the bus at every important stage in post-war history and then, to make matters worse, we per-
sisted in taking the wrong turn when the right way was before our very eyes.

1950 — We missed the golden opportunity of Integration. We could
have become the greatest offshore fiscal paradise in the world.

1960s — The spiritual terror of a corrupt church lacking any spirituality. An internecine war that has divided the country ever since between
two equally obtuse and equally mediocre parties.

1972 — A handful of votes gave Malta twenty years of squalid socialism.
Even today, Malta is the most socialist country in the world. A socialism in-
jected into our veins. A political poison that will take generations to transfuse.

1998 — A fresh Prime Minister who should never have touched politics froze us out of Europe. A blindness, a momentous masochism, a political suicide that still baffles.

2000s — A Prime Minister who should have known better after decades in power, calls an unnecessary, no-win referendum for European entry. Luckily, due solely to the political stupidity of the other side, he manages to scrape us in. In short, a concatenation of important events hinging on mere accident that have shaped our post-war history and brought us to this sorry state of affairs.

A parliament that resembles a circus run by clowns. Small men, fit only to manage a small bazaar, clowning their way through the nation's problems. Bureaucracy galore, confusion, cross-wiring, waste, white elephants — the list is endless.

Two parties with their eyes on the next election and nothing else. Politicians pandering to the lowest common denominator. The lowering of standards, the elevation of mediocrity. In short, a Mickey Mouse country!

And is there any substantial difference between the Maltese politics of these last decades, and the politics in any other 'democratic' country in Europe? No! A difference in regional circumstances, a difference in the timing of the blunders and the names of the blunderers — that is all. In principle, the same charade.

Yes, it is time to change course. We must devise new forms of government. We must end this Travesty of Democracy that has bankrupted our Island. What is the solution? We of *Imperium Europa* propose a Government of National Unity. A National Unity Government!

Both parties are in perpetual tug-of-war. They are like a driver with his feet on both brake and accelerator. We need to utilise the best men, so few as they are, on both sides. We must devise a new way, and one that works: a National Unity Government.

A National Government drawn from the best elements of society. Men above petty party politics. Men of stature who do not flinch from doing what has to be done, notwithstanding a certain amount of inevitable squealing. Men who mean what they say and say what they mean, and act in consequence.

Italy had a similar problem a few years ago. A long history of political instability, an underground economy, a ponderous government bureaucracy together with rampant crime and corruption. Two technocratic governments, that of Dini and Ciampi, in an incredibly short time placed Italy within the Eurozone and picked up the economy. We could do the same.

IMPLEMENTATION

What is needed is an emergency government, a government with emergency powers to act — since this is a real emergency. A government that gets things done. A government as in war-time, with war-time powers to implement far-reaching policies. In short, a government that offers real direction and leadership.

First, we need a referendum that gives parliament the power to enact a law electing the President of the country by popular vote. Anybody would be eligible to contest this Presidential election. Should the first ballot fail to consign a simple majority to anyone of the contestants, then a run-off between the first two would be held.

Second, the President would have the power to choose a cabinet from outside parliament. He would thus choose experts in their own field. The best from the university, business, science, the unions, the military and so on. A cabinet of competent men and women, ready to dedicate four years of their lives entirely to the country.

Third, the President and his cabinet of technocrats would serve a term of just four years. In the meantime, parliament with the present incompetents would remain. It would serve as a debating society and a point of contact with the people. Informing the nation of the cabinet's policies, explaining in detail what they entail and in turn, gathering feedback. A select handful of the sixty or so incompetents would serve as a link to the cabinet.

Fourth, after four years, the people would again be asked to vote in fresh elections. This time the nation would be asked a simple question: do you want the present system of Presidential power to be continued, or would you rather return to the old days?

Should the people choose the new system, then the President and his cabinet would carry on for another five years. The old parliamentarians would be sent packing, with a handsome pension to keep their big mouths shut. Thank you and good riddance!

Only our plan of a National Unity Government can work — can turn this island around in four years of honest, hard work. A system that rewards initiative and enterprise. A system ruthlessly cutting the benefits to the lazy and the incompetent. A Government of National Unity ending forty years of clowning and muddling through politics by petty politicians. Yes, we will heal this Island!

This system of government would be a temporary stop-gap for a few years. An emergency plan of action that will save the Island from total bankruptcy till the emergence of a new Europe: a *Nova Europa*. For once the New Europe is in place, once the Imperium rapidly starts forming, our Presidential system would transform itself organically into a Regional government within the coming *Imperium Europa*.

Our Sacred Island, Malta, this land of honey, Melita — would thus be ready for the exciting times ahead for the Old Continent. Ready to become the Apex, the Pyramidical Peak, the Focal Point, the Spiritual Centre for the coming, inevitable, unstoppable *Imperium Europa*.

IMPERIUM

0403

PUBLISHED BY THE **TIMES OF MALTA**

29 APRIL 2004

II

OTTO SETTEMBRE

NATIONAL UNITY

IN MY RECENT ARTICLE NATIONAL Unity I gave a general picture of the sorry mess we now find ourselves in. I gave a chronology of events, one wrong turn after another by two lesbian-prostitute parties cavorting in the same bed. I mentioned first the fundamental error: the missed opportunity that was Integration with Britain: 1950 — A few votes cost us Integration with Britain. Actually the pro-Integration vote was the largest, but failed an outright majority. The second largest vote was the abstentions, some 30 percent. And yet, Integration was lost and with it, Europe. For had Malta joined Britain, we would have been in Europe with Edward Heath, without the huffing and puffing that finally squeezed us into Europe thirty years later.

Instead, we opted for Independence; an unmitigated disaster. Within three years, every skyline on this once beautiful Island was ruined. Our valleys choked with hideous blocks of concrete. Our once blue waters, up to two miles out, a cesspit — so every summer the Maltese can 'Splash'n'Fun' to their hearts' content.

Standards plummeted all around and the opportunity to strike oil offshore, under the protective umbrella of Britain, was lost forever. A tinpot Arabic country, just across the waters, stopped our drilling operations with just a toy gunboat. That put paid to years of clowning by our socialist fools in power.

For Malta was unready for Independence. The Maltese showed themselves unworthy, undeserving of managing this paradise in the

Mediterranean on their own. What was needed was either Integration with Britain, or Integration with Europe. Left to themselves, the Maltese botched it!

Our politicians lacked the long-term vision of turning this island into a high-cultured haven. Our leaders had not the statesmanship to keep Malta securely positioned within the European fold.

Moreover, they abandoned wise leadership, pandering instead to the basest, day-to-day whims of the low-cultured. On the other hand, our intelligentsia lacked the moral fibre to act as a counter-weight, to hold the shallow politicians in check. Naturally, the masses simply followed and wallowed.

And as more time passes since Independence — as British influence recedes — our island, a rudderless raft in between two cultures, slowly drifts further away from Europe. Imperceptibly, genetically and culturally, Malta is being Africanised.

Our unnatural, imposed Arabic language: *il-lingwa tal-bigilla* ('the potpourri language'; *tal-bigilla* is a traditional Maltese bean recipe) keeps 80 percent of the population in servitude to an Arab mentality. Our *lingwa tal-kakkademja taċ-ċuqlajta* (language of our academy of shit-intellectuals) is the greatest hindrance to progress in every field. It is a lobotomy on our children — a cultural genocide. No wonder the low quality of our population — the abandonment, the vandalism even of our Paleo/Neolithic Sacred Sites.

IL-FESTA FARSA!

(THE FARCICAL FEAST)

Then came *il-festa farsa tal-Ħelsien!* Freedom Day — but freedom from what? The British occupied the islands at our beckoning. We asked them to help us oust the French. The Brits did their term and left according to a signed agreement. They left quietly and in dignity, as they did when they left Singapore and Hong Kong. In fact, the Maltese people in their great majority were sorry for the termination of over two hundred years of British presence. Huge crowds wept openly as the navy sailed out of our Main Harbour.

A socialist, economic mentality: the haggling for over one year over rent! The socialist myopia! They can never change — a socialist stands always at the basest level of mentality. Instead of copying the Sultan of Brunei, who actually pays the British to remain in his country and guard his huge oil reserves, our socialists painted themselves into a corner. A peripheral island, 200 miles south of Tunisia, bereft of any defence, was left to the mercy of a Libyan toy gunboat.

Together with the discovery of oil, under the protective umbrella of the British, we could have turned this island into the Channel Islands of the Mediterranean. The Cayman Islands in the Middle Sea. Instead, we opted for *il-festa farsa tal-Ħelsien*!

And we have a monument for this feast. The most grotesque, ugliest monument in the whole of Europe. A monument without a focal point, of no artistic value whatsoever. Four figures and a flagpole: *erbgha pasturi tal-presepju* (the crib).

OTTO SETTEMBRE

Now that we are in Europe, both National Days, Independence and *il-festa farsa*, will lose all significance. They will rapidly be forgotten. These two, bogus National Days will make way for the *Otto Settembre* (8th of September): the only day worthy to be our National Day.

That day when, 500 years ago almost to the year, our forefathers, after an epic siege, consecrated our islands of Melitae to Europe. When our ancestors chose to remain European: genetically and culturally, notwithstanding the Ottoman threat.

They could easily have changed sides, like the Albanians did. The Maltese could have turned against the few knights manning the forts and then joined the Turks, thereby earning privileges and tax concessions. They did not. Against all odds, they chose to remain true to their genetic and cultural identity. Five hundred years ago the Maltese chose to remain European. They chose Europe. They chose to remain true to themselves. *Otto Settembre* signifies all of this.

IDENTITY

The Mediterranean race does not exist. That lie, that 'we are not Europeans but Mediterraneanids', uttered by our first socialist prime minister, did more harm to our people than all the bombs dropped on us during WWII. It deracinated us. It confused our people. It literally shattered our sense of nationhood.

There exist two distinct races: Europids to the North of the Mediterranean — and Semites to the South of the same sea. The Europids consist of NW Europids (Germans and English), NE Europids (Finns) and the Sud-Europids; Portuguese, Spanish, Italians, Greeks, Balkan Slavs, Romanians etc.

In fact, most European populations (Germans, English, Finns and Italians) have exchanged genes during the past four thousand years and are very closely related and compatible.

On the other hand, Semites — or, as they are generally known, Arabs — are either pure Semites (Saudis) or mixed with Berbers and/or Negrids (Anwar Sadat of Egypt comes to mind).

Thus the Mediterranean, even at the Gibraltar point, just ten miles wide, is the great divide between these two races: The Europid to the North, the Semitic to the South. And we Maltese are conscious, proud to belong within the Europid fold.

And we have to take care of our genetic affinity. We must not contaminate our race. We must not mix with Arabs and worse, much worse, with sub-Saharan Negrids. We must not listen to those communists and pernicious priests. Those who control the media and who want to destroy our people, our race, and our identity.

These communists and pernicious priests are moved by a self-hatred, an envy that pushes them into invoking racial suicide. We must expose them for what they are: traitors! Traitors to their race, the race of biological aristocrats, the Europids. Traitors to their civilisation: the greatest to have graced this planet and grazed the moon. Traitors to their very own ancestors who kept them as they are, Europids, through thousands of years of racial discrimination. Traitors to their people who naïvely gave them trust. Traitors to our children, malignantly and maliciously pushed, blindfolded and brainwashed into a multi-racial future full of horror. And finally, traitors to themselves, for deep down, they know what damage they are doing: it is their self-hate that makes them persevere in their diabolical plan.

BATTAGLIA DI CULTURA

It is a battle of cultures that we are facing and fighting. We of *Imperium Europa* are fighting this fight conscious that there is nobody else. Our people have been left to themselves. They are leaderless, confused and blind. We are the few manning the wide breaches, the unguarded beaches.

No wonder we have the heroic notes of *The March of the Spartans* as our signature tune. Like those three hundred heroes at Thermopylae, we have to do our duty, irrespective of the outcome or the chances of success. Whether victory or annihilation, we have to fight — and fight we will! And God help those traitors upon our victory!

We must save this island. We must heal this island. We must prevail, as otherwise thousands of years of history, of racial consciousness, of identity will be lost. Otherwise, we will bestow a Haiti to our innocent children — and this must not be.

Yes, we will fight! Like our ancestors during The Great Siege, we will choose to remain true to our identity. No matter how few we are, no matter what the odds, we will fight! We of *Imperium Europa* have become the only focal point left on this island abandoned to itself, misguided by traitors: politicians and priests. We are those 300 Spartans fighting on till our last breath. That Athens and civilisation as we know it will be saved.

Costi quel che costa, we will fight till Victory!

IMPERIUM

0403

PUBLISHED BY **THE TIMES OF MALTA**

27 MAY 2004

AFTERWORD — 8ᵀᴴ SEPTEMBER 2005

On this, our only National Day, *Otto Settembre*, 440 years ago, Malta saved Europe! Malta shone with courage and honor.

I have been warned by the authorities that I would be arrested if I set foot within our capital city. Our government, spurning 97 percent of the Maltese, is forbidding me, Norman Lowell, from honouring our ancestors. Me, whose parents are both born in Valletta — me, born and bred in that Gentleman's city.

9ᵀᴴ SEPTEMBER 2005

Together with other Patriots we placed a wreath at the National Monument in Valletta a day later. Spontaneous applause from crowds that happened to be there.

III

REFLECTIONS ON AN ELECTION

MEP (MEMBER OF THE EUROPEAN Parliament) elections June 2004. Extraordinary elections, negative elections that returned a macabre result. These elections were extraordinary in that the Maltese people could, for once, vote free from the bondage of their party. They could afford to intelligently choose individuals best suited to the task in Brussels, without directly rocking the government or opposition. For these elected individuals did not necessarily belong to the voter's own party. A considerable number of voters did liberate themselves from their party's vice-like grip. They did vote 'freely' — but they voted negatively. Indeed, the single most obvious factor in these elections was the negative vote: from the NP (Nationalist Party) to the AD (the Greens). A negative, incoherent vote from nationalists belonging to a declared centre, to a centre-right party (albeit, a bewildered party now reeling to the left) — towards the far left, that are in effect the Greens. A vote that reveals the confusion of our people. A vote that makes no political sense — except as punishment for an inept, incompetent government.

For what do the Greens stand for? More taxes, eco-taxes, especially on top of the overburdened, over-taxed people of Malta. We are the most taxed country in Europe. And worse than this, they stand for the accommodation of and automatic right to work for aliens who should never have been here in the first place. Here is what the AD manifesto says about immigration, though they never discuss it openly with the guileless public: 'Refugees and their immediate families should be granted the right to work automatically and should be granted all the rights that are granted to the Maltese citizens.' Is this what those befuddled NP voters supported with their negative vote?

Some MLP (Labour Party) voters cast their vote in our favor: *Imperium Europa*. There was a negative element in this, in that they are tired of a leader who can never, ever win a general election. With their vote they hoped to inflict another defeat on their own party and pave the way to a change of leadership. Whether there is anybody to fit the role, after their best men left in disgust, is another matter. The MLP are indeed a poor party: poor both in leadership and in ideas. But at least their vote for us had a positive aspect, in that the MLP voter sensed that we are the party against immigration. We are the only party speaking on behalf of the worker, the small worker and his fear of losing his job to cheap, immigrant labour. The MLP supporter who voted for *Imperium Europa* voted coherently: work and dignity.

THE RESULT

The general result was macabre. A party that up to six months ago was all against Europe garnered three seats in Brussels! A party with no European consciousness, no sense of belonging to an emerging political giant forged by cousin peoples, won a surprising result. A party pandering to the lowest level of debate during the run-up sent three Eurosceptics to Brussels! O Malta!

This apparent MLP victory is in effect a long-term loss. The leadership, an inarticulate, repetitive, boring leadership, was reinforced by the result — and this will mean certain defeat at the next general elections. For the floating voter, an increasingly determined voter, will never, ever vote for the MLP leader: never! The floating voter will tolerate anything, will forget everything — except abdication. And Dr. Alfred Saint abdicated in all but the formality of abdication when he went to the polls after less than two years in office. Inexcusable! Unforgettable! Unforgivable!

And this is the tragedy of our island: there is no choice. On the one side, an ineligible opposition, and on the other, an incompetent government. And the people: the ham in the sandwich.

ALL LOSERS

All emerged losers from the result: the Government was the biggest loser. We are lumbered by a tired government, notwithstanding a Prime Minister fresh in office but already showing all the symptoms of mismanagement and an inability to project and impinge himself on the national consciousness. One remembers his very first interview as PM at his home — seated at the kitchen table! A Prime Minister who was quoted by the party secretary as having sent his regards to all candidates, including Independents — except for Norman Lowell! How petty!

A Prime Minister who looks increasingly like that sea-captain rearranging deck chairs on the Titanic. Cabinet Ministers playing musical chairs — and in the meantime the requiem of the nation intones: political paralysis, environmental eczema, ecological damage, cultural cretinism, economic exhaustion, devouring deficit, unending unemployment — the list is endless.

The Nationalist Party, on the other hand, may be said to have emerged as a relative winner. Now they will dust themselves down, improve their image somewhat, recoup their lost sheep and arrive in time to win the next election against a no-leader opposition. The MLP, as already explained, are the net losers. They are now destined to another nine years in opposition. Will they ever learn?

The Greens are euphoric — and why not! But this is their flash in the pan. The last gasp before they fade out from the political scene. They are in effect a bunch of renegades who spat on their glorious past (right-wing origins and ideology) and who embraced ex-communists and anarchists. *Chi rinnega — va rinnegato!*

All the Independents lost, with no exception. But most of all, the greatest losers were we: *Imperium Europa*. We, who knew what the stakes were. We, who had a European agenda, as against the petty village-pump politics of all the rest. We, who had solid, ideological foundations envisaging a Europe of Regions and Peoples: a *Nova Europa*. A wave, a surging wave swept past. We missed the wave — we lost — we all lost.

Granted, we made mistakes. I assume primary and ultimate responsibility for the innumerable votes lost through my gratuitous rashness. Unfortunately, I can never be a political fox — I can only fight and die like a lion.

All is not lost. This is just the beginning, the opening shots of a far bigger struggle. *La nuova ondata ci sarà. E noi saremo lì, pronti a cavalcare la tigre!* (The next wave will come — and we will be there, ready to ride the tiger!)

We will not abandon those who placed their trust in us. We will never quit — never. We stand here, those few thousands that voted for us. It is reckoned we had 9,000 second-count votes. We will wait for the next wave. It will come — sooner than anyone thinks.

IMPERIUM

0407

This article appeared in the Times of Malta a few weeks after the MEP elections held in June 2004.

The author obtained 1,600 first preference votes and thousands more second preference votes.

IV

POLICY 14-14

THE LANGUAGE PROBLEM IS THE Fundamental Problem for our people, our Nation. It is of singular importance because, unless we solve it, we will remain the low quality people that we have become.

The Maltese are a low quality people culture-wise. One only has to stomach the *vox pop* on TV to realise how limited, how ignorant our population is. Monosyllable answers to the simplest questions — so inarticulate. Stupid answers to childish enquiries. The lowest level of conversation and debate at the highest forum of the land: parliament.

Why is this? Simple! Because we have a poor language. We are divested of the currency with which to buy ideas. We are bereft of that power to dream, to think, to act!

How did this come about? What made our people, a hardy people, a courageous people in times of adversity — a people that can reach high craftsmanship in diverse fields — so poor in the ability to express itself? It all started with the British, specifically their Policy 14-14.

In the early 70s I was a great, personal friend of Padre Milne. He was the Church of Scotland vicar in Malta for many years. He held rank of Squadron Leader with the Royal Air Force. For years I used to have breakfast with him, ringing his doorbell at Old Bakery Street, at 6am on the first Saturday of every month. We would discuss world affairs, stroll around Valletta, admiring the fortifications, ending up at the *Lantern Bar* for a huge steak — and more spiritual inspiration!

I visited Padre Milne at his house on The Bents, at Montrose, Scotland just a few months before he passed away. He was a superman if ever I met one. Right out of the SS! In fact, he studied at Tuebingen University in the 30s and was an admirer of Hitler and the Germans. He always referred to Churchill as 'that old fool' who squandered an Empire in just four years: 'fighting the wrong war, at the wrong time, against the wrong enemy!'

Padre Milne revealed to me British policy since their arrival on the island. They called it the 14-14 Policy towards the Maltese. It was very simple and effective.

The Brits immediately noticed that the Maltese, like the Catholic Irish, bred like rabbits. Maltese girls married at fourteen years of age — and they normally had fourteen children! Of course, some half of these usually died at infancy, but the survivors, in turn, kept marrying at fourteen and reproducing fourteen. In short, a demographic disaster for such a small island: a constant fornication and fecundity, an endless propagation, pro-creation and proliferation.

This would not do, of course. Something had to be done about it. One couldn't have such a beautiful island, a paradise in the Med, overpopulated by the Natives, who spoke, or rather mumbled, an Arabic dialect — and worse yet, with an elite that spoke Italian! Hence, Policy 14-14.

The males, those stallions, had to be separated from the women — so off to Australia cutting sugar canes!

Cut jobs to a minimum, thereby forcing the Maltese to emigrate to Algeria, Egypt and wherever, in search of a better life. Basically, a policy of forced emigration — or in reality, exile.

Second and most important: convince *il-Ġaħan Malti* (the Maltese village idiot) that he had a language of his own, equal to if not better than Italian! — And why? Because the British knew, as they still do, that language is power. That it was the miraculous English language that gave them domination over the globe. That even today, with an impoverished Britain, it is this language that still gives them the clout to influence world affairs.

The Brits convinced the gullible Maltese that this *ċuqlajta* (clack) is our true language — when of course, it is not, never was, and never will be! The Brits lobotomised the Maltese and ruled these islands for centuries with the greatest of ease — *għaliex lill-Maltin ġabuhom bergħut fil-jamjar!* (They reduced the Malts to fleas in a jam jar!) Only one man clearly saw, at inception, this policy and the threat it posed to our real identity: Fortunato Mizzi, in my view the greatest politician Malta has ever seen. He immediately, fearlessly challenged the Brits with his constant cry: *Ma perché state facendo questo, perché! Cosa volete, che noi diventiamo arabi? Volete che rimaniamo latini, o che diventiamo arabi? Ma perché, maledetti inglesi, volete questo?* (But why are you doing this! What do you want, that we become Arabs? Do you want us to remain Latins, or to become Arabs? But why, accursed British, do you want this?) And the Brits had their way — and we had our *ċuqlajta!* — And we are still lumped with it! And to this day we have fools who do not realise that this is an imposed language, an alien language, forced on us by the Arabs during their four centuries of occupation. In reality, we are still a colony, a cultural colony of the Arabs.

That is why Arabs are so arrogant in Malta. That is why they treat us so contemptuously when we visit Libya, for example. Customs officials greet Maltese roughly, never helping with the filling out of forms in Arabic. They make us Maltese open our luggage on the floor, then examine the contents by shuffling their feet inside. Ask anyone who has been there. We have to be honest with ourselves. We have to solve this problem once and for all. We have to liberate ourselves from this Catch-14 situation. We have to find ourselves again. *Be! Essere!*

IMPERIUM

0502

V

MELITA
SPIRITUAL CENTRE TO
IMPERIUM EUROPA

I AM IN POSSESSION OF AN original document that is possibly unique. As far as I know it has never been published or commented upon before. I had published it in my book, *CREDO: A Book for the Very Few*, and therein I had left it to speak for itself.

It does so with uncommon candour. Bonham Carter, the Governor of these Islands at that crucial time just before the Second World War, describes British feelings towards the Maltese. He mentions how important, strategically, Malta was for the survival of the British Empire.

Lastly he reveals the racial dynamics underlying politics — and that the British considered the Maltese as Europeans in every sense of the word: geographically, culturally and most important, racially.

That is why Malta was privileged, alone within the whole Empire, to have been offered Integration with the Mother Country. Britain gave this ultimate recognition to Malta, far more precious than any George Cross, for a simple, fundamental reason.

The British truly respected and loved the Maltese. They did not mind integrating with us, since they saw that Malta was White and presented no problems of assimilation.

Britain could never, ever dream of offering Integration to millions of Nigerians, Indians or Hondurans. We were indeed honoured to have been offered this golden opportunity — and, to the eternal shame of most of our politicians and church leaders of the time, we missed it.

We had a socialist prime minister, married to a Bentinck, who inculcated into the uneducated that we Maltese are not European after all — that we are Mediterraneans, cousins to the Libyans. The cultural devastation that this lie has wrought on our island is incalculable. It deracinated us. All the German and Italian bombs dropped during WW2 on this beleaguered rock would not make one percent of the Cultural damage brought about by this fallacy. A damage that will take at least three generations to heal — for as Napoleon so rightly said: 'To educate a man, one has to start from his grandfather.'

A lie that completely unhinged the Maltese. A cultural dislocation bringing disorientation as the nation lost its bearings. For up till 1972 we knew were we stood. We were poor, but proud to be Europeans. The ultimate insult to a Maltese would have been to tell him he was Arabic. It had to be a Prime Minister to instil this cultural catastrophe. A man who, through his education — an Oxford scholar, the English woman he married coming from a renowned family, among whom there was an excellent Member of the House of Commons — should have known better. He should have foreseen the disastrous consequences.

THE FACTS

A race of brunettes, non-Nordic, non-Alpinid, whose habitat stretches from Portugal to Bangladesh, from the Alps down to the Sahara — this race does not exist!

The well-known study by Bosch reveals that:

> The most striking results are that contemporary NW African and Iberian populations were found to have originated from distinctly different patrilineages and that the Strait of Gibraltar seems to have acted as a strong (although not complete) barrier to gene flow... The Islamic rule of Spain, which began

in AD 711 and lasted almost 8 centuries, left only a minor contribution to the current Iberian Y-chromosome pool.

Now, different population groups differ genetically — proving the existence of biological race. The study of the highest importance by Nei and Livshits in 1989/1990 found that Africans split off from the rest of humanity first. They moved to the Indian sub-continent and then to Southeast Asia, where there are still pockets of populations with African traits (Philippine Negritos, Andamanese, Dravidians).

The resultant population absorbed most of its gene pool from the Mongoloid group but retained the genes for dark skin, frizzled hair, etc. from the Africans — this because of natural selection in tropical conditions. This Africanised population moved to New Guinea and Australia some 40,000 years ago.

The next major split was that between Caucasians and the general Asian cluster. Both these groups demonstrated further splits.

It is of interest that English, Germans, Finns and Italians are all clustered together in the European group, distinctly separate from non-European Caucasians such as Iranians and North Indians, as well as Lapps. Thus, in contrast to the Mediterranean Myth, the Italians are firmly in the European group, distinct and apart from non-European Mediterraneans of North Africa.

Latins, according to Carlton Coon, the leading American anthropologist and president of the American Anthropological Society for over fifty years, are very much akin to the Nordics, whom he calls 'partially depigmented Mediterraneanids'. 'They are very similar since they have the same origin. Nordics and Mediterraneanids are the same people, with the same racial origins.'

The Race of the 'Battle Axe People' have left incontrovertible proof at Val Camonica, Italy, that they were Indo-Aryans, with genetic affinity to the Nordic-Atlantic, Franco Cantabrian Cro-Magnon, as well as with the Scandinavian Fossum Civilisation. This means that the Achaean-Dorics were the originators of both Sparta and Rome.

Apart from the genetic factor lies the language: Latin, the tongue of ancient Rome. It is an Indo-European language. Not only that, but Latin, quite apart from its vocabulary, has the same articulation, syntax and declension as the German tongue. So much for the vaunted, so-called 'incompatibility between Latins and Teutons'!

That same Aristocratic, Noble Spirit that was Rome, Sparta and Athens; a common origin, genetic, lingual and religious; the same 'Solar' veneration and cremation of the dead, as against burial. That same ethos of sternness, discipline, distance, bravery in anonymity, virility, love of order, sense of measure and spirit of sacrifice — all this, the Europids, from Swedes to Germans to Spaniards, innately have in common — and must rediscover in themselves, within the coming *IMPERIUM EUROPA*.

Permit me to be specific. I hail from Malta, in the Mediterranean. A tiny island, but of great Spiritual significance for the Europid. In this context it is relevant to note the findings of Dr. V. Wyatt, an expert on poliomyelitis, as reported in the *Times of Malta* of the 23rd July of 1982. Dr. Wyatt found that although the climate in Malta was similar to that of the Middle East, the disease affected its Maltese victims in the same way as it affected Europeans and North Americans (North Central Europeans NCEs). It was quite different from the symptoms found in Middle Eastern and African patients.

We Maltese know, and are justly proud, that we form part of that distinct sub-species: the Caucasian or Europid or White Race, the envy of the rest of humanity. The race that gave the world everything it has. That inventive, creative race of great explorers, scientists, musicians, composers. In short the race of Aryans: the builders! — and we Maltese, have the finest Aryan prehistoric temples to prove it!

Maltese are an assimilable minority of this great, Europid race. What is an assimilable minority? As Wilmot Robertson in his *The Dispossessed Majority* explains, it is simply a minority that can genetically integrate, naturally and harmoniously, with any segment of this great Europid family.

A Maltese female who cohabits with a German, an Englishman or a Norwegian, would give offspring to the most beautiful example of such people. The fact that we are the southernmost Europeans seems to redouble nature's result, make the bow tauter so to speak, with increased freshness, virility, brains and beauty.

I know of a particular case of an ordinary Maltese girl from a small village, married to an Englishman, whose firstborn son, a veritable angel, was chosen by SMA, the baby-food producers, for their first TV advert.

There is no Mediterranean race. That race does not exist, nor has it ever existed.

Why is this myth propagated when it is clearly so false? Well, ignorance is a factor here. But there is a more sinister motive as well; it is an expression of animus against Sud-Europids by our eternal enemies. They are the ones propagating the Mediterranean Myth, for in so doing, they make it easier for Sud-Europids to lower their guard and mix with North Africans.

The Mediterranean Myth is very dangerous in that it delegitimises Sud-Europids, their racial identity. It promotes the lie that Sud-Europids are in fact no different from North Africans. It denies the existence of the Sud-Europids and thus enhances the chances of their extinction by miscegenation: the soft-suicide of all races.

We Maltese are proud to form part of the Sud-Europid sub-race. We have nothing against the Arabs, but we have to be clear to them that we are not of their kind — nor do we ever want to be. We are Europeans and that is what we want to remain!

PIE

The Aryans were semi-nomadic Nordic Whites, perhaps located originally on the steppes of southern Russia and Central Asia. They spoke the parent language of the various Indo-European languages: the *Dnghu*.

Sanskrit, Latin, Greek, Hittite, French, German, Latvian, English, Spanish, Russian etc. are all Indo-European languages. Indo-European, or more properly Proto-Indo-European (PIE), is the lost ancestral language from which those languages ultimately derive. The 'Proto' indicates that the grammar and vocabulary of this long extinct language, probably spoken up until 2000 BC, are a hypothetical reconstruction by modern philologists. Just as Romance languages like Italian and Spanish derive from Latin, so Latin derives from PIE.

Indo-European philology traditionally used 'Aryan' both to denote a people, understood racially or ethnically, and the language group itself, 'Aryan speech', irrespective of the race or ethnicity of the people speaking its various branches. Arya, meaning 'noble', appears in various Indo-European languages. Its plural form (Aryas = 'nobles') was probably the name the Aryans used to describe themselves prior to their dispersal, and it may survive in Eire (Ireland) and certainly survives in Iran (*Airyanam vaejjo* = 'realm of the Aryans'). The discovery of thousands of such cognate words in widely separated languages, along with similar grammatical structures, led philologists to conclude, early in the nineteenth century, that most European languages had evolved from a common proto-language. This must have been spoken millennia ago by a distinct people, who gradually left their original habitat in a series of migrations, carrying their language with them.

Traditionally, Sanskrit, Ancient Greek and Latin were considered the closest languages to PIE, and much of the reconstructed Aryan proto-language is based on them. Modern Lithuanian, however, is the most archaic living language, closer to the original Aryan speech than any other. There is even a PIE language, Tocharian, attested in Chinese Turkistan, which indicates that Aryans must have made an appearance in the Far East — a long-standing piece of linguistic evidence which has been recently confirmed by the discovery of the physical remains of a blond-haired people in China's Tarim basin.

Perhaps the most famous proof for the prehistoric existence of PIE is the word for king: *rex* in Latin, *raja* in Sanskrit, *ri* in Old Irish, along with a host of other cognates. All are obviously variants of a common word for king. None of the peoples speaking these various languages were in physical contact with one another during the historical period — i.e. at a time for which written records exist. Comparative philologists have therefore inferred that their respective languages must have evolved from a single proto-language, which is the only way of explaining the presence of the same word for 'king' among such widely dispersed peoples. The Romans clearly didn't borrow *rex* from the Irish or the Indo-Aryans; each had instead inherited their own for 'king' from a common ancestral language.

The Aryans were remarkably expansionist, imposing their languages on the subjugated peoples. Hence the Latin world *malus* or bad is derived from the Greek *melas* which means black, or dark. This could be derived from the blond Aryan conquests of the darker, subjected races. Likewise the Gaelic *fin* means good, noble, pure and also blond. In English, *fair* is both the opposite of dark and the opposite of foul.

Aryan invasions, a long sequence of different invasions by speakers of Indo-European languages, swept across Old Europe as early as the fourth millennium BC, and over time, both conquerors and conquered melted into specific peoples with distinctive languages. Most of the contemporary inhabitants of Europe, along with their respective early national cultures, are the result of interaction between successive waves of Aryan invaders and the culture of the particular White people that they conquered, and with whom they later intermarried.

The birth of a European culture, however, predates the arrival of the Indo-Europeans. The cave art of Lascaux, which some have identified as the first flowering of Western Man's creative genius, was the work of Old Europeans, as were Stonehenge in the North and the ubiquitous Old European reverence for the Mother Goddess with its centre in Malta — the Sacred Island of Melita.

LATIN

The Latin language is the bedrock of Western Civilisation. Without Latin, nothing would have been possible. Language is power — and the power to express conceptions in Latin was the vehicle that carried European Man along his progress.

Latin is not a dead language. It is anything but. Young people everywhere are studying Latin with an enthusiasm which is amazing. Conventions of Latin speaking enthusiasts are held practically every month all over Europe. Even the Finns broadcast a weekly news review entirely in Latin on Radio *Nuntii Latini* (available on the internet). This is heartening. We must ensure that our progeny master Latin — not in order to be able to better understand English, French, Spanish, Portuguese, Italian or Rumanian, but in order to safeguard the continuity, the preservation of the integrity of our High Culture. As in the past, the hallmark of an educated man will be his mastery of Latin. The successful man of the future will be able to reply 'I am a computer expert — I studied Latin!'

After thousands of years of dispersal and persecution, the Jews were able to build Israel. Why? How? They did it because they had kept intact their ancestral language: Hebrew. It was the unifying tradition of Jewish thought. It enabled them to survive — and thrive! (They could have easily adopted Yiddish, a German-Jewish dialect that most founders of Modern Israel spoke, but instead they chose something that was uniquely theirs.)

And so too, it must be for the Europid. As the Old Continent moves towards political unity, it must acquire linguistic unity. Imposing English as the common language of a politically, United Europe would be a strategic mistake, cutting us from our roots and ensuring future strife. No German, no Frenchman, no Greek would accept such an imposition — and rightly so!

Europids in the future *IMPERIUM EUROPA* will be conversant in at least three languages: German, English and French. The reason is simple; a new idea would be first discussed in German, a language as rich, as mysterious, as creative as the sun's rays piercing the shadows of the Black Forest. The concept would then be lit by the full sunshine of luminous English, which enables all thought to be presented with a unique, complete clarity. Finally, the subject would be concluded, reduced to lapidary French, which for good reason is used in international treaties and on other occasions, when thought and language must be exact.

But our *lingua franca* for the Imperium must undoubtedly be Latin. That tongue of the Europid, lying dormant like a seed, ready to sprout to life again! That spoken word that will bind Europeans, wherever they will be, anywhere on the planet and out there, in outer space. Yes! We will restore that most clear, precise and dynamic language to its former glory. It will be our medium in our galactic quest towards our final destiny. Latin — *lingua Imperialis!*

We Maltese may choose English for the time being, since most of us speak it anyway. But ideally, as it supplants Maltese as our everyday language, we must revert to our natural, original language, that spoken by our forefathers right up to the time of the Arabs: Latin! We will be the first to adopt it nationally, before it becomes the common tongue within the IMPERIUM. We would be the first Europeans to speak it again — and what a first!

THE POWER OF LANGUAGE

At the beginning, at least the beginning we know of, the inhabitants of these islands must have been the Aryans — the builders. Our magnificent temples at Mnajdra and elsewhere testify to this. The Islanders must have spoken an Indo-European tongue.

In the 1920s, the well-known British anthropologist L. H. Dudley Buxton studied the Maltese ethnicity. He proved conclusively that the Maltese are ethnically European, of the Eastern Alpine type, who settled here around 2500 BC during the Bronze Age. These were certainly Indo-Europeans, pre-Doric; the Battle Axe People (this is interesting, as the Minoans were Battle-Axe people, and sent colonies to Italy and I believe naturally, to Malta, from their centre in Crete). A warlike race at the Bronze Age stage of development, they cremated their dead instead of following the custom of burial.

Later, with the coming of the Phoenicians, who traded continuously all over the Mediterranean and who spoke a Semitic language, we may have adopted or used their tongue for the sake of commerce. We certainly did adopt their gesticulations: the signs for no, yes, *hekk u hekk* (more or less). The *tsk*, which actually is the refusal of the mother's nipple. We adopted their 'don't be daft' by bunching our fingers and shaking them — and all the rest of it.

All this came from the Phoenicians; but we don't know for sure whether we adopted their language. However, this is highly unlikely since they never actually colonised the islands. To them, Malta was simply a free port.

What we do know is that the Maltese spoke a language akin to Latin prior to the Arab conquest. When St. Paul got shipwrecked here and regaled us with Christianity, it took just three months for him to convert the entire population. And why? Simple! Because the aristocracy, the rulers spoke Latin, a language which Paul, being a Roman subject, knew very well. All he had to do was concentrate on Publius, the leading citizen, and then the rest would follow. This he did with a resounding and lasting success, testifying once again to the power of language.

Indeed, during the relatively short Punic conquest of the islands, the Maltese clung to their Indo-European tongue. The Carthaginian conquest of the island was loose and weak. The Carthaginians never vigorously promoted a dominant cultural penetration, since Malta was considered peripheral to them.

Later, when Rome took over Malta in 218 BC, the Island, for all practical purposes, was considered Roman. This became a fact when sometime later the Maltese were granted Roman citizenship. The recorded proof is the Arab chronicler al-Himyari who confirms that the inhabitants of Malta 'were Romans'.

As the nobility with the masses, conquerors impose their language on the vanquished. The British imposed English on the sprawling sub-continent of India with its teeming millions. The French did the same throughout their North African and Central African Empire. Germans even managed to impose their language on pygmies in South West Africa!

In Malta this is exactly what happened. During the two centuries of their occupation, between the 9th and the 12th century, the Arabs divested the Maltese of their original, European tongue and imposed their own — and we are still lumped with it!

Harsh, cruel, with the whiplash constantly in hand, the Arabs forced the Maltese to adopt a slave language. A language just barely sufficient to enable the slave to execute the commands of his master. A poor language divested of the power to conceive. Not even high Arabic, but a meagre jumble of words. It was a forced lobotomy on the entire population — a *1984* Orwellian nightmare of the limited dictionary for the masses.

With the departure of the Arabs the Maltese leading citizens, eventually the nobility reverted to the European tongues: Italian, French and English. This is understandable since they must have felt that the political liberation from the Arabs could only be total with the liberation from the yoke of their language. Not only that, but as ethnic Europeans they must have felt the unnaturalness, the incompatibility of this imposed, low Arabic with their genes, their very being, their culture, their desire and urge to communicate effectively. In short — the Maltese wanted to be themselves!

The lower classes unable to read or write, and too lazy to start afresh, were quite content to carry on with what the Arabs had forced them to use. After all, monotony is the spice of life for the uneducated, and Maltese fitted them admirably!

The Master-slave language also suited the nobility, who simply stepped into the shoes of the former masters. The Maltese language was just what was needed in the new Master-slave relationship. The nobility spoke a European tongue amongst themselves and communicated with the masses in Maltese. The intelligentsia did the same.

Later on, when it became convenient to translate Maltese into writing, in order to settle contracts of land for example, this low-Arabic language was simply written in Roman form: lock, stock and vowel.

THE CLEVER BRITS!

And here, the genius of the clever Brits, their ability to manage peoples with so few men on the ground, came into play. In Malta, they adopted a policy of what they called '14-14'. It was simple and effective:

First, they drew around them a tiny minority of intelligentsia and nobles and, in tandem with the powerful Roman Catholic Church, used them as megaphones to transmit their policies towards the masses. The Brits never, ever spoke directly to the people.

Second, the Brits realised the Maltese were like the Irish Catholics, breeding like rabbits. Clearly the island would be overpopulated in a short span of years and that, of course, was not cricket!

So the Brits embarked on an aggressive policy of emigration to Australia. Thousands of Maltese were shipped off to start a new life. And they did — some very successfully too.

Third, and the most important part of their policy, they conned the Maltese language in written form. They reasoned, quite correctly, that with such a poor, limited language the Maltese would never be a threat to them. The masses would never be able to articulate their desire for freedom from colonialism.

And here they used an idealist: Mikiel Anton Vassalli, an extreme Francophile. As they had done to Napoleon, the Brits imprisoned him, watched him wither away as his health sapped — and when he was taken to hospital, as it was clear he was dying, he was kept chained to his bed. Like Napoleon, the Brits then exiled him. We do not know whether, like Bonaparte, he was poisoned while in custody — but his health certainly deteriorated badly.

What we do know is that the British callously used Vassalli to translate the Bible (the only book the ignorant Maltese masses would be interested to read), into Arabic in Roman script. This, Vassalli did for two reasons: his genuine interest in Semitic languages, and more pragmatically, his desperatation for money at the time. With this concoction of an artificial language, Arabic written in Roman form, Vassalli quite unknowingly performed an invaluable service to the British in their determination to hold this strategic rock for as long as possible.

Of course, had Vassalli witnessed the present cultural devastation he brought about with his concoction of this crude Semitic language, he would be horrified. He would have preferred French to anything else, or another European language of Latin derivation — but certainly not this clack! Like Livingstone, who lived and travelled all over Africa — and who would be horrified today if he had to visit Bradford, Brixton, Birmingham or any other multi-racial town or city in England — Vassalli must be turning in his grave!

One man, one man alone, saw through the British policy at its very inception: Fortunato Mizzi — clearly the greatest politician Malta has ever produced. He realised and recoiled in horror at the cultural catastrophe the British were callously inculcating on our people. In the 1880s Mizzi used to defy them, openly and without fear. He struggled unceasingly, till his death in 1905, for Maltese self-rule, and in the defence of Italian culture and language. He risked exile (his son Nerico Mizzi was exiled during World War II — later to return and become Prime Minister). Directly defying British designs, Fortunato Mizzi had the courage to define as 'the curse of our people' the limited, rasping, Arabic-based Maltese language.

Clearly, it was the British who were the chief culprits for the infusion of our Arabic, low-culture language amongst our guileless people. And why? Well, as Bonham Carter himself admitted, the Italians were making inroads here.

Italian influence was gaining prestige in Malta. Umberto Primo School was an elite institution. Scholarships were offered to Italy, while smartly dressed Italian teachers were increasingly visiting the island. The *Casino Maltese* was, and still is, the top gentlemen's club: '*Presto vediamo sventolar il tricolor dal balcone*' ('We shall soon see the tricolour flying from the club's balcony'). In short, Fascism loomed across the waters and it was necessary for the British to distract, dazzle the Maltese with something that kept Italians out. It was important to find a red herring, and the British, old players at this game, sprung the Maltese language, white rabbit from their top hat! — How we applauded!

Why EUROPA Needs MELITA

Now, on the verge of joining Europe as full members, we Maltese have to discover our true identity: our latent European identity. Our forefathers fought the bloodiest siege in history to remain Europeans. Not one single Maltese changed sides and joined the Arabs, though they could have done and gained great favours. After that epic siege, the Maltese victors consecrated this island of Melita to Europe. They were ready to shed their blood, give their lives so that their progeny remain European — for all time.

Europe beckons us. We must shed the folly of the past forty years since Independence and go back to basics. We simply have to *be* ourselves.

Europe wants us not for any military, strategic advantage it may gain. Europeans want us in their fold because they know of the possible score or more buried temples that lie as yet undiscovered. Europe is conscious of the Spiritual power embedded in this Sacred Isle. Europe knows it lacks a soul, and that only a Spiritual focal point can infuse it with one.

After Charlemagne, the two great Supermen that Europe brought forward — Napoleon and the Hero — both spoke highly of Malta. Napoleon Bonaparte on his deathbed stated: 'Who but myself has ever conquered Malta?' They were practically his dying words.

And in 1942, the Hero told Goebbels: 'With the Maltese, we are not dealing with the usual Semitic people. These are the direct descendants of Hannibal — and Mussolini can have anything he wants: Nice, Corsica, Cyprus, Crete, Tunis, Egypt, the Sudan, anything — but not Malta! That island I want for myself. I want to retire there and spend the last years of my life on that Sacred Island' (archived at the Golders Green Library, London; as reported by Mr. Dougall, BBC correspondent to Malta).

THE REAL ANSWER

The urgent need for the White Man today, be he Swede, German, Russian, Spaniard, Greek or Italian, is to band together — or else risk disappearing from the history books. We are too few, too scattered, to permit ourselves the luxury of divisiveness, ethnic exclusivity, ethnocentricity by a minority of a minority, inter-Aryan rivalry or worse, feuds and fratricides.

The four European cousins: the Anglo-Saxons, Teutons, Slavs and Latins can together form the mightiest Imperium ever seen on earth. An *IMPERIUM EUROPA* on a planetary basis that would ensure the survival of the Europid. Once the Imperium is in place, then we may proceed with a eugenics programme, a judicious mixture amongst the cousin Europid, sub-races. This can only fortify the Europid race as a whole.

One should remember that, just a few centuries ago, the Ottomans reached the gates of Vienna, and that the Arabs overran Spain and large tracts of France. One should remember that, should the Europids of the Mediterranean Northern Littoral become separated from the rest of the White World, it would be only a matter of time before we would all be submerged and perish piecemeal.

MELITA — SPIRITUAL CENTRE

Malta, this jewel in the centre of the Mediterranean, *Mare Nostrum*, will become the Spiritual, mystical Mecca for the Aryan. Our pre-historic sacred sites, Neolithic temples, medieval bastions, at once awesome and inspiring, will be the destination for millions of discerning Aryans, yearning to discover their genetic and Spiritual roots. Yes, we Maltese will be the guardians and curators of these unique, sacred sites on behalf of the Imperium. We will defend them with our lives.

Of course, the population would need to be drastically reduced. This island was never meant to accommodate 400,000 people. The maximum ideal number would be 200,000 — a high quality people raised through a eugenics programme. The very low IQs would not be permitted to breed, while high IQ persons would be encouraged to sire at least three children.

Euthanasia, as practised by the pre-Dorics, the Athenians, the Spartans and the Romans, would again become a natural and normal process in eliminating the weak, the bungled and the botched. These would get progressively fewer as the genetically defective become bred out over a few generations. We have to move on, beyond two thousand years of morbid, Christian-Catholic cretinism.

Every single building on the island post-dating 1800 will be razed to the ground. Olives and rubble walls will again cover the island. The Three Cities, Mdina and Valletta and one revolving, Sky-High city, will be quite enough to comfortably house our population. Solar and wind energy will ensure our needs, while an underground transport system will girdle the island. Not one single vehicle will be allowed to pollute this Sacred Island.

The manufacturing base, except for the most specialised and sophisticated of niches, would be gradually eliminated. Our quality population would move up the notch to a cultural-oriented way of life. This would include both workplace and leisure time.

Endemic fauna and flora will again thrive: giant owls, ferrets, the wild rabbit. The unique and exceedingly rare, Maltese ox and the wild boar will again be introduced in the wild.

Only tourists of the highest quality would be permitted to set foot on our Sacred Soil. The whole island would be listed as an Imperium heritage area.

One huge university, drawing students from all over the Imperium, would serve as an intellectual magnet for the Elite, High-Culture Bearers, specialising solely in the Spiritual origins of the Europids. They would study the scores of temples buried under tons of concrete that forty years of 'progress' have dumped on our tremendous past. Special submarines would serve as moving observatories of the other, numerous temples, submerged offshore around our beaches and cliffs. Indeed, Malta would become the focal point, the Spiritual apex of the coming *IMPERIUM EU-ROPA*.

Tarxien Temples, Malta, the original world centre of the Cult of Great Mother, the progenitors of whom are the two virgins, both from Ephesus, Diana and Mary. The huge Mother Goddess statue, representing the central role of the all-powerful Mother-Mother Earth-Yin.

Mnajdra, Skorba, Xemxija (*Shem-shi-sunny*), and our other magnificent temples, all facing South-East; so precisely aligned to the penetrating rays of the rising sun at the winter solstice, they bear testimony to the previous 'Solar' veneration of our Aryan forefathers — Yan.

Melita — the future centre for an authentic, nature-oriented belief for the Europid. The fundamental importance of a high White birth-rate of healthy, intelligent Europids; explorers, astronauts, adventurers.

COSMOTHEISM

A Spiritual outlook on politics, government, Imperium, life; a mysticism, a new Belief; Divine Guidance for the White Race. For we are an expression of Cosmic Forces. The Earth has a skin, and its antenna, its sensory organ is Man. The White Man, the Europid, as the Earth's attunement to the Cosmos.

A Creed in conformity to Nature. Man viewed as a functioning aspect of the Cosmos in its great, eternal rotational process of growth and decay. A continuous cycle of death and birth.

A transformation, whereby the decomposition of one life-form results in the composition of new forms of life — and the beginning of a new cycle. Man, originating from the soil and its atmosphere which is part of him — and to which he returns in a never-ending cycle of life.

A Cosmic conception of Man. His struggle for ever higher forms of being, of identity. His courage against adversity, his self-overcoming and a higher form of happiness and fulfilment. An ascendancy towards ever higher forms of existence, ever higher forms of life. A galactic quest to the furthest reaches of the universe — till we come face to face with Godhood: and finally, fully realise ourselves!

A Creed propounding an Organic State with a Racial outlook of the body, mind and spirit. The Sacred Gene Pool — the kernel of our CREDO.

Malta will be to the Imperium what the Easter Islands were to the pre-Colombians: a Sacred Space, a spot, an island beyond the horizon to where the Europid would do pilgrimage and discover his Spiritual roots. Where each of us will discover that primordial, pre-Christian, pagan purity, potentiating our predecessors. A purity profaned and polluted through two thousand Christmases.

An *IMPERIUM EUROPA* based on Spiritual, Aristocratic, Elitist principles is the only way for survival for the whole Aryan race. Melita as a Spiritual Centre for the Imperium — Melita as the Spiritual focal-point for the Europid Race—attuned to the Cosmos. Melita, as Mecca for the coming, inevitable, unstoppable: *IMPERIUM EUROPA*!

MAGNA EUROPA EST PATRIA NOSTRA!!
IMPERIUM
0306

ADDENDUM

I have decided to include Bonham Carter's Confidential Memorandum. I consider it revealing of British policy just before WWII: completely Thalassocratic.

See illustration 2 http://www.imperium-europa.org/thebook

CONFIDENTIAL ADDRESS BY H. E. THE GOVERNOR TO THE OFFICERS OF UNITS ARRIVING IN MALTA

Malta was in the occupation of the Knights of the Order of St. John from 1530 till 1798. During that time they combined the two duties of the Order, which were firstly to oppose the Turkish Fleet and to suppress the activities of the Barbary pirates from Algiers, Tunis, and elsewhere, and secondly to act as Hospitallers. They were far from considerate masters of the Maltese.

On the 12th June, 1798, Napoleon on his way to Egypt captured Malta and turned out the Knights. After spending an active week here tightening his hold on the Island and gathering loot, he left on the 16th June and passed on to Egypt, leaving a garrison in the Island. There he met his first severe check at the battle of the Nile on the 1st August, and lost all his loot at the same time, the *Orient* sinking with two million pounds worth of valuables from Malta in Aboukir Bay.

Naturally the importance of Malta as a harbour, easily defended, and as an admirable base for ships of war, from which the Mediterranean Sea could be dominated, was realised in England as well as in France, so that when, not long after Napoleon left, the Islanders rose against the French, they received some support, chiefly in the form of moral encouragement, from the British.

The French were driven into Valletta and there besieged. Though contributions of arms and food were arranged for by Nelson it was not until February, 1800, that any serious contribution was made by the British to the strength of the besieging force when 12,000 British troops were landed. Most of the work of the siege, therefore, was carried out by the Maltese themselves. On the 5th September 1800, the French capitulated and the island was handed over the British Commander, Major-general Pigott.

By the Treaty of Amiens, March 1802, Malta and Gozo were to be restored to the knights, but they were never handed over as it soon became clear that peace would not last long. In fact, in May, 1803, war broke out once more between England and France. After the end of the Napoleonic wars it was not unnatural that the British Government should be unwilling to take the risk of releasing their hold on the island. The Islanders themselves were also anxious to retain their new protectors. If you will look at the Latin inscription over the Main Guard in the Palace Square you will see that it says: — *'Magnae et Invictae Britannicae Melitensium Amor et Europae Vox Has Insulas Confirmat. AD 1814,'* which by very free interpretation means; — *'To Great Britain, unsubdued, these islands where entrusted by the powers of Europe at the wish of the Maltese themselves, AD 1814.'*

I am not going to give any more history because what I have told you already will illustrate to you the two points I wish to make. One is that we British have been responsible for the government of Malta for 137 years, and secondly, that we have never conquered Malta.

The Maltese are a European race, probably of Phoenician origin; their language is Semitic and the root-forms are very like those of Arabic. Their origin is similar to that of the inhabitants of other countries of Southern Europe, who in ages past were overcome by the migrations from the East. I was told by a great scholar that he thought that the Maltese language was probably as near that spoken by Hannibal as any now existing.

The record of our Government of Malta can scarcely be called one of our greatest achievements. We have regarded Malta as an important Naval base and Fortress in the first place, and have sometimes forgotten that we owed to its people something more than only peace and protection.

In the 19th century it was accepted principle of all British Governments that there should be as little interference as possible with the private lives and activities of their citizens. They considered it their duty to follow rather than lead public opinion. As a result, in Malta social services became backward. Since then much has been done, but much remains to be done. As an instance at the present time we are educating only 27,000 of 44,000 children of school age, and I could mention others. Our Government of Malta for 137 years has always shown sympathy but has lacked of imagination. Our personal conduct has frequently lacked both.

When I first came here and was trying to learn as much about the island as I could in a very short time. I sent for a very able Maltese civil servant, a man of remarkable attainments and character, and was discussing his race with him, and he said: 'You will often find it difficult to get our true opinions — we all of us suffer from an inferiority complex.' I asked him why, and he said; 'There are two reasons: first, if you ask us to give our opinion on a subject of which Malta gives us little experience we are naturally somewhat diffident; secondly, we are never certain that we are going to be treated with courtesy.'

The Commanding Officer of a Battalion that was here during the time when our differences with Italy were acute, gave me, at my request, his views on the situation in Malta. He wrote: — from the very start I have been tremendously impressed by the charm and friendliness of the Maltese and their loyalty to the King and Empire, but there was a characteristic that at first I did not understand; I now realise that it is diffidence and lack of self-assurance, and I feel convinced that it has been fostered by the attitude of many British people towards the Maltese in the past, and that is only by the development of the change in this attitude that is being encouraged now and is already showing good results, that the Maltese will become enthusiastically British. A few nights ago it was forcibly brought home to me what extent this inferiority complex has been caused by us even among the best-born Maltese. A charming Maltese lady unburdened herself to me on the subject and obviously felt that no Maltese were ever treated as equal by the British in Malta. She told me quite openly that not only had she been frequently rebuffed by British, but had actually been insulted.

It is partly the lack of manners by British men and woman that contributed to the very serious situation that existed here some two years ago or more ago. You will remember that in 1935 there was great hostility in the minds if the Italians against us owing to the application of sanctions by the League of Nations; and it became clear that during the preceding few years it had been possible for the Italians to make inroads on the good feeling of the Maltese towards us by propaganda. The mass of the people, probably 99%, or even more, were always loyal, but there was a small group, infinitesimal in numbers but noisy and active, who were definitely pro-Italian politically, and a considerable number of others who were feeling that after all Great Britain was not altogether such a pleasant master and was not worth active support if it entailed discomfort. That situation came about far more as a result of the bad manners of the British than any other reason, and I can assure you that if we had given the Maltese more sympathy and understanding, even from motives of good breeding and courtesy only, the fortress would be stronger from a defensive point of view.

We have every reason to be proud of our race, and while that might rightly give us self-confidence, it should never make us domineering. I can assure you that evil results of rudeness, or even more thoughtless lack of considerations, by members of the British community, both in their social life and their dealings with shopkeepers, working people and others in similar positions, have been very serious.

Let me give you one small example of what I call thoughtless lack of consideration. It is common failing of English people to refer to the Maltese as 'Malts'. This term is regarded rightly by the Maltese as contemptuous, and I urge you never to use it. Why hurt unnecessarily the feelings of our fellow-subjects and thereby incidentally do an injury to the Empire?

It is not difficult to suggest reasons for the attitude so often taken up by British Officers of all services, and their wives, in the past. The first cause of all is that most of us are terribly ignorant about Malta and many of us do not trouble to learn. May I urge you therefore, to take an interest in the history of Malta and in the treasures it contains. Much can be learnt from guide books, but to those who care to read more deeply, Sir Themistocles Zammit's *Malta* is the best general work, and there are others. Another cause is that we officers have so often adopted in Malta the same attitude towards its people that we do in other colonies and military stations. In practically all other colonies the inhabitants are coloured and non-Christian, so that social intercourse with them is often difficult and sometimes impossible.

It is worth remembering, however, that in India our lack of manners did much to foster and strengthen the political agitations of past years. Some of the most violent anti-British agitators in India, took the first step in their

careers as such owing to some slight or rudeness by British officers. Zaghlul
Pasha in Egypt began his political careers as pro-British and as the friend of
Cromer.

In Malta no such excuse can be urged. Malta is, for all practical purposes,
the only colony in the British Empire in which the inhabitants are European, for one quarter of the people of Cyprus are Turkish; the inhabitants of
Gibraltar are Spaniards, but their position in relation to us is somewhat different; and the Falkland Islands are unimportant as having a population of
only 2,500. There are no others. As regards language, Maltese is the ordinary
tongue of all classes, but the educated classes, with practically no exceptions,
now also speak English. There is, therefore, now no difficulty of language in
social intercourse.

When you meet the Maltese you will find them to be friendly and easy to
get on with. I urge you to take every opportunity to make friends with them.
Naturally you will not get a great number of opportunities of meeting them to
start with, but a good many will call on your mess — and among the officers
of the Royal Malta Artillery and of the King's Own Malta Regiment, which is
a Territorial unit, you will meet many very pleasant men and keen soldiers.

It is of enormous importance to the Empire that Malta should never be in
danger of capture by an enemy.

If we were to fail to hold Malta, our position on the Suez Canal and in
Egypt would be precarious, we should probably lose the Sudan and have to
withdraw from Palestine, if it were possible. I am convinced that a failure to
hold Malta would mean the end of the British Empire.

If all the Maltese were British in feeling, not only from self-interest but
also from devotion to British institutions and affection for the British people,
as indeed a great number are, one danger would be removed permanently.
There would be no fear for the spread of Italian influence in the island and
Italian propaganda would lose all power.

The Maltese would soon become aggressively British if our Government
and those of the Dominions were to treat them exactly in the same way as we
treat each other, in fact, as in every way our equals, and if friendships between
ourselves and them were more common.

So I urge you all (including your wives) to guard your tongues and watch
your manners and to let us make some amends now and repair the evil which
our predecessors in Malta have wrought by a racial exclusiveness that did

much harm. If you do so, I am sure, that your advances are met more than half-way, you will make pleasant friends and acquaintances, and you will be doing a service of great value to the Empire. I can assure you that there is no people more responsive to friendliness than the Maltese.

CHARLES BONHAM-CARTER

VI

POLITICS
ARE
OFF-CENTRE

At the lowest level, people talk about other people. At the medium level, people review current affairs and events. At the highest level people discuss Ideas.

— LAO TSU

LAO TSU LEFT THE EMPEROR'S court and lived as a hermit away on the fringes of the empire. He happily fished by the riverside every day. When the Emperor sent two emissaries to call him back to ministerial duty, Lao Tsu replied: 'Go and tell the Emperor that I cannot possibly come back to the Imperial Court, I am so busy — I am watching the turtles grow older!'

When the furious Emperor again sent his messengers, this time with a warning that should he refuse, they would have to bring Lao Tsu's head back with them, the sage simply bent forward and uncovered his neck, ready to die. Such was Lao Tsu's revulsion for Politics — he had had enough of it.

THE THREE LEVELS

The realm of Spirituality, the highest level, is the realm of Ideas. The world of all High-Culture Bearers: the world of Aristotle, Plato, Goethe, Mozart, Nietzsche, Wagner and the other torch-bearers of our race.

Then come High-Politics: Alexander, Charlemagne, Napoleon — and, I would include, the Hero. All these personages had an element of the Spiritual within them, but were shackled, impeded by the world of current events. They were burdened and slowed down in the implementation of their Vision by the middle level of current affairs: the Economic, Financial and Social level.

Here, at this middle level, successful businessmen, idolised and projected as heroes, hammer out an ever increasing array of goods, at maximum efficiency. The aim is one: maximising production. Time and motion, economies of scale, constant rationalisation is the world they live in. They are the dwarfs of the underworld, the blacksmiths in Wagner's opera, hammering out their glorified junk in a cacophony of shrill sounds and deafening noise.

DER UNTERGANG

At the very end of his life, on the brink of defeat, it is to Speer the artist that the Hero turns. He tells him: 'Speer, I am sick of politics. I do not want to make politics any more.' They both admire a scale-model of the Berlin they had planned together. Hitler the artist reminisces about his dreams for the Germania he had in mind: splendid cathedrals, monuments, Parthenon and Pantheon. 'It is not only with skyscrapers and shops that the people live.' The Hero's heart craved for the Artist within him, for the Spiritual. — Like Lao Tsu, he had had enough of politics.

ART OR POLITICS

The eternal question: art or politics — which comes first? Within the bowels of the Lascaux caves lie wall-paintings that are as fresh and dynamic as any of Picasso's works. These were painted 16,000 years ago — and where was politics to be found then?

Clearly, Art comes before politics. And rightly so, since it is Art that fills that craving within us for the Spiritual. That void that no amount of politics, economics or finance can ever hope to satiate. It is Art that serves as the final bridge towards the ephemeral, the Spiritual.

And this is the Rubicon that each of us, especially the artists amongst us, must cross. Those few free spirits seeking the highest spiritual level of self-realisation. This is their gravest problem, their dilemma: To leave the world of art and creativity and wade into the dung heap that is local politics. And after that sordid battle is won and the decision taken, to then take up the fight with the hidden enemy at the world level.

This is the decision that the most creative, sensitive, honest amongst us must take. For politics throws the individual off-centre. He loses his rootedness, his purity of mind, his life of frugality and fulfilment. From the highest level, that of Spirituality, the individualist must by necessity descend into the world of petty politics, economics and day-to-day affairs.

It is only after the battle for power at the planetary level is won, that there will be a fusion between Spirituality and High-Politics. For at that level, the two will converge and become one. Within our *Imperium Europa*, the Elite of Supermen will elevate High-Politics to Art, to Spirituality. The three will become one: a Trinity of the Divine!

For now, at this stage of the fight, the Artist has to hold his nose and wade into a pool of slime. This is the ultimate sacrifice for every

Artist: to leave Art and enter the political arena. Yes, this is the supreme decision each one of us has to take in his innermost self — for, politics is off-centre.

IMPERIUM

0504

VII

RACE NATION STATE

THERE IS A LOT OF confusion in the minds of the common people regarding the concepts of Race, Nation and State. The three are indiscriminately used and abused, lumped together with no precise understanding of their true definition and delineation. Our opponents use this confusion to their own ends and, of course, muddy the waters still further in their pursuit of the destruction of races and peoples. Knowledge of the true meaning of the three concepts is therefore fundamental in our fight for survival.

RACE

The human species — *Homo sapiens sapiens* — is sub-divided into six major races. These are Europids, Mongolids, Indianids, Negrids, Khoisanids and Australasids. In turn each race is divided into many subraces; mixed groups also exist. It is essential to emphasise that, as distinct from species (i.e. horse/donkey), races and subraces are interfertile in their natural state; in other words, members of two different races can produce fertile offspring. It is this fact that leads so many to confuse the issue and claim, quite erroneously, that the differences between the races are only skin deep.

Ironically, colour variations, although the most visible, are not in themselves the most important criteria in determining variability amongst the various races. In fact they are among the least important, and the most truly 'skin deep', of differences. Skin pigmentation is determined by the activity of melanin present in skin tissue. Skin colour evolved over the ages as a protective measure. In hot climates dark skin affords essential protection from ultra-violet radiation present in sunlight. In cold climates, pale skin permits absorption of the sun's rays and favours the accumulation of vitamin D, thus preventing rickets.

Believers in racial equality are either unaware of or else completely ignore the truly astonishing number of scientifically catalogued physical differences between one race and another. These differences range from the glaringly obvious — like odour, shape of skull, facial features, size and shape of genitalia — to the microscopic — like blood groupings and susceptibility of certain races or subraces to certain diseases.

A few examples will suffice. The primitive characteristics of the Australasids skulls set them apart from all other races. Their long muzzle and small brain-case is distinctly pongid, while the overall shape of the skull — wide below, narrow at the top — is reminiscent of that of *Homo habilis*, one of man's early ancestors.

Another pongid feature are the teeth, which do not overlap but snap together. The nose, like that of the orangutan, is flat and wide. Significantly, the brain weight is 85 percent of that of Europids, while the brain gyres are less tortuous, and the sutures the simplest of all the Races.

The Khoisanids consist of two subgroups, the Hottentots and the Sanids, better known as Bushmen. Both subraces display unique physical features. The Sanids, for example, retain paedomorphic (juvenile) features into adulthood. The skull is infantile in shape while the hair is aggregated naturally in tufts. The legs are very short in proportion to the trunk, and the female buttocks are enormous and of a strange form. The genitalia of both male and female are also unique. The male penis maintains a horizontal posture in its flaccid state, while the female labia minora are enormously lengthened, somewhat resembling the penis.

Another important distinction between the races is odour. The difference is most pronounced between Negrids and Europids. The former can distinguish Whites by their aroma alone, while to the latter, Negrids have a fetid smell. Both smell strongly to a Mongolid. Body odour is mostly produced by so-called auxiliary glands (A-glands), situated in the anal-genital area and on the armpits. In the case of the aborigine, A-glands are also found in front of the ear. Body odour is almost completely absent in the Mongolid races. The Japanese have it only to a small degree, while the Ainuids in their midst, being partly Europids, smell strongly to them.

It is no accident that both men and women of the same race produce the same odour — and that within the same race this odour has a sexually alluring effect. Between different races it has the opposite effect and acts as a deterrent to miscegenation.

Another difference which can be of importance in distinguishing the races is their relative susceptibility to certain diseases. It is now becoming increasingly obvious that the Negrid Race is the most vulnerable to AIDS. American Columnist Fred Reed recently reported that responsible medical men in the Pentagon put the figure of AIDS infection at 30 percent for soldiers in Zambia and Zaire — and as high as 50 percent to 80 percent for the Zimbabwean army.

Enrique Jose Zelaya, chief epidemiologist for the Honduran Ministry of Health, stated that the geometric rate of progression for AIDS in his country will likely cause the 182 reported active cases in October 1988 to balloon up to 14,000 in three years.

Dr. Robert Remis, epidemiologist at the Montreal General Hospital, notes that the city's large Haitan community has a far higher rate of active AIDS than the rest of the population. As of May 1989, 116 Haitian natives in Quebec province had come down with the disease. Back in their mother country, Haitian AIDS figures are around 6,000 cases per million, with vastly more still in the dormant phase.[1]

Likewise Jews, which of their own admission form a distinct racial group, are prone to some 102 inherited diseases which affect them much

---

1   Since Mr. Lowell wrote this article, the HIV infection rate has vastly increased among Blacks: In Haiti it is now six per cent., or ten times what it was in the early 1990s — D.S.

more frequently than non-Jews. This is amply recorded in a massive 494 page-study 'Genetic Disorders Among The Jewish People' by Dr. Richard Goodman, at John Hopkins University in Baltimore. He is now professor of genetics at Tel Aviv University School of Medicine.

Prof. Goodman states that Ashkenazi Jews, who make up 82 percent of world Jewry, and Sephardic Jews, who make up the remaining 18 percent, suffer from such hereditary diseases as Abetali-poproteinemia (failure to grow), Bloom syndrome (dwarfism), Familial Dysautonomia (affects strictly Jews and results in instability and slurred speech; it is carried by 18 out of every 1000 Jews), and of course, Tay-Sachs which is the best-known Jewish disease.

This last is so prevalent amongst this racial group that Jewish couples are urged to take a test before marriage to insure that they are not carriers. Symptoms start to show after six months of age, and by eighteen months the victim becomes blind and unable to hold up his head. The skull becomes enlarged and the hands become pudgy. Over 90 percent of Tay-Sachs victims worldwide are Jews.

It is noteworthy that there is not one hereditary disease that affects exclusively the Europid race.

Again one is reminded of the findings of Dr. V Wyatt, an expert on poliomyelitis, as reported in the *Times of Malta* for 23 July, 1982. Dr. Wyatt found that although the climate in Malta was similar to that of the Middle East, the disease affected its Maltese victims in the same way as it affected Europeans and North Americans. These symptoms were quite different from the symptoms found in Middle Eastern and African patients.

The world of sport also provides a glaring example of racial differences. All competitors are supposed to have an equal chance of winning, but in reality specific subspecies do best at different games or events. Thus the long-legged Dinarids, with their slim bodies, dominate the high jump. Europids, with Nordics at the forefront, dominate the heavy field-events like putting the shot, throwing the discus, the hammer, or the javelin. They also excel at swimming, not to mention Grand Prix car racing, with its demand for lightning-quick reflexes.

Running is a sport that is of great interest in the racial context. The marathon and other long distance races, with their demand for stamina, are the preserve of Europids and Ethiopids (think of Kenyan domination in long-distance events). The shorter events generally fall to the Negrids. Thus, in the 1984 Olympics, the most successful 'British', 'French', and 'Canadian' competitors in these events were all Negroes!

It is to be noted that the Japanese, who are by no means unsuccessful at sports in which tallness is not important, have never won any medal for high jumping or running at the Olympic games. Their genetically determined small stature precludes such success.

The even smaller stature of the African pygmy has made him invisible at the Olympic games as they are currently held. However, were a track event to be included in which the contestants would have to crawl through long narrow pipes, then the pygmy's day in the sun would finally have arrived!

One hesitates to term as a sport so intellectual a pursuit as chess. It is, however, a game in which all contestants start off as 'equals'. One has yet to hear of a Negro grandmaster. The game is completely dominated by Jews and Europids.

It is clear that significant differences between the various races of men do in fact exist. These differences are obviously due to genetic factors. Science has also shown that variations in intelligence between individuals are also mainly due to such genetic factors.

Is it therefore unreasonable to ask how it could ever be possible that any two races could be exactly the same in all the genes that affect intelligence and the nervous and sensory system, yet so different from one another in other structural characteristics?

Not only is it not unreasonable, but it is glaringly obvious, to all but 'equality' bigots, that races are as different from one another mentally as they are physically. Logic makes this conclusion inescapable: the facts devastatingly prove it.

NATION

Nation is 'flesh and blood'. It is people. It is a common consciousness of an identity. A consciousness of a people's characteristics. Nation is language, culture, customs, religion. It is common perceptions, fears, and phobias. A common identification of who is the common enemy, or perceived friend. Nation is the knowledge of a common history and a common yearning for a common destiny.

A cat born in a stable is not a horse. Thus a birth certificate does not make a Nigerian Negroid a German, a Frenchman, or a Maltese. Race determines everything. Nations are the various subdivisions of the race.

Thus, in simple language: Germans, Frenchmen, British, the Swedes, and the Russians are all nations within the White race. Within these nations are further subdivisions: In Britain there are the Scots, the Irish, and the Welsh. In Spain the Catalunyans, the Basques, and others. In France the Bretons, the Germans, Italians, and the Cottienniese. There are the Tyrolese, the Ticini, Italian minorities in Istria, Dalmatia, and even in the Ukraine. The Balkans are a myriad of various sub-nations all living cheek by jowl, mostly in animosity amongst themselves: a tragedy.

STATE

State is the juridical set-up of a nation. It is law, civil service, army, police, etc. State is a completely different entity from either race or nation. The U.S. government is a glaring example of a state representing neither the race nor the people. It is a government-juridical system taken over, hijacked, by a pernicious minority of aliens. These enemies of the White race, through their hold on the state government apparatus, thus control all the various branches that make up the state. They can bamboozle the captive population, composed of various nationalities and races that make up the USA, and march them off to war — whenever it suits their purposes.

Imperium Europa

That is why we have been divided for so long. Nation versus nation, state against state, sub-nation opposed to sub-nation and other configurations of all these; a tragedy for the White race. A continuous fratricide. A spilling of precious blood of this small minority of biological aristocrats, spread so thinly amongst the billions of the Third World. Not only that, but the breeding of these aliens within our midst, our heartlands: White women cohabiting with primitive Blacks; a planetary dysgenic disaster. Why?

Because our enemies cleverly interplay the three concepts: Race-Nation-State. They have confused us as to their real definition and delineation, to the point that Blacks play football for Britain and Germany, represent France and Sweden at the Olympic games, and so on. Yes, oh yes, our people are confused!

Only the vision, the *IDEA* of *Imperium Europa* can save the White race. Only this unifying *IDEA* can solve the riddle of Race-Nation-State. An Imperium, acting as a state on a planetary scale, encapsulating the various nations and sub-nations of the White race. Nations and sub-nations, cousins living in harmony with each other, conscious of a common history and destiny.

Magna Europa Est Patria Nostra!
Imperium
0411

VIII

THE THREAT
OF
GLOBALISATION

Millions of Television viewers around the world watched with amazement the Genoa riots by thousands of seemingly idealistic youths. The message that came across from the world's controlled media was that these youngsters were protesting against the G8 and Globalisation — in favour of the oppressed and downtrodden of the Third World.

In another part of the world, the Seattle Youngsters, as they were called, screamed their demands to the world's leaders:

Abolition of debts owed by the poor countries of the world, billions of dollars, loaned by banks, owned by shareholders, all of us, who will have to forsake our earnings and further investment. In a nutshell: money down the drain.

Investment of billions of dollars to stop the spread of AIDS — so that the world's poor nations can carry on with their feckless fecundity and then demand more aid of us, more loans to prop them up. And of course, further abolition of these future debts.

The opening of our borders to the burgeoning billions because 'the world is big enough for all of us'. And once we open our borders, the automatic right of immigrants to free hospitalisation, schools, jobs, welfare and everything we Europeans have worked for and achieved, in our battle for survival and evolution.

The whole thrust of these demanding demonstrators was that Globalisation is a sinister tool employed by the rich nations, namely White countries of Europid stock, against the poorer populations of the world. Nothing could be further from the truth.

THE THREAT

Globalisation aims at the gradual, total liberalisation of the market on a global level. The freedom of Movement of Labour on a world scale. This means that Labour will soon become a commodity as any other: tomatoes, steel and computers. Labour would become expendable, to be bought and sold, disposed and acquired, hired and fired at will — as the propriety of the market demands. *Il mercato del lavoro.*

This obviously presents a threat to the best-paid, best-qualified persons on the planet, in whatever field they may operate. More, planetary liberalisation of movement of Labour and Capital, added to the liberalisation of Labour Laws, would mean a lowering of wages, salaries and standards, as capital and productive means move to less demanding areas of the globe.

At the same time Liberalisation would induce a massive immigration by the have-nots into the Europid nations. Such immigration would bring direct labour competition, forcing down the wages and standards of the Europids. Eventually, it would mean massive unemployment of Whites.

Socially, all the above would turn into a racial time bomb which would make Oldham, Bradford and Liege seem but minor riots. More awesome yet is the genetic catastrophe which the inevitable miscegenation with the immigrants would bring about.

It is obvious from the above that the real threat of Globalisation is not directed at the poor, downtrodden nations of the world. The threat, and a very real one, is directly against us: the Europids — that biological aristocracy of the planet. That minority of five percent of the world's population that has given humanity everything it now enjoys. The threat is nothing less than the physical elimination of the White Race.

Cui Bono? Who gains from all this? Who gains from all this confusion and chaos? Who is behind the wilful destruction of the highest civilisation ever to grace this planet and graze the moon? What is there to gain from the lowering down of standards, wages and the very rule of law?

Well, as Disraeli himself once said, 'The world is ruled by unseen hands. The politicians we see strutting about on the world stage are but passing stooges, puppets in the hands of immensely powerful clans, who are in power not for a mere four-year democratic term, but for generations.'

The world's leaders we saw wining and dining at Genoa are mere passing politicians. Small fries doing the bidding of those behind them: the plutocrats. — Those international-manipulators whose dream is a one-world government with themselves lording over a multiracial, planetary mess. A tiny group of plutocrats would become master of the planet — picking and choosing the right Labour for the right job wherever it suits them — paying the very minimum wage which cut-throat competition will permit them to impose.

A group with a burning sense of mission for world power. — An incredible disdain for the rest of humanity: a humanity reduced to a world population of rootless, obedient slaves with no sense of ethnic identity, squabbling amongst themselves and ruled through the incessant filth of the media. Lemmings, couch-potatoes with no mind of their own, ready to acquiesce, to sink ever lower: to procreate, consume, and obey.

In this regard, it is noteworthy that the world's media, controlled by the international-manipulators, racially exclusive and ethnocentric themselves, pushes miscegenation both in the entertainment field as well as in the news. The targets are young White women who are induced to cohabit with Blacks. White male youths are deracinated, morally disarmed of their ethnic and racial pride.

Mixed couples are made to look 'cool'; they are doing the 'in thing'. Crime by Blacks on Whites, statistically overwhelming wherever the two races live together, is covered up or downplayed. White crimes on Blacks, though few, are exaggerated and overplayed. Whites are made to look cruel, callous, stupid and mean in the media, while Blacks are portrayed as heroes, victims, and role models.

Throughout the news, the tribe, who form the majority of the international-manipulators, are portrayed as oppressed, a long-suffering people to whom the world owes an eternal debt. Palestinians are 'terrorists' who must be hunted down and exterminated — even if this should mean a real holocaust of six million Palestinians.

THE SMOKESCREEN

The smokescreen for this sinister plan are the Third World — Famine — The World's Poor — Debt by Poor Nations — AIDS — Racism of Whites towards Blacks.

A close look at the front-row demonstrators on TV, the ring-leaders, reveals that the Seattle Suckers protesting against the G8 are led by young, vicious and venomous members of that same international tribe, the usual mischief-makers, acting as Judas goats. In Italy, it was the same, with Casarini (Khazars) inciting youths, calling out for war.

For those of us who remember, it was just the same in the USA in the sixties. Then, the smokescreen was the Vietnam War, and the terrorist organisation at that time was the Weatherman Underground Movement. Its members planted bombs all over the USA killing dozens of innocent people. The Weatherman leadership was almost entirely tribal — all rich members of the tribe, young university graduates with affluent parents living in exclusive suburbs. A case in point was Dohrn, convicted for twenty-five bombings which killed and maimed many. Tribal Judge Suria gave Dohrn three years probation stating that 'she has already suffered much'.

Today the Seattle Dupes unwittingly aid their very enemies. Those young Suckers do not realise that it is themselves and their children who are the target of this sinister world force: this Moloch. It is they themselves who will be the first out of a job. Their children who will see their standards of living plummet to that of the Third World. The Seattle Youngsters are today's prime lemmings.

APEX OF CAPITALISM AND COMMUNISM

Two senseless World Wars: instigated, manipulated, and perpetrated by the same international-manipulators, left the Europid bled white. The emerging victorious ideologies were Liberal-Capitalism and Bolshevism, two sides of the same coin. For Liberalism, parliamentary-democracy, socialism, communism and the modern tyranny of plutocratic capitalism — ostensible enemies — have the same matrix, the same goals: anti-Hierarchy, anti-Spirit.

For today, Communism and Financial Capitalism meet at their highest point. The apex of Communism today is nothing else than the multinationals. Huge conglomerates, with an unseen, multiracial, board of directors, more often than not manipulated by one or two of the usual tribe, operating from some unreachable, hidden headquarters. And below them, far, far below them, millions of shareholders, blind as to the operations, the machinations, the goals of their all-powerful, mysterious Moloch. The quarterly document denoting the dividend keeps the millions of minions contented and quiescent. Today's multinationals are nothing else but the meeting point, the convergence, the apex of both Communism and Capitalism!

In the approaching global free market, millions of Whites will go unemployed. The first to be hit will be the best paid, and so on until the effects of globalisation finally trickle down to the very bottom of the barrel. Waves of Third Worlders will swarm in and take over our jobs, only to be replaced by even more destitute populations, till the lowest level of wages and salaries would be reached for each category of jobs.

This is already happening everywhere. In Assam, India the native population, though one of the poorest in the world is losing jobs to neighbouring Bangladeshi immigrants. The Indian police do not have the means to track the thousands crossing the frontier every week. Indian capitalists regularly corrupt the police force, which turns a blind eye. Assam Indians, jobless and in desperation, are hacking the Muslim intruders to death by the hundreds. A clear case of ethnic cleansing ignored by the controlled media.

And in Europe? Look at any high street where the butchers, the bakers, the grocer, the fishmonger, even hardware shops are hard to find. In the country areas bank branches are closing, small manufacturers can no longer compete and they go out of business. Everywhere the original inhabitants are being elbowed out by swarming immigrants, ready to work longer hours at lower wages.

SOLUTION

What is the solution then? What is the solution to the G8, to Globalisation? Simple! The answer is — Globalisation! But a Globalisation with a difference. A Globalisation of the Europid Race. A Racial globalisation! An *IMPERIUM EUROPA* on a planetary scale, uniting the four Europid cousins: the Anglo-Saxons, the Teutons, Slavs and Latins.

An Imperium reserved solely for the Europid — and nobody else! Two White rings will encircle the globe, North and South of the Equator. To the North, the Imperium will stretch from Ireland to Vladivostock. Across the Bering Strait it will join a Nova America, or Vinland, comprising Alaska, Canada and a re-dimensioned White USA.

In the South, the White Man will be the undisputed lord over White Africa, South of the Congo River and the Great Lakes. Australia and New Zealand will become a White continent reserved solely for the Europid. The sub-Amazonian White-cone, as well as the Panama Isthmus and its adjacent territories, will be the White Man's sole preserve.

Thus the Europid will control the food growing areas of the planet. This is our ultimate weapon — the White Man's ability to grow a food surplus. No other race is capable of this. The Imperium will trade food for all it needs from the rest of humanity. We will barter enough food to keep them from starving — nothing else!

Latin will be our common tongue and capitalism our economic ethos. Capitalism and Racism are not inimical. The former is our creation — we will uphold it amongst ourselves only. We will not trade or transfer our technology, the fruit of the White Man's genius, outside the Imperium.

Indeed, we will have a free market throughout the Imperium — with fair, straight competition between productive Europids. Every region will find its niche of productivity, its optimum produce. Productive man will again assume the economic high ground as against the speculative financier. We will go back to basics!

We will again adopt the Gold Standard — this time on a planetary basis. All Euro issuance will have to be backed by Gold mined from within the confines of the Imperium — or bartered for food from without. All-White South African mines and the Urals are more than enough to keep pace with the volume of currency in circulation. The price of gold will automatically and directly relate to the Gold reserves and currency. Inflation would finally cease to plague the European Man.

We will reduce our income tax to a 10 percent flat rate for everybody — without distinction as to his wealth. No tax should be more than this. For our so-called progressive taxation penalises the rising entrepreneur. Capital accumulation is impossible for him.

Meanwhile the established rich are already there. They do not need to accumulate new capital. What they need is shelter by the tax collector from competition. The established rich in our present system are the staunchest advocates of progressive taxation — for others.

Tax collection will be used to operate the Imperium: the army, the police, the regional government. It is for these purposes, and for very little else, that the Imperium will collect the 10 percent tax from all. For when a growing percentage of tax collected is used, not to operate the government, but for the express purpose of redistribution of wealth, then that is a flat rejection of the concept of freedom and private property. We will reduce government to a minimum in the Dominium sphere.

Socialism as a frame of mind will be finally extirpated. There will be no welfare in the future Imperium, no social benefits, no minimum wage, no children allowance. Nothing, but nothing will be free — except the minds of Men!

Instead there will be a steady reduction of working hours in preference to wage increases. A continual increase in technology to compensate production. And most important of all: an investment in the Lifetime Education of Europid workers, transforming them from mere productive citizens into persons! We will finally achieve that most ambitious of all goals: the reversal of productive man, *Homo economicus*, into the complete man, the Super Man!

Yes! Capitalism in a racial context within an *IMPERIUM EUROPA*. A Europe not of merchants, bankers and bureaucrats — but an *IMPERIUM EUROPA* of high, planetary politics and peoples. All the different regions and peoples of the White World. Then we can turn our full attention to harnessing nature and conquering space. We will carry the Imperium to the furthest reaches we can strive for.

Imperium

0202

IX

TWO WEIGHTS - TWO MEASURES

SOME MONTHS AGO JÖG HAIDER wrote me a letter complimenting my *CREDO: A Book for the Very Few.* I had offered him my movement's solidarity with his Freedom Party of Austria (FPÖ), then under vicious attack from the corrosive forces of world subversion. As always, under the direction of the usual mischief-makers: the international-manipulators.

In Vienna itself there were violent street demonstrations, described by police chiefs as 'unseen in Austria before' — meaning, of course, that professional street-fighters were imported from neighbouring countries especially for the purpose. Haider himself was spotted at an Italian restaurant and surrounded by a screaming mob. He would have been killed had the police not intervened in time. Such was the hatred, the atmosphere generated.

The reaction against Haider's Freedom Party was shrill, deafening, world-wide. The mass media, the politicians, the leaders of the Christian churches and the wimp-brigades, the rest of the many-too-many, all howled their worth. Even the local *Ġaħan* (village idiot) group added its little voice. Our illustrious journalists and correspondents flooded the press with letters, solemnly urging our government to recall Malta's ambassador from Vienna. Thankfully, we did not.

Some countries did — Israel first and foremost! They had done the

same years ago, when they closed their embassy here in Malta. Good riddance! We are so much better off without them.

The EU shamelessly froze diplomatic contacts with Vienna. Trade and
tourist embargoes against Austria were threatened. There were even rumours that pressure would escalate — the Milošević treatment?

And the reason? Haider had broken some taboos by making statements the international-manipulators didn't like. He had said that there
had been many decent people fighting on the German side during the
Second World War, including people in the SS. He had also said that some
of Hitler's economic policies in the 1930s had made good sense. And
worse yet in the eyes of our hidden enemies, he had called for a cut off of
immigration into Austria.

Now, Haider is not exactly an extremist. Previously, when he had been
criticised for his statements, he had apologised and back-pedalled. But,
of course, his apologies had not been enough. Nothing can ever satisfy
those pushy, insatiable, relentless enemies of ours. I had advised Haider
against ever retracting again. He replied that he would follow my advice
and would try never to apologise to anybody in the future.

This seems to have worked well for him. Vienna's mayoral election
of March 25th was a concentrated and concerted campaign against the
FPÖ, organised and orchestrated by the usual tribe, led by Ariel Muzicant. Haider's Liberal allies slyly participated in this political lynching,
while the Austrian Greens, showing the whole world how clever they are,
fielded an African! Naturally, the ones that gained from all this were the
Socialists.

Notwithstanding this barrage of vilification, Haider held his own and
the FPÖ remains Vienna's second party. It represents a solid body of Europeans who have had enough of present, party politics. We shall see more
of Haider — as President of Austria. Imagine the aria of the Musicians!

SAME TREATMENT

And a few weeks ago the same thing happened with regard to Italy. The

Belgian Government, controlled and ridden by the international-manipulators, a corrupt government accused many times of collusion with pederasts and paedophiles, stated that the Haider treatment would be meted out to Italy, should Berlusconi be elected! Why? — Simply because Alleanza Nazionale, the moderate right-wing party, forms part of Berlusconi's coalition.

Some years back, one Belgian minister, of Italian-Jewish parents, had vowed he would never shake hands with Tatarella of Alleanza Nazionale, then a minister in Berlusconi's short-lived government. Barely had a month passed, when the same 'Belgian' minister was forced to ignominiously resign. It was revealed that he had indirect links with pederasts and paedophiles associated with Dutroux, the notorious child abductor and murderer.

MASS MURDERER

Having observed all this, certainly one of the more significant things that has occurred lately was the world's reaction — or lack of it — to the election of Ariel Sharon as Israel's Prime Minister. He set upon forming a government as if nothing had happened. Now wait — who is this Ariel Sharon?

Sharon is the man who, as Israel's minister of defence in September 1982, during Israel's invasion of Lebanon, was responsible for the slaughter of more than 3,000 Palestinian women and children in the Sabra and Shatila refugee camps, just outside Beirut. The Palestinian fighters had evacuated the camps, leaving their women and children behind, after being assured by the U.S. Government of Ronald Reagan that their families would be safe.

Who can ever forget that evil smirk on Sharon's face as he peered through binoculars, relishing the devastating effect of heavy artillery on defenceless Palestinians, including women and children?

As the army moved in, radio communications among Israeli military commanders were monitored in which they talked about carrying out 'purging operations'. The attackers surrounded the camps with tanks so no one could escape. For two days they kept the camps sealed while the slaughter went on, non-stop. That was Ariel Sharon's work: more than 3,000 murdered women and children—murdered in a characteristically treacherous way, after tricking the men into leaving their families unarmed and defenceless.

But the massacre of refugees in Sabra and Shatila that gave Sharon the nickname 'Butcher of Beirut' wasn't his only work. Long before 1982, when Sharon was an Israeli army general, he was notorious for the atrocities he and his troops committed. His tactic was to sneak into an undefended Jordanian village at night with his soldiers, then go on a throat-cutting rampage.

After the reaction to his butchery in Sabra and Shatila in 1982, Sharon was obliged to resign as defence minister and leave politics for a while. But when he decided to run for prime minister last year, he prepared the way by deliberately provoking the violence and killing which have been so much in the news in recent months.

At a moment when things were already extremely tense, he marched up to Jerusalem's Temple Mount with a large contingent of armed bodyguards. These chased away Moslem worshippers and caused outrage among Palestinians. This outrage predictably erupted into stone throwing by Palestinian children, countered by shooting, in cold blood, of Palestinian civilians by Israeli soldiers. Since Barak couldn't restore order, Sharon became Prime Minister.

So, first there was Begin: an assassin and a terrorist (Irgun gang, Deir Yassin).

Then there was Shamir; a homicidal dwarf, an assassin and a terrorist (King David Hotel).

Then came Barak; an assassin in woman's clothing (Beirut).

Now there is Sharon: the fitting Prime Minister for Israel and the majority that elected him: a mass murderer!

MASS MEDIA

And where is the outrage among the politicians who were wagging their fingers at Jörg Haider a little over a year ago? Where are the sensational media stories about Sharon's criminal history? Why are the church leaders who condemned Haider's 'immoral' statements now silent?

What country is threatening to recall its ambassador or to cut off trade with Israel?

The silence is deafening. Why? — Simple! The international-manipulators control the world's media conglomerates. They own the leading newspapers, magazines, TV and radio stations. CNN is a twenty-four-hour long, non-stop litany of lies, half-truths and outright cover-ups. Just recently, a mass-murder of five Whites in Wichita by two blacks was never even mentioned. Riots in Seattle during Mardi Gras, just hours before the earthquake leading to hordes of blacks attacking, beating up, robbing and raping White women, were never covered. One White lad, Kristopher Kime, who went to the rescue of a White woman victim, was savagely beaten and killed by a bandit bunch of blacks.

At CNN, behind Turner, who is there solely for the money, there lurk the two vice-presidents; Levin, the son of a rabbi, and Eisner, a self-described 'control freak'.

In Italy, at RAI, we had Gad Lerner and paedophilia shots on prime-time news. Now we have Zaccaria as Chairman, Cappon as Chief Executive and of course, that essence of nastiness, Luttazzi of Satyricon fame. It is the same the whole world over: the same tribe of mischief-makers.

With their control of the media, the international-manipulators dictate what we think and what we talk about. They set and impose the planet's agenda. They can create a diversion, a distraction — anytime, anywhere! Hence, the Falklands, hence Iraq, Kosovo (Sharon was spotted in Macedonia incognito, one month prior to the start of hostilities in Kosovo in 1999. When asked what a war-horse like him was doing in such a sensitive spot, he replied he was 'on a peace mission'!).

Anything would do to give Israel time and build more settlements in occupied Palestine — to gain the political time it needs in order to manipulate and control U.S. presidents.

Any distraction would do to suit their plans. Hence the farce of a single Cuban boy in Miami, capturing world headlines for weeks, while savage, primitive Blacks butchered White farmers in Zimbabwe. No film-footage here, no heart-breaking scenes, just scant, perfectly neutral news-coverage. Cold announcements that 'another white farmer has died in Zimbabwe, former Rhodesia'.

The international-manipulators' hold on the world's media must be broken — and it will be broken!

Only then, can we set our own priorities for the survival of our race and our progeny.

That is why the international-manipulators and their lackeys are screaming about the Internet. It has to be censored! Not sites spilling pornography or lewdness, but sites 'inciting racism'. The Wiesenthal Center, B'nai B'rith, the World Jewish Congress (WJC), and all the other manifold front organisations are wailing and hissing that the web should be censored — with themselves as censors, naturally!

The problem for them is that they have gone too far this time — they cannot and will not turn back. It is simply their nature. The more perceptive and prescient of them see this danger and are trying to salvage the situation. Alas, it is of no avail — it is too late! History must take its inevitable course.

Why has anti-Semitism existed for thousands of years? (The term is a misnomer really since the Palestinians, the Egyptians and a host of others, are Semitic peoples.) There is no word, attributable to any other people, comparable to this planetary phobia for this tribe. There is no anti-Hindu, anti-Indian, anti-Arab, anti-Eskimo, anti-Chinese term, as there is for this unique, tiny nation scattered around the globe: anti-Semitism.

Why have nations, peoples always detested this roving group? Why have a dozen popes condemned them, expressly forbidding gentiles from marrying them? Why have nations today, in the year 2001, after half a century of incessant brainwashing and lies, again turned against them? Why is history repeating itself?

Perhaps one can comprehend this world-wide reaction and aversion to this band of wanderers by understanding, or trying to understand, what animates these intruders — why they are so implacably hostile to the rest of mankind, especially to those who accept and enrich them. One can do this by searching for and reading that little known book: the *Talmud*: it explains it all.

IMPERIUM
0103

X

NO ONE ASKS
WHY

ONE COULD NOT HELP BEING moved by the heart-rending scenes of New York on 9/11. 'Shocking', 'unbelievable', 'indescribable' were words we heard over and over again on the controlled mass-media. After that came the calls, ever insistent and strident, for retaliation. Against whom? Against an unseen enemy? Against all Muslims? Against the Arab world? Palestinians? Iraq? Who? At last, the scapegoat was found, and every piglet in the farm dug his little hoof in — bin Laden the millionaire, hiding somewhere in Afghanistan and protected by the fuzzy-wuzzies!

We watched as the media ran crowds of blood-donors, Chinese, Negroes, Mexicans and Whites, all queuing up to donate their blood in support of non-existent patients. After what happened, real casualties were few — one was either very much dead, or else alive and well. Yet the controlled-media played the blood-donation scenes for all their worth, the message being of course: look at multi-racial America, look at how the nation's blood is mixed!

The same scenes of U.S. Marines bidding wives and children goodbye, as they boarded aircraft for war, on behalf of Israel. Prolonged shots of Blacks hugging White wives and their mixed-breed offspring. The message: look how beautiful multi-racial America is, how united, patriotic multi-racial USA can be!

Talking tough was the order of the day. Every Jew on CNN, from Richard Roth and Wolf Blitzer to all the rest, slyly worked the patriotic theme. They kept pointing the accusing finger at Afghanistan. The question on everyone's lips was: Who did this to us? How can we punish them? The tribe permitted no one, but *no* one to ask the question: WHY?

Indeed, why did all this happen?

WHY?

In 1982 Israel invaded Lebanon. During their invasion and eighteen-year occupation, an estimated 40,000 civilians died. Cities and villages were relentlessly bombed, as well as many hospitals and orphanages (as documented by the Norwegian Red Cross). The once beautiful city of Beirut, the Paris of the Middle-East, was devastated.

The current Prime Minister of Israel, Ariel Sharon, does not even dare to step foot in Belgium or the Netherlands, fearing an indictment of the World Court for war crimes. Sharon the assassin, the terrorist and mass-murderer, is responsible for the slaughter of three thousand refugees, mostly women and children at the Sabra and Shatila camps.

At about the same time, Israel shot down a Libyan passenger airliner over the Sinai Peninsula, killing 111 people.

Every day grinning Israeli soldiers, indulging in target practice with live ammunition, shoot at mostly stone-throwing Palestinian children. Armoured Israeli bulldozers, continuously level Palestinian homes in their own country! Psychotic Israeli settlers, arrogantly shooting at anyone they please with total impunity and immunity! This has become 'normal TV viewing'. People watch but do not perceive. We have been numbed to this very real holocaust of the Palestinian people.

If the U.S. Government really thought it worthwhile to wipe out the governments that sponsor terrorism or harbour terrorists, the government of Israel would be the first one on its list to be cauterised. Israel has sponsored terrorism and assassination from its inception and does so to this day.

America was attacked, and will continue to be attacked, because it has let itself be used to do all of Israel's dirty work in the Middle East. The USA was attacked because it supported militarily, diplomatically and financially every aggression, every atrocity Israel has committed against the Arab peoples for the past half-century. Everyone in the world, with even a minimum of brains and intellectual integrity understands that — except the U.S. Government, of course.

America does not have a government that represents the interests of the American people. For the past fifty years and more, it has had a tribe-controlled, corrupt government, doing the bidding of Israel and the international-manipulators. Until America regains control of its own news and entertainment media, and finds leaders whose sole concern is what is good for Americans, it will remain a nation adrift, hated by most, respected by none.

What happened in New York was a profound psychological shock to Americans. They never expected anything like this could ever happen to them. Should another attack take place, the USA would implode, disintegrating along racial lines, as I predicted in my *CREDO: A Book for the Very Few*.

America is not a nation, but a polyglot amassment of races all squabbling amongst themselves for resources and power. History has amply shown us that non-homogeneous societies succumb to hard knocks. The USA is in its last throes and a racial war is inevitable. Millions will perish — but a new, stronger White Nation, Nova America, or Vinland, will be forged out of this terrible, second civil war.

JEWISH TERROR

The West has also suffered from Zionist terror. In 1954 the Israeli government plotted to blow up American installations in Cairo and Alexandria, then blame it on Egyptian nationals. By chance the plot failed and was uncovered. It was called the Lavon Affair, after Pinhas Lavon, the Israeli Defence Chief. He resigned in 1955 over the incident.

In 1967, Israel intentionally attacked the *U.S.S. Liberty*, an American Navy intelligence vessel off the Sinai Peninsula, with unmarked jet fighters and torpedo boats. The Jews even machine-gunned the deployed life rafts. The attack killed thirty-one American servicemen and wounded over 170. Israel sought to sink the ship, kill all the crew and blame it on the Egyptians. The utter contempt of the Jews for *Boobus Americanus* is unbelievable! What *chutzpah!*

The attack on the *Liberty* was a vicious act of war by Israel against the United States. U.S. Secretary of State Dean Rusk and Navy Chief Admiral Moorer confirmed that it was deliberate. However, the all-powerful Zionist Lobby prevented a formal congressional investigation. The story quickly vanished from the news after a few short days. America kept up the billions of dollars in aid to Israel.

In 1986 Israel schemed and actually caused America to go to war and militarily attack Libya. The Mossad planted a transmitter in Tripoli and broadcast terrorist messages in Libyan code, indicating Libyan responsibility for killing two Americans in the bombing of the La Belle discothèque in Germany. It was later proven that Libya had nothing to do with the bombing.

It was American support of Israel's brutal invasion and occupation of Lebanon in the 1980s which led directly to that Arab suicide truck-bomb, killing 300 American young Marines.

Every Arab is aware that Israel's half-century of terror could never have occurred without the active financial, military and diplomatic support of the United States. Arabs know that the Jewish Lobby has control of American Policy and that the Zionists can get whatever they want from Congress.

Arabs know that almost every bomb that kills their people comes from America. Every bullet, every rifle, every fighter plane, every explosive is manufactured or paid for by American dollars. It is America's billions that have enabled the Jewish state to terrorise the Arab people.

America never threatened to bomb Tel Aviv (as it did Iraq) if Israel refused to obey UN resolutions to withdraw from stolen territory. How different was America's reaction to Iraq's invasion of Kuwait!

Iraq invaded Kuwait — Israel invaded Lebanon.

Some 3,000 Kuwaiti civilians died in that war.

40,000 Lebanese died during Israel's invasion and occupation of Lebanon.

Iraq disobeyed UN resolutions to withdraw from Kuwait.

Israel likewise disobeyed UN resolutions to leave Lebanon (for a full eighteen years) — and also refused to leave Palestine.

Iraq broke international conventions on chemical, biological and nuclear weapons, even though no weapons of mass-destruction were ever proved to exist.

Israel is a far greater offender, having one of the largest stores of chemical, biological and nuclear weapons in the world.

Iraq refused UN inspections for some time.

Israel has always refused such inspections.

For all these violations America bombed Iraq. Yet America would never dream of responding to Israel's crimes and violations. It never even threatened to cut off aid to this bandit, terrorist state.

America was once a great friend of Iraq, from whom it bought oil. America actually supported Saddam Hussein in the war with Iran. Iraq did nothing against the United States, but made the mistake of becoming a strong enemy of Israel. That was enough to turn it into an arch-enemy of the USA.

America dropped more explosives on Iraq in a few weeks than it had used in the whole of the Second World War. Hundreds of thousands of Iraqis, including tens of thousands of civilians were killed. A blockade and embargo followed. This led to the deaths of at least 1,200,000 children and hundreds of thousands of elderly through starvation and lack of medical supplies. A real holocaust!

The Jewish-dominated media are very careful not to let the American people understand the real reason why so many millions in the Arab world hate them. All the while the number grows larger every day.

CUI BONO?

But who really gained from the devastation of New York? The Palestinians? Surely not — for this terrorist act destroyed all the progress the Palestinians have recently made with world opinion. New York has blinded the world to Israeli terrorism. Israel is the only winner in this tragedy.

They will now have a green light to do anything they want. They can kill any of their foes when and where it suits them. Zionists will milk more money from the American people and no one will care about the on-going suppression, murder and human rights violations against the Palestinian people. The Zionists are the only benefactors of that horrendous day of terror on September 11th, 2001.

That is why the USA is in this mess: because a foreign tribe, imbued with an insatiable thirst for world power, an implacable hatred for the rest of mankind, is in control of the American government, through its money and majority control of the mass media.

The primary reason Europids are suffering from terrorism, in Europe and the United States, is because of the world-wide Jewish conspiracy for world supremacy. And it's right in the open for everyone to see.

And there are persistent reports that over 4,000 Jews who worked in the WTC Twin Towers abstained from work on that fateful day. The media reported only one, just one Jew dead in the attacks — and he was on one of the hijacked planes.

Indeed there are confirmed reports that billions of dollars have been profited in a few hours of speculative trading at the Milan and Berlin Stock Exchanges, through foreknowledge of the attacks, provided by the Mossad. The Jew Larry Silverstein who owns the 99-year lease on the Twin Towers was not amidst the rubble! With friends like these, America doesn't need any more enemies.

ZIONISM

Zionism has cost the Europid billions of dollars a year in foreign aid and weapons. Almost one third of America's entire foreign aid budget during the last half-century has gone to Israel.

Zionism has poisoned the White Man's relations with the oil-rich Mid-East nations. Actually, the Arabs are our natural allies. They have nothing except oil — we have everything except oil. It is the perfect symbiotic relationship. Yet, because of the Jews, Arabs have been turned into our enemies. They have been alienated and their actions against us have led to destruction, confiscation of billions of dollars of Europid property, the kidnapping of Europids and the instilling of hatred for Whites.

The powerful agents of Israel in the American media and government are ultimately responsible for this terror, just as surely as if they themselves had piloted those planes into the World Trade Centre and the Pentagon.

Now they cynically plan to use the terror they themselves created, to increase the cycle of violence against Israel's enemies. In the mad rush to 'punish those who did this', America and the usual British lackeys will once again be used to strike against whoever Israel wants.

The American response will ultimately produce even more hate against Whites. Terrorism will increase. This ever-increasing cycle of violence will produce exactly what the Zionists want: the White Man will fight Israel's wars. The spilling of Europid blood instead of theirs. Israel will always fight till the last American! Israel will be the sole beneficiary from all this tragedy.

That is why it is so important to understand why these events occurred and how we can heal the rift between the Arabs and us, once and for all. Once we understand the reason why, then the solution to this recalcitrant problem will become obvious. We must let Israel sink or swim on its own.

THE CRUCIAL FIGHT

We, the precious few, we the Elite, we who know and understand the fundamental issue, the nature of the struggle: this war of civilisations — 'questa battaglia di civiltà' — this struggle between Aryan order and chaos — we have a huge task ahead.

We, the bearers of the *IDEA* of *IMPERIUM EUROPA*, we who are spread across the entire White World, know that victory will be ours after 2012. It is inevitable. We know, with messianic certainty, why. It is written in the ancient Hindu texts. The Dark Age of *Kaliyuga* has just ended. The New Golden Dawn is with us: the age of *Kritayuga*.

The White Man will soon rule the universe for more than a million years!

And that ancient (2000BC and before) Hindu symbol of fortune, the Swastika, representing the sun and Ganesa, the pathfinder, will again illuminate the Aryan. It will be our banner, our symbol as we proceed with the terraforming of Mars and other planets.

Our task is difficult. At this point in time our progress is slow — but there is progress! The number of people understanding the fundamental problem of what is wrong with this modern world is increasing every day, as more adhere to the Imperium *IDEA*.

Ordinary individuals are recognising the internal enemy. More Europids are coming to a Spiritual-cultural-total-understanding-feeling. Recognition of what is truly alien, abhorrent and mortally dangerous.

Of course these are still a minority. But it is not composed of those slack-jawed, beer-bellied couch potatoes, those multi-culturalists, bourgeoisie who make up most of today's lemmings. Nor is money any more so important in this struggle for the minds of the best, within the Europid family of nations. We, the Elite, the bearers of the Imperium *IDEA*, now have the means to reach the masses, just as much, if not better, than the Jew-controlled establishment media does.

When we speak, the right people listen. They are bored stiff with the usual establishment platitudes and lies. They are keen for a new, fresh, honest message. Our people, the great stream of Europid life, can still be saved. They are yearning to be saved! They will yet scream for an iron-hand to lead them. As Lao Tsu in the *Tao Te Ching* says: 'When the people are in disarray, the country in disorder: loyal ministers and true leaders step forth.'

The whole world is entering a new era now, in which the Jew's continued hegemony is not guaranteed. What happened in New York and in Washington this week is just one small manifestation of this new era.

George Bush can order the bombing of every aspirin factory in the Middle East — but that will only hasten this new dawn.

Not everyone in the world is willing to be dominated by the Jews. What happened in New York is a direct consequence of the White Man permitting Zionists to control his government, and to use the White Man's strength to advance Zionism. When people are driven into a corner, as the Arabs have been, sometimes they will fight back. That is happening now, and it will happen even more in the future.

This was no gratuitous attack out of the blue by terrorists. The people who flew those planes into the World Trade Center and the Pentagon were certainly not madmen. They did not bomb Ireland or Switzerland! They knew exactly whom and where to hit. Nor were they cowards, as the American President foolishly described them. Bush repeated that the strike was an unprovoked attack — liar! He knows very well that those kamikaze martyrs acted because traitor politicians, at the behest of the Zionists, had pushed them into a corner.

One remembers that after the bombing of the Federal building in Oklahoma City, which clearly was a reprisal against the government for the mass murder of innocent civilians in Waco, the mass media ignored this linkage and tried to place the blame for the bombing on 'right-wing extremists'.

Now that same controlled media will try to keep the public from tracing the blame for the attacks on New York, back to the long-standing subservience of the U.S. Government to Israel. The media will prevent, by incessant propaganda, people from asking the crucial question: WHY?

But this deception is not going to work as well as it has in the past, because the reprisals against America are just the start. 'We ain't seen anything yet!' Many, many more innocent people will be killed, because of what Western governments have done on behalf of the Jews.

Certainly biological terrorism will be next. When it does come, the death toll will dwarf anything we've seen so far. At the same time, people who can think for themselves, who will understand the causes of this, will continue to grow. And with them the demand for a cure to this worldwide malady that has contaminated the world and bled white the White Man.

We, the Elite, the precursors of The Order, High Culture Bearers of the *IDEA* of *IMPERIUM EUROPA*, will see this fight through! We will lead, usher the White Man into a new era, a million years of peace, progress and Aryan order. This, from the year 2012, *Anno Zero!*

IMPERIUM

0110

XI

THE STRUGGLE
FOR THE
SOUL of MASONRY

At the very beginning of Man's appearance on earth, social groupings proved better able to cope with the fight for survival, in a harsh environment, than the individual. Within such groupings or tribes, there must have always formed further, inner circles, or secret societies. Such eclectic clans continue to exist in every culture right till the present day.

These fraternities were originally nothing more than those individuals who had proved themselves superior to the common fold. These supermen recognised each other and aggregated naturally to protect themselves from the envy and mediocrity of the herd.

The originators of fire for example, must have kept the secret for quite some time, since such knowledge, like any other innovation, gives power to the holder for as long as he manages to keep it his own.

Knowledge is power — and the quest for knowledge, and its safekeeping away from the many-too-many, is the *raison d'être* of some secret societies, including Masonry.

Origins

The history of Masonry stretches back at least to the Pharaohs, probably further back to the Sumerians. In the course of centuries, Masonry was heavily influenced by the Judaic Kabala. There is a strong dose of the latter in Masonic rituals, with a curious blend of Christianity at the intermediate levels.

Scottish Masonry dates back further than British Masonry. Recently discovered tombstones in Argyle, Scotland bear unmistakable Masonic markings. These tombs belong to the Knight Templars who fled Europe during the Papal persecutions of 1309. They are a testimony to the far-ranging geographical spread of the cult.

In Eastern Europe, Germany, Poland and Russia, the Teutonic Knights were likewise Masonic. These knights were formed by Papal decree in 1198 and escaped the persecution and torture by the Papacy and King Philip that befell the Templars. The Teutonic Knights welcomed some of the fleeing Templars who fled east, rather than to Scotland. These joined the Teutonic ranks and carried on as professional fighters.

It is only natural that the Masonic Knight Templars influenced the Teutonic Knights. The vast knowledge and the rituals of the former were shared with the German Knights. These in turn became the precursors of Germanic, nationalistic Masonry.

Purpose

The original purpose of Masonry must have been the quest for the answer to the fundamental question as to the origin of the Race — the White Race.

The question as to where we came from must have haunted us from time immemorial. The second query, which naturally follows the first, is: what are we here for? And the third — where are we heading? — completes the triangle.

All this, Masonry, as an elitist, eclectic and erudite group, has tried to answer.

Apart from such fundamental questions, Masonry gradually evolved a defensive mechanism to protect what had been achieved. Every heart-rending sacrifice, every achievement that benefited the race, had to be preserved, protected.

Masonry, as any leader-group or Culture-Bearer Elite would have realised, must have concluded that the preservation of the race as an intact, cohesive sub-species, is the *sine qua non* for the preservation of all knowledge hitherto acquired.

After all, the Arcane Tradition specifically teaches us as to what brought the destruction of our ancient forebears: the Lemurians. These had committed the unpardonable sin of bestiality — they had mixed with the Negroid race. This had not only brought them down, but also spawned the emergence of the other, inferior coloured races. These are today known as the 'under-developed world' and which no amount of help will ever lift from its eternal, genetically predetermined misery.

Masonry therefore became a two-pillar organisation. Through one part it sought, discovered the hidden knowledge, and on the other, acted as an inner layer, a defence-mechanism for the White Man. The *Broederbond* in South Africa, that for many years protected the interest and welfare of the White minority, was a microcosm of Masonry on a world scale.

This is borne by the simple fact that only White males are eligible into Masonry. In America, Negroes are excluded and have formed their own lodges, which are unrecognised by White ones.

Moreover, severely crippled or handicapped persons are barred from Masonry — a clear indication of the purpose of Masonry to act as guardian for the preservation of the best within the species.

Such noble aims must be the reason for Masonry's attraction to some of the best racial types: Charles Lindbergh, General MacArthur, Henry Ford and others, including George Washington and Benjamin Franklin. Such fascination prevails even today, and most of America's presidents like Truman, Nixon, Reagan and Bush Sr. were all Masons. Truman was for many years a high official of the Ku Klux Klan, testifying to the perfect compatibility between racialism and Masonry.

The unmitigated disaster is that today, individuals who have the preservation and improvement of the White Race at heart continue to join Masonry in the belief that the fraternity is still faithful to its original aims. But is it?

SUBVERTED

The battle for the control of the heart and mind of Masonry was fought and lost sometime between 1925 and 1935.

Edward VIII, the British monarch who was forced to abdicate in 1936, was a Mason who believed in true Masonry and its aims. He was an unashamed admirer of the Germans and von Ribbentrop, the German Foreign Minister, was one of his best friends. Edward was initiated into Masonry in a small Scottish village — by the village postman.

By and large the British people stood by their king in his terrible, personal dilemma. The international-manipulators however, conscious of the fact that with him on the throne there could be no war against Germany, put on the pressure through their hold on the world press and eventually, forced him to abdicate. As ex-monarch, he was a frequent visitor to the Hero's *Berghof* before the war.

As has been stated, Scottish Masonry dates back further than British Masonry and is ingrained in the Scottish culture. There are whole villages in Scotland whose every male member of qualified age is a Mason.

Scottish Masonry, unlike British Masonry, has by and large remained faithful to the original aims of the organisation. This is borne by the ingrained and strong feeling of nationalism and sense of race-consciousness of the Scots to this very day.

There is no doubt that in the decade just before the Second World War, British and French Masonry were taken over by the international-manipulators — lock, stock and gavel.

The Protocols of the Elders of Zion, written in 1897 (in Hebrew), translated and published by Prof. Nilus in 1905, describe in detail the sinister manipulation of Masonic Lodges, in preparation for the Russian revolution and the First World War.

As for the control of the press, Protocol 7 states: 'The world media, with a few exceptions which can be discarded, is already entirely in our hands.' All this as a prelude to the 'World Government emanating from Zion', or, in today's language 'A New World Order'.

In the decade just before the Second World War, British and French Masonry were used by the international-manipulators in their war against Germany. Chaim Weizmann, president of the World Jewish Congress, declared total war on Germany as early as 1933 — financial, economic and if need be, military.

The world media, by now firmly controlled, headlined Chaim's war declaration all over the Western world. The old lies of German atrocities in Belgium during World War One, fabricated stories of babies bayoneted and barbecued, re-appeared as facts in the mass media.

By now, many of the top Masons in Britain and France were Jewish.

Instead of serving as a protector, preserver of the White Race, Masonry from 1925 onwards became a hidden, subversive element at the pinnacle of power within the major European Nations. It now served a diametrically opposite end: it was a weapon wielded by the international-manipulators, in order to isolate National Socialism and lay the ground for the greatest fratricidal folly ever witnessed: the Second World War.

Since then English Masonry has been nothing less than a poniard, held by the international-manipulators, at the bared breast of the hoodwinked and noosed 'White Man'.

GERMANY AND SCOTLAND

Germany too has a strong Masonic tradition. Like that of Scotland it is intensely Nationalistic and Racist. The Hero, contrary to the lies we are told regarding his supposed persecution of Masons, was intimately connected with *Ostara*, the patriotic Masonry with lodges all over Germany and Austria. He knew both Guido von List and Lanz von Liebenfels and met the great English mystic, Houston Stewart Chamberlain in Bayreuth in 1923. He was also profoundly influenced by the *Thule* adept Dietrich Eckart, to whom he dedicated his *Mein Kampf*.

In *Mein Kampf* (Hutchinson's Original illus. Ed., p. 273) he writes, 'And in the freemason organisation, which had fallen completely into his hands, the Jew found a magnificent weapon which helped him achieve his ends. Government circles, as well as the higher sections of the political and commercial bourgeoisie, fell a prey to those plans though they themselves did not suspect what was happening.'

His deputy Rudolf Hess was a top Ostara Mason and an expert on World Masonry. He knew every single lodge in the world and kept records on them. He was in close contact with Scottish Masonry. In 1939 Hess flew all the way to Scotland in a final, desperate attempt to prevent war amongst racial cousins. He could easily have flown to Dover, Cornwall or Margate, but instead chose the hazardous, long solitary flight to the North of Scotland. His aim was to meet Scottish Masons and urge them to convince the British fraternity to avert the slaughter.

Churchill, an English Lodge Mason, was by now completely under the control of the international-manipulators. In 1938 Henry Strakosch (not a Zulu), had given him one hundred and fifty thousand pounds and shares in South African gold mines, in order to bale him out of his personal financial troubles. Churchill killed the Hess peace attempt. He even refused to meet him!

After the war Rudolf Hess, a true hero of Europe, the man who could have saved millions of slaughtered Whites, languished in solitary confinement for over half a century — a sentence not even fit for a murderer. We were led to believe that it was the Russians who had objected to his release throughout these long years; however, when Gorbachev assumed power, one of his first acts was to publicly call for the release of Hess.

Guarda caso, the British resolutely refused, and finally Hess died mysteriously at Spandau prison during the British term of custodianship. One autopsy hurriedly concluded that he died of strangulation with a telephone wire after jumping off a table. The second autopsy, by a foremost forensic expert of international repute, agreed that yes, death was by strangulation — but that Hess had been throttled from behind. There was no evidence of the telltale jerk produced by a fall.

Hess died just as world opinion was pressing for his release. A re-united Germany, just a year away, would surely have released him. Hess had to die. Why?

Hess had to die because on his release Europeans would have been told who were the real schemers, perpetrators and victors of World War II. We would have been told that Britain knew, conclusively and without a shadow of a doubt — that it had the proof, in writing and endorsed by a former monarch — that Germany would never attack her if left alone to crush Jewish Bolshevism. We would have known that World War II was nothing more than a struggle for the soul of Europe — won by the international-manipulators.

RACE and TERRITORY

Hess introduced General Karl Haushofer to the Hero. The general was a paranormal, a man of extrasensory perceptions. He lived years in the Far East, in Japan and Tibet. He stood for a Telluric Imperium. He was undoubtedly the greatest geopolitician of his time and, consonant with Bismarck and the Prussian General Staff, he was adamant that Germany should never, ever go to war against Russia. Haushofer was the Hero's foreign policy advisor till 1945. He was the architect of the Tripartite Act. He believed that Germany and Russia, a National Bolshevist Russia, could dominate the world, instead of the Thalassocratic powers.

However, the Hero had to attack The Soviet Union. Why?

He had sent his personal photographer, Hoffman, during the signing of the non-aggression pact in Moscow, to photograph Stalin closely. Photograph his lips and his ears, especially, to see whether he was a Jew. It was concluded that Stalin was not. He was a Georgian.

So why Barbarossa? After all, the Russians were supplying Germany with all it needed. Rubber, steel, iron-ore, oil, whatever — and Germany could pay later! — Why the attack?

Because the Hero was convinced that Stalin was alone, isolated, the only Russian amidst the tribe of poisoners, international vipers. At any moment, Stalin would be assassinated, and then: the Soviet Union, Jewish, strengthened and a world power, would attack Germany — in alliance with the Jewish-dominated USA.

The Hero, reluctantly, had to attack Russia.

And let us remember that General Haushofer was a student for two years, along with Stalin, under Gurdjieff. They were intimate friends. They had vowed that their respective *Patrias* would never, ever, go to war against each other.

And let us also remember that on the night of the launching of Operation Barbarossa, Bormann, the Hero's trusted secretary, ashen-faced at 3:00am, drove from the Chancellery to Arno Breker's studio. They were friends and, according to the artist, Bormann just said: 'All is lost, all is lost — the Thassalocratic powers have won the war.' Then he left — and the White World lost everything!

In 1945, Haushofer, first poisoned his wife, then, dressed in Japanese noble, ceremonial garb, committed *seppuku*. He could not stomach a world dominated by the sea-powers, pawns in turn in the hands of the international manipulators.

ROSENBERG

Alfred Rosenberg the philosopher of National Socialism, whose book, *The Myth of the Twentieth Century*, written in the early 20s, underpinned the Hero's political and racial philosophy, says nothing against Masonry — not a word. This proves that top National Socialists, up to this time, viewed Masonry as a positive factor in the survival of the race.

Rosenberg states only that National Socialism will solve the problems of the *Volk* 'not through the humanism of Free Masonry, but through National Socialist political philosophy' — that is all.

Rosenberg too was an *Ostara* member of high rank, and an expert on world Masonry and religions, including the Eastern ones. He read all the Indian sacred books—in the original language. He had intimate knowledge of the *I Ching*, studied Confucius, whom he admired greatly, and also Lao Tsu. Nobody who reads his books can have any doubt as to his great erudition.

He was also the world's first 'Green', writing about the long-term effects on the race by increasing mechanisation and even skyscrapers! He advocated the de-industrialisation of Germany, by concentrating industry in clearly defined and limited areas. He was the first to tackle the problems of pollution and its effect on future generations—this in the early 1920s!

It is significant that the present-day Greens were founded by August Haussleiter, a veteran of the beerhall *Putsch*. In 1980, Rudolf Bahro, the East German dissident, discovered the positive side to Nazism and launched his idea that Europe needs an eco-dictatorship, an ecofascism—a Green Adolf! A Green Party that would stand for the preservation of every species—including most of all, the racial preservation of the White Race.

THE SS

Rosenberg's Masonic affiliation and wide knowledge of most religions influenced Himmler, the high priest of the SS. Members of this elite, the *Waffen-SS*, were simply the best fighting units during World War II. This was not through their better training or equipment, but through their ideological and *Spiritual* underpinning.

Himmler created rituals for aspiring SS officers. He had a medieval castle in the forests of Wewelsburg, Westphalia, a castle once the property of the Teutonic Knights, turned into a veritable temple for the SS.

One ritual included the burning of clothes of the twelve disciples formed in a circle. The drinking of each other's blood mixed with a potent alcoholic concoction from a common chalice. The 'raising' of the naked young men to the upper chamber, where elderly SS officers awaited them with their new uniforms and rank.

By now the Hero was portrayed during these rituals as a Messiah, a saviour of the race — and put on a par with Christ and Mohammed. Had Germany emerged victorious from the conflict, there is little doubt that a new, nature-oriented belief, befitting and benefiting the White Man, would have supplanted Christianity.

The Bond forged amongst the SS during such rituals made them formidable fighters throughout the war, amazing the Russians who greatly outnumbered the Germans on that particular front. The French are fascinated by the cult of the SS right up to this day. Books on this fighting force are published in all languages every year.

A special SS department was formed to study world Masonry and upon the conquest of France, this unit took up as headquarters the Lodge of the Grand Orient at 18, Rue Cadet, in Paris. The international conspiracy against Germany became evident from the files discovered within the Lodge.

FINAL STRUGGLE

World War II was nothing more than the continuation, by military means, of the struggle for the soul of Masonry and hence, the Soul of Europe. It was a struggle between German Masonry, with the tacit approval of Scottish Masonry on one hand, against both British and French Masonry. By 1930 both the latter two were firmly under the control of World Jewry.

The struggle continues to this very day and European patriots, new leaders are rekindling the embers left after that epic, but premature struggle that was World War II. Anyone who travels to either Germany or Scotland cannot fail to notice the inherent nationalistic and racialist attitude of both peoples. This has been inculcated through centuries of Masonry — authentic Masonry.

In 1939 German and Scottish Masonry stood for Race, Nation, Family and Aryan order. British and French Masonry, subverted from within at the highest levels, stood for universalism, equality, fraternity, multi-racialism, liberalism and chaos.

We shall soon witness another, final, life or death struggle — a last heroic attempt to wrest world control from the hands of the international-manipulators. A struggle between two eternally opposing forces, two irreconcilable concepts of life. A supreme struggle for the *Soul of Europe*. There is no doubt who will emerge victorious.

Magna Europa Est Patria Nostra!
Imperium
Dec 1994–Updated Nov 2004

XII

RHODESIA -
MY
EYE OPENER

I<small>N THE LATE SEVENTIES AND</small> eighties I travelled extensively in Southern Africa, from the Zambezi to Cape Agulhas, from Windhoek to Umtali and Beira. This was an eye opener for me. I could observe first hand the sinister forces of international finance, the international-manipulators at work in the destruction of the White Race in that part of the world.

I travelled to Rhodesia and South Africa as a fervent anti-communist, ready to help in whatever way I could for the survival of that White plant that was showing sturdy growth on the Dark Continent. I thought the battle-lines were clearly marked and the issues fairly simple and straight-forward — I was a very young man. How wrong I was in my assessment of what the Cold War was all about!

True, before I even travelled, I had begun to notice that something was wrong with the way world politics was evolving. It was obvious to me then that both World Wars had been fratricidal and of no benefit to the West. The betrayal by the Western Democracies of the Hungarian uprising was perplexing. Then came the 'wind of change' and the undignified exit by Britain from the colonies, followed by the Cold War, with one blunder after another, handing out territory and raw materials to communism, from Angola to Mozambique.

This could not be chance. This could not be stupidity. But what was it? Why was communism being aided, helped on its way to world conquest? Why were Britain, America and the rest of the White World so dead against their racial kith and kin in Southern Africa? Why, but why did the Western Democracies seem hell-bent on destroying these peaceful countries?

Indeed, why?

A DIGRESSION

Before I flew off to Johannesburg, I learned that a retired Maestro Vella, living at Tignè, Malta and considered one of our island's top violoncellists, had a daughter living in Rhodesia. I sought Mr. Vella and he was delighted, asking me to present his daughter in person with a special, waxed string for her violoncello. He gave me her husband's office number and urged me to phone him upon my arrival at the airport.

This I did when I eventually touched down at Salisbury airport. When I asked for Mr Trindell, a voice at the other end replied: 'Yes, Mr. Lowell, we've been expecting you — I will put you through to the Minister.' — He was the Minister of Immigration!

Minister Trindell invited my New Zealander friend and me for dinner that Saturday evening. The Trindells lived outside Salisbury, twenty kilometers down Enterprise Road, a military road linking the capital with Umtali at the border with Mozambique, then groaning under a brutal communist regime and at war with Rhodesia. When I nervously asked how we were to find his house, he replied with a chuckle: 'Just drive, eventually you will see!'

Come Saturday, we set off at 7pm and within a little while it was pitch dark. A lonely road, no traffic except military convoys. The occasional, cowardly ambush by communist terrorists made it advisable for motorists to step down on the accelerator. We sped on, the cats-eyes in the middle of the road our only guide. We were somewhat apprehensive, then, suddenly, out of the darkness a luminous, large wooden board: *Għajn Tuffieħa!* — O Malta!

The Trindells (Maltese wife née Vella) greeted me courteously and were perfect hosts. Their Black Portuguese cook presented us with the best Wellington Roast Beef I have ever had. *Għajn Tuffieħa* was an oasis of tranquillity. Acres of lawns, gardens, trees, a huge swimming pool, splendid ridgebacks (Rhodesian lion dogs), everything one could desire. The staff, some five or six, were all happy, at the same time terrified at the thought that one day, soon, there would be a black government. For they knew very well what this meant for them and for Rhodesia.

In the early hours, over liqueur, the Trindells recounted what their beautiful, once peaceful country was going through. The sanctions, the betrayal by Western governments, the treason by those who should have known better: primarily the churches and the do-gooders. Sadness overtook me — why? But why?

It was soon to dawn on me.

The next day we set off for Salisbury again. Then onwards to Kariba. It all started to become clear to me when I was at the Victoria Falls Hotel, a magnificent Edwardian grand hotel overlooking the Falls. One morning, as I sat sipping a glass of white South African Nederburg, I noticed a Rhodesian train, a mile long, slowly moving towards the bridge dividing Rhodesia from Zambia. This Black-ruled country was then harbouring communist terrorists like Mugabe.

Just as the train reached the bridge the engine was unhooked, sidetracked and the convoy of wagons pushed forward slowly by another locomotive at the rear. The first wagon inched its way to the middle of the bridge, where a white line divided the two countries at war. There, the whole convoy stopped and the rear engine was pulled away.

Some half-hour later a Zambian locomotive backed slowly to the centre of the bridge, hooked the Rhodesian wagons, then moved towards the Zambian hinterland and disappeared on its way to Lusaka.

Now, I wondered why Rhodesia was supplying all those goods: food, spare parts, whatever, to an enemy country that harboured communist terrorists who fired mortars at night, at the very hotel I was staying. I asked an obviously military man, late fifties sitting on the table beside me, what was happening. He introduced himself and gradually I got to know he was in the Rhodesian secret service (he was keeping an eye on us!). He nonchalantly explained that since Western democracies aided Zambia with grants, in dollars — and that Rhodesia was starved of foreign currency — it had to perforce sell its products, and those of South Africa, to the enemy, since the enemy paid in dollars — and with those dollars, Rhodesia could buy the weapons needed, again from Western Democracies, in order to shoot back at the Zambians!

Later that week I was back in Salisbury and, strolling down Jameson Avenue, the main street, I noticed the offices of a medium, privately owned American Oil company with its base in Houston, Texas. As I peered through the large windowpanes at the spacious offices inside, a polite secretary came out and asked me if there was anything she could do to help. One word got another: Malta and the Mediterranean and all that — and within a short time I was introduced to the company chairman himself, who happened to be in Rhodesia at the time.

Later that evening we had dinner together at the Park Lane Hotel, Salisbury's equivalent to our Phoenicia in Valletta. I asked this oil magnate, an obviously very rich man, why he was drilling for oil there, when it was obvious that no oil lay in that region of Africa, but only towards the West, in Southwest Africa and Angola?

Wallace replied that he was, like me, an ardent anti-communist and he was doing his bit for Rhodesia and the White Man. 'You know, Norman,' he said earnestly, 'if we were to find oil here, in appreciable quantities, the war would stop forthwith — the six sisters would immediately put a stop to this communist nonsense!'

So there it was: international finance controlling communism. And it was true, for just next door in Angola, a terrorist war was raging between South African-backed rebels led by Savimbi and the communist government, aided by thousands of Cuban troops. During this protracted, vicious war the American oil companies at Cabinda carried on pumping as if nothing was happening. While Angola burned, the flames at the oil wells signalled that all was well with production and profits!

And who was guarding these American oil installations against the SA anti-communist forces? — Elite Cuban troops, naturally! So there we have it — Communism and Capitalism, two sides of the same coin, joining hands against patriotic, nationalist, racialist forces all over the world.

This cooperation has a long history. It is now common knowledge that the French Revolution, that satanic cataclysm that destroyed an Aristocratic view of life, was financed by the Rothschilds, at that time the richest family in Europe.

The First World War saw Germany, Imperial Germany, protecting and secreting Lenin (part Jewish: grandfather Israel Blanck) into Moscow to foment the fall of the Imperial Czar. Lenin sojourned in the sumptuous villa on the lake Lugano in Switzerland, biding his time to enter Russia. Money was never a problem to communism — capitalism ensured that.

The height of this collusion between these seemingly opposing forces, Capitalism and Communism, was reached in the Second World War. Then, it became obvious to all that these two systems are not polar opposites, but merely two sides of the same coin: Economic Materialism. During World War II, they put aside their superficial differences to gang up and oppose the one force which threatened both: Racial Idealism. After the war, they reverted to their mock boxing.

But who ultimately controls the twins? Who lies behind, manipulating one and the other? Who controlled every move of the Cold War that sent millions of Whites to their early death? Who is this Moloch?

Well, while in Rhodesia I came to realise the uselessness of conservatism: 'we are fighting for our blacks' and all that. I remember that a conservative organisation, the 'Save Rhodesia Campaign', had invited Gary Allen, a 'right-winger' from the USA, to give a series of lectures in SA and Rhodesia, which I attended. I noticed that he reserved his most sarcastic retorts at question time for the most honest, patriotic Afrikaans who spoke openly about the need for the continuing separation of the races. An over-bloated gourmand, Gary admitted to me one evening after a typical gastronomical orgy of his, during which he kept wiping his soiled fingers on his shirt, that he was Jewish! It suddenly dawned on me what we were up against.

At that time I sought and spoke with valid persons, one of whom was SED Brown, editor of the SA Observer, an erudite man who had been in the intelligence game for years with the British Army. He opened my eyes to this worldwide malady affecting the White Man, what it was all about: that Capitalism and Communism are two sides of the same coin, flipped regularly by the same international-manipulators. From then on, I resolved to join the fight. From a bitter young man, groping, hitting out in all directions, I started formulating a plan of action and a philosophy for combating the Decline of the West.

The cancer started in the pestholes, the ghettoes of Poland. For communism is indeed a Jewish creation, based on the Jewish kahal, a communal living system later known as the Kibbutz. It is a completely different socialism to that National Socialism of Germany, or the socialist side of Fascist Italy that flowered briefly in the *Repubblica di Salò*. The fundamental difference is Race.

While National Socialist Germany placed an enormous emphasis on race, even to the point of ethnocentricity, Fascist Italy only regarded race as the White Race in relation to all the rest. A much more sensible, pan-European approach. On the other hand, the Jewish-created Communism de-emphasises race altogether and promotes miscegenation. Communists throughout their history have fought for racial equality and miscegenation of the races. Of course, the creators of communism: Them! They are the staunchest racists anywhere!

The International Banks are largely Jew-controlled. They create money out of nothing and loan it to governments — with interest! Money today is not backed by gold, as it should be. This Jewish system of trillions of dollars in national debt, started with the Federal Reserve — and has enabled this tiny minority, the Jews, to control both Marxism/Communism and 'Modern Capitalism'.

On Marxism & Modern Capitalism's unity, one may read *Western Technology & Soviet Economic Development* by Anthony Sutton, published by the Hoover Institution Press. He details the behind-the-scenes support of the Soviet Union from its very beginnings through the Vietnam War, by 'Western Capitalist' corporations!

Suffice it to say that the Kama River heavy-industrial plant, turning out armies of the best trucks and military hardware for the Russians, was entirely financed by such names as JP Morgan, FNCB, Chase Manhattan and a bevy of others. Most of these trucks and army vehicles finished up in Vietnam — used against American boys of course!

These points are taken from the Communist Manifesto:

1) Abolition of property in land and application of all rents of land to public purposes.

2) A heavy progressive or graduated income tax.

3) Abolition of all right of inheritance.

4) Confiscation of the property of emigrants and rebels.

5) Centralisation of credit in the hands of the State, by means of a national bank with State capital and an exclusive monopoly.

6) Centralisation of the means of communication and transport in the hands of the state.

7) Extension of factories and instruments of production owned by the State, the bringing into cultivation of waste-lands, and the improvement of the soil generally in accordance with a common plan.

8) Equal liability of all to labor.

9) Combination of agriculture with manufacturing industries; gradual abolition of the distinction between town and country.

10) Free education for all children in public schools.

And

Communist Rules for Revolution

(Captured at Düsseldorf in May 1919 by Allied Forces)

1) Corrupt the young; get them away from Spirituality. Get them interested in sex. Make them superficial; destroy their ruggedness.

2) By specious argument cause the breakdown of old moral virtues; honesty, sobriety, continence, faith in the pledged word.

3) Encourage civil disorders and foster a lenient and soft attitude on the part of government toward such disorders.

4) Divide the people into hostile groups by constantly harping on controversial matters of no importance.

5) Get people's minds off their government by focusing their attention on athletics, sexy books, plays, and other trivialities.

6) Get control of all means of publicity (media).

7) Destroy the people's faith in their natural leaders by holding the latter up to contempt, ridicule and obloquy (disgrace).

8) Cause the registration of all firearms on some pretext, with a view to confiscation and leaving the population helpless.

Now compare all the above to *The Protocols of the Elders of Zion*. The same message in different words! — Same source, same sinister force of prime evil, same black octopus, with tentacles greedily clutching the whole world in a deadly embrace. Same originators, same mischief-makers: Them!

And if anyone you meet asks you whether the *Protocols* are a fake, as the controlled media screams that they are — just reply calmly that there is one, only one, categorical proof that they are authentic: the Jews insist that they are not!

RHODESIA AND MALTA: THE SAME ENEMY!

The same sinister forces that destroyed Rhodesia are now besieging Malta, our Sacred Island. The same mischief makers, Kissinger foremost amongst them, the most evil man alive today, with thousands of killed Whites on his blood-soiled hands. That same tribe has now vowed to take away our happiness. They want to wipe that innocent smile off our children's faces — just as they had done to the Rhodesians. They want to turn this homogeneous and proud people, the Maltese, into an island-dwelling race of half-castes and Africans. Them! Always Them! — Behind it all.

An American Orion plane able to pinpoint a floating football amidst the wide, open sea, continuously circles our island, covering Sicily, Malta and Tripoli. It spies everything, every single boat leaving North Africa, laden with disease-ridden Kaffirs heading for Europe. As soon as the boat enters

Maltese waters, a vast area covering the centre part of the Middle-Sea, the American Navy alerts the Italians who in turn order our lickspittle government to send off our operetta navy to salvage the aliens.

And so, day by day, boat by boat, Malta, our beloved island, is being taken over. Our job market is being undermined as vile capitalists employ Blacks and fire Whites. Our women are being seduced, raped and left to bear the stain of Africa. Malta, betrayed by the American Government. And who controls the USA Government? Them! Those same international manipulators who sent Rhodesia down the path to oblivion. Them!

Them! Who manipulated and insinuated Lewinski, who branded the hot-irons on Clinton's hot-pants! Who made him bomb our Serbian brothers. Madeleine Albright, one of Them, born in Prague, Czechoslovakia, repaid the Slavs' hospitality in the only way they ever do: by biting the hand that feeds them.

Them! Who made the stupidest President in the history of America, Boobus Bush, lead the country into a senseless war on Iraq. An insensate war with no valid justification — till, that is, one realises it is a war waged solely and simply on behalf of that abomination called Israel.

My Country — My People

But this is not Rhodesia. I am not in Rhodesia lending my limited support. I am in Malta — my island home! My country! My people! — And by God I will do everything in my power to save both.

We of *Imperium Europa* will fight these international vipers. We will eventually vanquish them and their fellow travellers. Those servile, traitorous Maltese who have betrayed their kith and kin, betrayed their forefathers and children and generations to come. We will be merciless with the traitors!

And who are these treasonous vermin? Well, the priests, the Jesuits, the monsignors all wailing and bleating so that we welcome more illegal Africans within our midst. A corrupt Catholic church serving as lackey to the international-manipulators.

Those newspaper editors who have sold their soul and their people. A Green Party that would stand for the preservation of every species under the sun — but cares not a whit the racial preservation of the White Race. Those vile columnists spewing and spinning lies and treason. TV presenters and obnoxious TV hosts promoting traitors and vilifying patriots.

Malta's whole intelligentsia and political class have betrayed their country and their people. Shame on you, you traitorous bastards!

We will be merciless with them all!

IMPERIUM

0501

XIII

RACIAL PRESERVATION
IS
GREEN

THE GREENS! — ONE HAS to admire their idealism. You will find them campaigning for the preservation of the shark, the whale, a snake or spider in the depths of the Amazon, or some little-known lizard in New Caledonia.

Yet, when it comes to the preservation of the White Race, the Greens are virulently anti-racialists, screaming abuse and chastising anyone who dares defend its preservation and its progeny. That White Race which has given humanity everything: from the wheel to space ships and computers.

Greens are on the forefront of every anti-racist demonstration, always alongside the 'downtrodden Blacks' — no matter what. Often, not even having the decency to check the ever growing complaints of alleged 'discrimination' — by Whites against howling Africans of course. A blindness, a self-hate seems to afflict the Greens. They have become today's leading ethnomasochists.

Greens do not mind the mixing of that most civilised and advanced race, the White Race, with that most primitive and savage of all races, the Negroid. In fact Greens remain unconcerned about the burning issue of unlimited immigration. Whenever they can, Greens actually promote and encourage racial miscegenation. And it is always the same: Black males with White women.

Vienna's mayoral election of March 25th 2001 was a typical case. As I have noted before, it was a concentrated and concerted campaign against the FPÖ, organised and orchestrated by the usual tribe, led by Ariel Muzicant. Haider's Liberal allies slyly participated in this political lynching, while the Austrian Greens put up an African as their candidate.

Most of the Greens, as I said, are idealists. They go about in their wilful destruction of their own race out of ignorance. They are what Lenin used to call 'useful idiots'. However, a few in leading positions within the party know exactly what they are doing. They are the conscious tools of the international-manipulators: our hidden, most implacable enemies. Always scheming behind the scenes for the destruction of the White Race. Cohen Bendit, son of the notorious 'Nazi-hunter', heads the Greens in the EU Parliament in Brussels.

NATIONAL SOCIALISTS

Many Greens do not know the origin of their Party. It may come as a bit of a surprise to them that the founder of the present-day Green Party is none other than August Haussleiter. A National Socialist of the old school, a veteran who stood by Hitler's side during the beerhall putsch in Munich, at the start of Hitler's political career.

Haussleiter formed the Green Party in 1974, organised it, was its first chairman, imbued it with the principles it now embraces — and was then booted out for his troubles due to his Nazi past! He was replaced by left-wing extremists and ex-communists of the Joschka Fischer type.

National Socialists were indeed the ultimate Greens. Their legislation for the protection of animal rights was the most advanced in the world. Hitler was a vegetarian since he could not bear the thought of slaughtered hens and cows. All those who knew him intimately, or worked closely with him, testify to this truth. He was a non-smoker and a teetotaller, a fanatic for the preservation of the countryside, to the point that a mere cottage spoiling a skyline or a valley would upset him.

Rosenberg, the party ideologue, was undoubtedly the world's first 'Green', writing about the long-term effects on the race by increasing mechanisation and even skyscrapers! He advocated the de-industrialisation of Germany by concentrating industry in clearly defined and limited areas. He was first to tackle the problems of pollution and its effect on future generations — this in the early 1920s!

In 1944–45 Germany stood alone against much of world. Bombed mercilessly by thousands of Allied planes, its industry and economy crumbling, National Socialists still doggedly refused to send German women to work in factories — as the Americans and the British did not hesitate to do. Germans had a noble, mystical view of womanhood: women as bearers of the race. They would not envisage German women performing a simple, mechanical operation thousands of times a day.

National Socialism was indeed the ultimate Green Party.

ORIGINS

Today's Western environmental movement didn't begin in the '60s. It actually took root in the late 19th century among individuals in Germany, who today would be targeted by watchdog groups dedicated to monitoring the 'extreme right'. Whatever their political orientation, these hopeful romantics were no less dedicated than their modern-day standard-bearers.

Perhaps the most influential of these pioneers was scientist Ernst Haeckel. Considered by many to be the father of modern environmentalism, this fierce German nationalist and avowed Social Darwinist is credited with introducing the term 'ecology' into public discourse. In 1866, he defined this new field of study as 'the science of relations between organisms and their environment'.

Haeckel published a number of books articulating his Darwinist view that humans were intrinsically tied to the soil. His ideas resonated beyond his borders and years. The celebrated British author D. H. Lawrence would consider Haeckel an early influence on his thematic development and naturalistic prose style.

Haeckel was highly critical of Christianity for exalting people above wildlife. He reverently believed that the magnificent forests of his beloved Germany, provided an ethereal bridge to a higher state of awareness. Yet his contribution to environmental consciousness cannot be dismissed. In her remarkable work *Ecology in the 20th Century*, Dr. Anna Bramwell declares that the well-known naturalist 'enabled ecology to become a viable political creed'.

THE FIRST WORLD WAR

Haeckel's Earth-centered *Weltanschauung* took on greater importance following the horrors of the First World War. Millions of soldiers were slaughtered or horribly mutilated and permanently disabled. The war also left massive chunks of sublime countryside barren, pockmarked and infertile from artillery barrages. Thus did the 'war to end all wars' realise the worst fears of the environmentally minded.

For many, technology was the villain in this Greek tragedy of international proportions. The horrifying combat debut of large-scale artillery fire, machine guns, hand grenades, land mines, poison gas and other manufactured instruments of death, provoked a widespread distrust of humankind and an aversion to industry.

By the 1918 armistice, many veterans, shell-shocked and reeling from the ghastly images of war, sought redemption in the only way they knew — by turning back the clock to the agrarian life of their grandparents.

This reaction to the war was manifested in Britain by the growth of many 'back-to-the-land' movements, such as John Hargrave's crypto-fascist 'Green Shirt' movement of the '20s and '30s. But after unsuccessfully attempting to gain support via the electoral process, the Green Shirts and other like-minded organisations were quickly doomed to obscurity.

This wasn't the case in Germany, where support for ecological views became widespread as salvation was sought in the anti-cosmopolitan, anti-technological 'peasant movement'.

BLOOD AND SOIL

Amidst the resentment and disillusionment that marked the interwar Weimar Republic, a newly aroused Green awareness took hold. This loose amalgamation of new ecologists comprised a cross-pollination of Haeckel admirers, popular German youth movements, and adherents to Rudolf Steiner.

This new 'peasant movement' took as its slogan a simple phrase: *Blut und Boden!* or 'blood and soil', celebrating the virtues of heritage and the nobility of the pre-industrial agrarian way.

Steiner, an influential lecturer, firmly opposed artificial farming methods. He served up eloquent encomiums celebrating the peasant's role in Germany's glorious future. His writings would greatly influence SS Chief Heinrich Himmler, Rudolf Hess and the man Bramwell considers the 'Father of the Greens': German environmentalist Ricardo Walther Darré.

DARRÉ

Darré, author of *The Peasantry as Life Force (1928)* and the seminal *New Nobility from Blood and Soil* (1929), was a little-known figure who quickly rose to prominence as leader of the postwar *volkisch* revolution. While he is now considered suspect at best for his pan-German racialism and links to groups supporting eugenics, Darré's environmental program is progressive even by today's standards. The World War I veteran wanted to see his world transformed into a planned society based on environmental ethics.

Charismatic and possessing a rare gift for organisational ability, Darré's radical influence among rural Germans quickly gained the attention of deputies of the National Socialist German Worker's Party (NSDAP) by the early '30s. Asked to promote National Socialism in the countryside, where the NSDAP then lacked popularity, Darré completed this task with alacrity, his efforts easily gathering peasant support for the Nazi party in North and East Germany. His successes were rewarded in 1933, when he was named Minister of Agriculture and Reich peasant leader.

Darré set up a peasant capital in the town of Goslar with progressive measures that empowered the farmer while preserving the soil. By 1940, Darré had accepted Steiner's belief in biodynamic farming and funded several such experimental farms. Darré continued to espouse the benefits of organic vegetation and soil conservation, but he was soon muzzled.

In 1942, completely out of favour with the party cadre of hand-picked advisors, he lost his cherished position as Minister of Agriculture. Nevertheless, up until the end of the war, he continued to criticise German agricultural methods and spoke passionately of creating his envisioned peasant state.

Darré was subsequently tried at Nuremberg for his demands that his countrymen be allowed to occupy the newly conquered Polish countryside. He was sentenced to seven years imprisonment by the tribunal, but he continued to urge the merits of organic farming up until his death in 1953.

His advocacy was not in vain. Our ongoing concern with the detrimental effects of pesticides and artificial fertilisers proves, not only that Darré was correct, but that he was well ahead of the curve, espousing these beliefs some four decades before the issue became in vogue (the modern 'Bio' foods movement could easily be attributed in origin to Darré).

As is to be expected, today's liberal-minded Greens show very little admiration for Darré, although they continue to promote his collectivist beliefs and other elements of his agenda. The mere mention of his name provokes a combination of anger and resentment. However, even left-leaning environmentalists must grudgingly pay lip service to his contributions. 'It was largely Darré's influence in the Nazi apparatus which yielded, in practice, a level of government support for ecologically sound farming methods and land use planning, unmatched by any state before or since,' notes Peter Staudenmaier in his cautionary *Ecofascism: Lessons from the German Experience*.

In a 1984 *History Today* article that Staudenmaier describes as 'repugnant', Dr. Anna Bramwell goes further, noting that without Darré, 'the ecological movement would have perished in his time and place.'

THE FUTURE OF OUR MOTHER EARTH

'There's no way to preserve a species that's programmed to kill the planet,' explains the manifesto of today's extreme Greens, represented by the Finnish Linkola. He advocates involuntary sterilisation, comparing the planet's population to a sinking ship clumsily attempting to seat 100 passengers on a lifeboat built for ten. 'Those who hate life try to pull more people on board and drown everybody. Those who love and respect life use axes to chop off the extra hands hanging on the gunwale,' he ruthlessly advises.

To wield the axes, the onetime pacifist envisions the rise of a ruthless 'Green Police' patrolling the wilderness, undeterred by what he derisively termed the 'syrup of ethics'. A fierce opponent of both Amnesty International and the Vatican, he advocates an end to economic aid for starving Third World nations. Linkola favours an immediate reversal of open-door immigration policies — specifically so that millions might perish.

Of course, this would constitute a mountain of human corpses unseen since the dark days of Mao's People's Republic of China, or Stalin's planned famine in the Ukraine and the Gulags. But to Linkola, a few million deaths are of little importance when the entire planet is at stake. 'We still have a chance to be cruel, but if we are not cruel today, all is lost,' he admonishes.

Linkola outlines the central tenets of his credo: an unyielding scepticism of egalitarian democracy, an unwavering belief that unchecked overpopulation will kill our once-bountiful planet.

The latter contention is not without merit. Recent estimates by the United Nations Population Division project a growth of over three billion people within the next 50 years. If the acceleration of births continues at its current pace, by the year 2150, an additional six billion inhabitants will threaten our imperilled ecosystem and obviously limited resources.

Therefore, Linkola would shed few tears if a few billion of us were to meet a quick demise. In the name of conservation, he consigns democracy, conventional humanism, and the principle of non-violence to the waste bin.

Child limit would be enforced on all households. A fierce anti-capitalist, Linkola insists that fishing and organic farming constitute the two primary occupations. Manufacturing would be overseen by the state, which would openly discourage technological research. Ozone-killing automobiles would be confiscated, so that roads could be cleared for additional forest growth.

Consequently, bicycles and limited public transportation would return as the most popular modes of locomotion. Products would be created to last several lifetimes, with no exports allowed. As he has often stated, individual rights would give way to the rights of the Earth. His 'Green Police' would punish miscreants who violate our beloved *Gaia*.

Like the National Socialists, Linkola would strive for a 'return from unthinking consumption to a pre-industrial agrarian society'. However, for most of today's Greens this is too violent a change to envisage. Today, Linkola stands alone but determined. A one-man force of will, undaunted in his quest to end the desolation of the Earth. Although branded an 'eco-fascist' by detractors and openly despised by the more image-conscious activists, he is actually more of a traditional ecologist than his critics would care to admit.

From a historical perspective, Linkola's books and articles resurrect a legacy of environmental consciousness that began over a century ago, in the dark forests of Germany. There, the first systematic environmental philosophy was formulated.

CONCLUSION

In 1980, Rudolf Bahro, the East-German dissident and later a leading exponent of Green views, discovered the positive side to Nazism. He launched his idea that Europe needs an eco-dictatorship, an eco-Fascism — a Green Adolf!

A Green Party that would stand for the preservation of every species — including and most of all, the racial preservation of the White Race.

For one cannot be Green and *not* be a racialist. Unless, that is, one is either incoherent or intellectually dishonest — or both.

Racial preservation is Green!

Imperium

0102

XIV

THE REFUGEE
TIME-BOMB

In 1977 Jean Raspail in his novel *The Camp of The Saints* chronicles the arrival of millions of Indians packed on scores of aged, rusty ships, descending locust-like on Europe. Weak politicians, imbued with two thousand years of Christian platitudes, cannot muster the courage to order the army to shoot them at sea or as they land ashore. Eventually, the so-called refugees disgorge themselves on top of us and the dark ages settle over Europe. His description of the voyage is at the same time both erotic and frightening:

> Life at sea had turned vegetal, at best. They ate, they slept, they saved their strength. They pondered their hopes for the future, and their paradise of milk and honey, with its gentle rivers thick with fish, whose waters washed fields fairly bursting with crops, growing wild for the taking. Only the children, the turd runners — darting, dashing, hands cupped, in and out — gave any signs of life in that stagnant throng, lying on deck like battlefield corpses laid out at day's end. But in time, very slowly, the flesh began to seethe. Perhaps it was the heat, the inertia. Perhaps the sun, pouring druglike against the skin and into the brain, or that tide of mystical fervour it swam in. Most of all, the natural drive of a people who never found sex to be sin. And little by little, the mass began to move. Imperceptibly at first. Then more and more, in every direction Soon the decks came to look like those temple friezes so highly prized by tourists, prurient or prudish, but rarely touched by the beauty of the sculpture

and the grace of the pose. And everywhere, a mass of hands and mouths, of phalluses and rumps. White tunics billowing over fondly, exploring fingers. Young boys, passed from hand to hand. Young girls, barely ripe, lying together cheek to thigh, asleep in the languid maze of arms, and legs, and flowing hair, waking to the silent play of eager lips. Male organs mouthed to the hilt, tongues pointing their way into scabbards of flesh, men shooting their sperm into women's nimble hands. Everywhere, rivers of sperm. Streaming over bodies, oozing between breasts, and buttocks, and thighs, and lips, and fingers. Bodies together, not in twos, but in threes, in fours, whole families of flesh gripped in gentle frenzies and subtle raptures. Man with women, men with men, women with women, men with children, children with each other, their slender fingers playing the eternal games of carnal pleasure. Fleshless old men reliving their long-lost vigour. And on every face, eyes closed, the same smile, calm and blissful. No sounds but the ocean breezes, the panting breaths, and, from time to time, a cry, a groan, a call to waken other sprawling figures and bring them into the communion of the flesh

Today, 2002, this prediction has turned to stark fact. In Europe, the White Man is being besieged in his heartland. In the past he used to smite his enemies ruthlessly, as did Martel in France with the Arabs. Now the Europid is armed with the most sophisticated weapons of mass destruction, yet he is defenceless, powerless to use them, since he has been disarmed ideologically by the enemy within. That tribe of mischief-makers who infiltrated, steadily and stealthily, for well over two thousand years. That tribe who, through their control of the mass media, influence our behaviour and stance for survival.

The French Revolution, that demonic cataclysm, wrenched out the feeble last vestige of the Aristocratic view of life. Then, World War I bled the old continent white. It replaced the landed aristocratic gentry, an organic aristocracy, with plutocracy, an aristocracy of money. Millions of Europe's best sons perished senselessly in that fratricidal slaughter.

Our hidden enemies then completed the holocaust with World War II. Millions of Germans, Russians and hundreds of thousands of the best of Britain and France, were once again offered as human sacrifice to the Great Moloch of international finance.

The victors that emerged from these three cataclysms were the international-manipulators, their hold on the world's financial centres and stock
exchanges consolidated. The tribe then imposed its mercantile view of life
and the mystification of labour on the Europid. Gradually, especially since
World War II, we have seen the transformation of a productive mentality,
the hallmark and genius of the White Man, into that of the speculative
financier. In fact, finance today utterly dominates and controls production
and determines all its factors: location, machinery, workforce, etc.

GEMEINSCHAFT vs GESELLSCHAFT

Tribal, and later national (*Gemeinschaft*) societies enjoyed harmonious
collaboration and development due to their common genetic and cultural
identity. Later, especially after the Industrial Revolution, this cohesion began to unravel and the *Gesellschaft* type of society began to predominate.
Collaboration among humans now rested, not on common heritage but
solely on economic exchange and profit. Society became a fight for survival
amongst isolated, egoistic individuals with no sense of kinship — a war of all
against all. A system of simple horizontal exchanges and interactions.

Paradoxically, both the Marxist and Liberal view of life coincide perfectly with this *Gesellschaft* system. In both systems, at their extreme
forms, mankind is reduced to a vast faceless proletariat, instead of a rich
diversity of nations. Both destroy historical memories, eradicating man
from history and placing him on the production line. Their goal is the
same: material well being. There is no place for any communal myth that
gives that mystical union to kindred people.

At this point the politician serves as puppet of big business. Politics
become a delivery service, accommodating the strongest lobby within
the melee. Government is reduced to a servicing tool for special interest
groups, while the nation sinks to a mini-market.

FRONTIER CAPITALISM

We have now reached a stage when unbridled consumerism is necessary to the survival of a financial capitalist system — one that needs an ever more frantic cycle of production and waste, with the concomitant despoliation of nature. A capitalism that needs a new frontier to attack and despoil — ever new forests to be cut down, new mines to be gouged out, new ocean floors to bore, new seas to overfish. Financial Capitalism has rapaciously raped Mother Earth.

A Financial Capitalism that has now reached its highest stage: Globalisation. A world market where labour is treated just as any other commodity — where the multinational conglomerate has become the apex, the highest stage of both Financial Capitalism and Communism. Where millions of minions, shareholders holding a slip of paper entitling them to a dividend, quiescently await their quarterly handout, without any inkling as to the aim, goals, machinations of their hidden, unreachable board of faceless, multi-racial directors idolising their money-Moloch.

Finance Capitalism has coerced productive capitalism, through the total competition that Globalisation brings, into accepting the suicidal policy of importing millions of aliens in White heartlands. These migrant workers take over White jobs through a gradual lowering of wages and standards. All desperately seeking the mirage of an easy life, secure in the comforts of an ever increasing array of material goods.

More ominously, these invaders are outbreeding the Europids in their own countries.

Globalisation: an ever increasing race for the optimum production (anything), location (anywhere), optimum labour (anybody) and lowest wages (rock-bottom). The gradual closing down of the Europid's manufacturing base (motorbikes 99 percent Japanese) and its supplanting with non-Europid (mostly Asian) produce. The utter dependence of the White Man on others for his very survival and defence. A strangulation process which can only mean the disappearance of the White Man, that biological aristocracy constituting just 5 percent of the world's population. In London, to cite one example, ethnic minorities form 40 percent of the population. White British are already a minority in their own capital city; very soon, Whites as such will be.

This is the tragedy unfolding before our eyes. This is what our hidden enemy has in store for us. Their aim is a world dictatorship by a tiny homogeneous group with an implacable thirst for global power, vengeance and hatred for the rest of humanity: a world human-mass of rootless, raceless, coffee-coloured zombies.

OUR ISLAND

Up until forty years ago, there was only one black *Pawlu it-Tork* (Paul the Turk), pushing a trolley of fresh bread all over the island. That was the entire non-Europid population in Malta. We were a homogeneous population, a materially poor but proud nation. We were strong in moral fibre and knew where we stood.

Then came the gradual infiltration of Arabs and Blacks, masquerading as refugees. First they came in tens, in little boats. Then they started coming in hundreds. They found hospitality from a naïve people, misled by those two pernicious enemies within. A combination of rapacious capitalists seeking cheap labour and the eternal Christian do-gooders, providing the greedy capitalist with what he needed. An incongruent symbiosis between, on one side the Dun Challies, Dun Joeys, the sly monsignors — and on the other, the crude capitalist with his Mercedes-Benz.

The religious collectivists, those who have lost their bearings, their original message, have now become indistinguishable from the communists. In fear of the international-manipulators, who lash them mercilessly through the controlled world press and TV, these pathetic-political-priests lay the groundwork, the psychological predisposition of our naive population of village idiots (*il-Ġaħan Malti*) to accept, even to aid, these hordes of aliens. The pernicious-political-priests then channel these intruders to employers, those callous capitalists who exploit them to the full. These

Catholic-capitalists in turn, assuage their conscience by donating massive amounts of cash to the do-gooders. Luxury hotels are made available as venues for the political-priests to hold seminars for simpletons. A symbiosis by two evil traitors of our race: the political-priests and the Catholic-capitalists.

The so-called refugees, after appropriating our jobs are now increasingly cohabiting with our women. TV brainwashing depicts Blacks and minorities as role models or heroes, or else poor displaced persons to be pitied. Our women eventually succumb to this incessant poison and are breeding an ever-increasing army of half-castes. Senglea is a case in point. A black African was admitted into the island to play with one of our football teams. He married a *Żeża ta Bubaqra* (village wench) and became a Maltese citizen. Immediately, he called in his three 'brothers' and they too, married Maltese goats. They are breeding like rabbits and, I am told, we shall soon see them elected as town councillors!

No, clearly this cannot go on! Unless drastic measures are taken to stop the rot now, within fifty years, Malta will become the Haiti of the Mediterranean. Is this what we want? Is this the future we are handing over to our children? Is this fair to them?

However, both these traitor Catholic-capitalists and political-priests will soon come to regret what they are doing. They are the betrayers of their race, that race of Aryans, the builders. Betrayers of their civilisation, the greatest this planet has ever known. Betrayers of their country, that Sacred Island of Melita that has given them all they need to live a fulfilling life. Betrayers of our children, who will be faced with a monstrous problem within a lifetime — and the greatest betrayal of all: of themselves! For most of them know the evil they are perpetuating. It is their self-hate that makes them do it.

The Final Struggle

There is a fight underway for the soul of the Europid. A fight on a planetary scale pitting Aryan order against chaos — a life or death struggle between two, irreconcilable views of life. A fight for the survival of the

White Man. On one side the few White patriots fighting valiantly against incredible odds: controlled TV channels, world press, political-priests and obnoxious opinion-formers. But by the grace of the *Cosmic Force*, we will win and then, as the Italians put it: *Faremo i conti — con tutti gli interessi!* (We will settle accounts — with interest!)

Malta is indeed a microcosm of Europe. Malta's fight against alien immigration from Africa reflects the same struggle facing Europe and all Europids. Should Malta lose, then Europe is lost too. The fate of Europe is inextricably tied with that of our Sacred Island.

Malta will not, cannot ever lose this fight for survival. The Spirituality of *Melita* can never be vanquished. As did La Vallette, who resolutely defended Malta against all odds and saved Europe in 1565, so will this brave people prove once again their valour. Malta will act as a beacon for the rest of Europe. It will ignite a spark that will set Europe ablaze. And at the end of this planetary struggle, involving all Europeans, this island will be recognised as the Pinnacle Peak, the Spiritual Focal Point of the Imperium.

We, the precious few, will emerge victorious! The traitors and their masters have had their innings and at last, they are rapidly coming to an end. They will yet regret they were ever born. We will be like ferrets and seek them out, wherever they may hide. We will go after them even to the end of the world, hauling them out by the neck from the deepest, darkest recesses they may try to hide in.

Then we will build our Imperium. An *IMPERIUM EUROPA* on a planetary basis, uniting all Europids wherever they may be. We will not tolerate one single non-Europid within our ever-expanding borders. All aliens will be expelled. With them will have to go their Europid spouses and mixed offspring, the innocent victims of racial treason. Only then will we Europids rediscover our true nature and live according to it. We will return to our way of life. We will again be attuned to the cosmos, to that primordial, pre-Christian, pagan purity, potentiating our predecessors. A purity, profaned and polluted through two thousand Christmases.

The gentleman-farmer, *il Signore contadino*, will provide all the wholesome, healthy, organically farmed food we will ever need. We will have ample surpluses that we can barter for whatever we want from outside the Imperium. The producer will again assume the high ground over the speculative financier. The military will have a higher status than the bourgeoisie. And above all, there will be the Elite. An Elite beyond parliaments, parties, politicians, prostitutes and pernicious political-priests. An Elite of a quarter of a million men. High Culture Bearers. An Order of Men as were the Templars and Teutonic Knights. They will be the guardians of the Imperium. Their sole concern will be Spirituality, High Politics and Race. This Elite will usher in the Golden Dawn of a new era; the age of *Kritayuga*, the age of harmony and Aryan order.

IMPERIUM

0111

XV

CALAMITY - CHRISTIANITY

A BELIEF, A RELIGION CAN BE pro-life or anti-life. A religion can act as the philosophical underpinning towards the survival of a race or civilisation. In general, polytheistic religions are pro-life, affirmative, positive, having sprung naturally out of man's observation of nature in all its forms. In polytheism there is a God for everything: thunder, lightening, water, mountains, war or struggle, and innumerable others. In polytheism Man sees the Divine in a Himalayan mountain — and in a dewdrop.

Monotheistic religions are synthetic, man-made, artificial, anti-nature and anti-life. They negate the here and now and instead take as their fixation the after life, the pie-in-the-sky. Certainly the most dangerous of these monotheistic, synthetic religions is Christianity. With its pandering to everything that is weak, pathetic, reliant, bungled and botched, it has brought Western Civilisation to the brink of destruction. Two thousand Christmases have led us to the end of our survival as a species on this planet. The dosage of masochism, the suicidal poison that this perversity propagates, increases every year.

Christianity glorifies all that is weak, defective, putrescent. It condemns all that is virile, healthy, affirmative, pro-Life. It is inherently an anti-noble, anti-master morality, one indeed that evolved in the ghettos of Rome and proliferated largely amongst the lowest strata of society throughout the Roman Empire. To the Roman nobility it was a detestable religion with its appeal to humility, forgiveness, tolerance and resignation to any situation.

Beneath its message of 'love and peace' lay another: the snarling hatred for the strong, the noble, the competent and the truly good. And it was this message that attracted the many-too-many to its fold. Within a few centuries, like a virus infecting the whole body of Europe, it managed to supplant the old gods, who had become worn out. By the second century even the emperor had converted. The cross triumphed and stood on the Roman hills, where formerly the imperial eagle had surveyed the Empire.

Christianity is the greatest calamity to befall the White Race. If one had to add up all the slaughters and genocides in all civilisations, the Aztecs, Maya, Patagonian, Indian and Chinese — if one had to add up all the millions slaughtered in the name of all dictators, Genghis Khan, Attila, Stalin, Mao and others — the total would not make 1% of the numbers slaughtered, tortured, and murdered in the name of the founder of Christianity, the Lamb of God.

Even Buddhism, the other slave religion preaching universal salvation, does not stoop so low as Christianity. At least, when faced by oppression, the Buddhist retreats 'a few miles down the river to fish. In time, he sees the corpse of his aggressor floating down before him'. Thus the Buddhist sins by omission.

On the other hand the Christian sins by commission. He actually turns the other cheek to his tormentor. Thus, Christianity is anti-life. It is the greatest aberration of the instincts. If really taken seriously and adhered to, if followed to its logical conclusion, Christianity would kill its believer.

How can one turn the other cheek to trousered apes rioting in San Francisco or Watts? Where would present-day Christians be had our forefathers not fought bloody battles that stopped the Arabs in Spain or the Turks at the gates of Vienna? They would be wearing sandals and turbans.

Two thousand Christmases later, this disease has debilitated us to the extent that the White Man has come to carry a guilt complex for his very existence. Examples are too many to enumerate; White girls, healthy, of child-bearing age, forsake motherhood and follow an emaciated Albanian 'sister of the poor' to the pest holes of Asia, tending to the festering wounds of starving Hindus. Christianity is a Chandala religion.

Young men and women, bereft of a vision, of a philosophy of life, embrace Christianity and depart as missionaries to Africa to save Black babies from being devoured by fellow Blacks. They scream at us and demand that we admit these inassimilable aliens within our midst.

And just in case we ever run out of enemies, the Pope encourages these Third-Worlders to keep up their feckless fecundity, admonishing them against birth control.

Some years ago, we relished the edifying spectacle of the African Bishop's synod, at the Vatican in Rome. There, in the kernel, the centre of Christianity, the very seat of Peter, we witnessed the simian spectacle of Blacks dancing to the tune of the limbo! How low can you go!

All this would not be a real problem if our young people had a vision of an *IMPERIUM EUROPA*, underpinned by an authentic religion fit for the White Race. A vision that would not leave the vacuum that Christianity now fills. The unfortunate thing is that the most honest, the most idealistic of our youth are the ones who are taking Christianity most seriously.

They are the ones poring, thumping and flipping continuously through that most evil book ever recorded in the annals of literature. A book brimming with hatred, penned by a bloodthirsty tribe of psychopaths, imbued with a burning sense of mission for world power. A tribe describing themselves as 'The Chosen Ones.'

A book describing in gory detail every kind of murder: deicide, regicide, patricide, matricide, fratricide, infanticide — the sacrifice of the first born to an implacable God. The mass slaughter of entire nations together with their domestic animals. The murder of every first-born in every household in the quiet of the night. The slaughter of all babies under two years — cannibalism — real horrifying holocausts.

A book written by a psychotic people at the best of times — raving lunatics proclaiming themselves messengers of God and bearing the usual litany of self-abnegation, self-torture, self-denial, self-immolation in order to quieten the most natural feelings and impulses. A book listing every kind of sexual perversion. And the *pièce de résistance*: the wild cabalistic imbecility of the Revelations.

One must admit that the least harmful of all Christian denominations are the Catholics: at least they don't take it seriously! All the rest: the Evangelicals, the Born Again thumpers, the Baptists — they actually believe the nonsense!

Luckily for the White Race, Catholics only go through the motions of Christianity. They attend mass every Sunday, wearing decent clothes as they do, and that's about all. The Catholics are not so stupid as to turn the other cheek to an aggressor — they'd blow him up! They are not ingenious enough to bleed themselves white by 'giving their all and following Jesus'.

The White Race has survived, in part, because of Catholicism, but in spite of Christianity — certainly not because of it.

NEW BELIEF

It is obvious that this ideological-religious debilitation of the White Race cannot go on. We have reached a nadir. A few more years and it will be too late to save our civilisation from the deadly effects of this malady. We must either take the road to atheism or — we must devise a new belief.

The atheist is a man who recognises that he is alone, with no one, nothing above or surrounding him. The deist is a man who submerges himself into nothingness, in order to justify a deity above, all around him. Ultimately — and this is the real reason — a deist wants something, someone to blame for his failure.

Though adequate for that minority of individuals who are educated, enlightened and mature enough to live by it, atheism is not the answer. Our people, the biological aristocrats of the planet, would be terrified without a God. We have to create a new faith.

Mysticism and science are not antagonistic. They are complimentary. When one rises a notch, the other follows. The White Man may go to the furthest stars — but there he will still need a belief, a *CREDO*.

We need to create a belief adequate for our survival, strength and will to power. A religion that fits our genetic makeup, our very being.

And what better God to serve this purpose than: *THE SACRED GENE POOL.*

No one knows exactly where, when or how it came into being; whether here on Earth or, as is probable, in outer space. In the Arcane Tradition this human-soul-energy was the harbinger of Lucifer, the Bringer of Light, later identified with Prometheus.

What we do know is that today its bearers are a declining minority on this planet. This inestimable precious *Sacred Gene Pool* may irremediably disappear — for eternity.

Etheric and vaporous in the Polarian and Hyperborean Epochs, the human-soul-female/male body gathered density in the Lemurian age and took shape in our forefathers, the Atlanteans. Now it is our turn: the Aryan Age.

The law of heredity holds sway. Children carry the characteristics of their fathers. Likewise the White Race carries on within itself a process of *Spiritual*-soul perfection. If it is lost — then all is lost.

Everything that today we take for granted will grind to a halt. Airlines will not fly, nor trains run. Skyscrapers will tumble down, electricity will fail. Dams will burst open while deserts encroach upon whole continents.

The primates left inhabiting the Earth will simply revert back to the cave. Our racial enemies cannot hope to survive without us, for they have progressed only through copying us. Without the *Sacred Gene Pool*, without the White Race — there will be nothing!

We must breed a new religious caste. The members of this Elite will be experts in cosmology, the Arcane Tradition, genetics, genetic engineering, anthropology, eugenics and medicine.

They will forge a new *Science of the Spirit.*

They will research and study the distant origin of our race and the insoluble bond between the White Man and the Cosmos. This bond is the fundamental basis of our existence and evolution. They will help the White Man discover himself. These future priests will underpin the goals of the Europid and urge him onwards to both racial and individual self-realisation. Race and Individual — an indissoluble bond.

A race-mind, a race-consciousness gripping the *Volk*, the Europeans — linking them to a distant past and an ever-present, all-encompassing Aryan identity.

A truly individual mystical experience; a mystical ecstasy. A momentous attunement with the cosmic-force; the *Vril* — the Divine.

A Religious Elite forging an esoteric, healthy, nature-oriented new belief that befits the White Race. A primordial, substratum, pre-Christian, pagan wisdom for that Elite attuned to it — conscious, through personal experience, a direct perception of transcendent realities, of the Eternal Truths that express the essence of the universe. A strong, indomitable caste of veritable Supermen on Earth — living Zarathustras.

A new warrior-priesthood that will attempt a final, supreme struggle for the soul of the Aryan. A struggle against the Judeo-Masonic-Christian cabal choking the White Man. A religious caste that will rekindle the embers left after that epic, but premature struggle of half-century ago, by that great political genius and leader: the Hero.

We will breed the best, in increasing numbers, by a judicious mixture within the Europid family of peoples; through a well-planned and well-executed eugenics programme. A humane plan, that will include the sterilisation of the very low IQs, as well as euthanasia for those born bungled and botched.

Moreover, through recent breakthroughs in genetic engineering, we could identify and cauterise the mutant genes, thus eliminating deformities and degeneracy. We could consciously breed ever Higher Forms of Life. We could gradually breed those Supermen Nietzsche dreamed of — those *Übermenschen* of the future.

Not only that, we will resurrect the Hellenic Heroes! We have sarcophagi of all the best of our glorious past. We will resurrect the Roman nobility, the perfectly preserved Tocharians, those most beautiful redheads with green eyes. We will search for the best genes amongst the Vikings, the Visigoths, past Caesars and Medieval knights, Florentine artists. We will exhume the best and, through our genius, through our recent break-throughs in DNA, we will infuse those genes, that DNA into our present, living, highest-IQ sons and daughters. We will get the best of the past, infused in the best of the present to create the best of the future!

The number of children per couple would be commensurate to phys-ical excellence and level of intelligence. For it has been amply proved that low achievers tend to have large families. In this way, we will populate the Heartland and Europe Overseas, the coming Imperium, with the most healthy, the most intelligent specimen of our race.

Then we will start to colonise space. We will live in huge, clean orbit-ing cities and the habitable planets within our solar system. We will turn the planet Earth into an ecological museum for our grandsons to visit and learn about their origins. We will heal this planet.

It is high time to adopt this new belief in *THE SACRED GENE POOL*. Only thus can we be assured of the continued survival and strengthening of the White Man — and the accomplishment of his sacred mission within the Cosmos.

IMPERIUM

0105

XVI

RACE
AND
TERRITORY

THE INTERACTION BETWEEN *RACE AND Territory* is all-important in the survival of a species. In the animal world, most animals are territorial, instinctively realising that their survival depends on the amount of territory they control. Here in the Yorkshire Moors where I am writing this article, I am living on a farmstead and every evening three vixen come quite close to my window. They scavenge for any food or scraps left by the farm dogs. Each comes from a different direction, from an area clearly delineated. They call at different times and stay clear of one another. It is the way of survival. It is *the Way of Nature*.

How different to our stupid way: greeting aliens to our shores, admitting them amongst us. Allowing them to devour our limited resources in an orgy of Christian piety and self-destruction. Instead of defending, tooth and nail, our territorial integrity as those vixen do, instead of following the way of Nature. And since this is not the way of Nature — it is the way of death.

Hardly any country today can survive on its own, cut off from the rest. The balance between people and territorial area has been upset. Population growth is no longer organic but explosive, due to the interference of man upon Nature.

FRANCE

One of the few countries that can survive on its own, even should all imports be cut, is France. It is undoubtedly the largest, strongest country in the world. Its area relative to population is ample, vast. The country has most resources: from bauxite to coal, to iron and steel and more. Its agricultural land is more than adequate, is fertile and most crops can be grown on it with ease.

France covers a territory many times over the actual native French territory. Its former African possessions were, and, notwithstanding independence, for all practical purposes still *are* colonies. Some are huge and laden with resources. French interests exploit them to the exclusion of all competition.

But it is in the oceans that France is truly vast. Islands strewn across the globe, in every ocean and sea, span an almost limitless area. The potential in resources and fish is immense. Counting both the native territory and the overseas possessions and maritime areas, France is actually bigger than the former Soviet Union.

JAPAN

The Island of the Setting Sun on the other hand, is in fact a weak island. It is incapable of living cut off from the world. It depends completely on imports and value added manufacturing. Japan's economy is one of the most precarious. If Japan were quarantined for just fifteen days, its economy would collapse.

An oil crisis, a downturn in imports by the rest of the world, and the Japanese would be jumping off roofs, committing suicide in droves — as they have already started doing. They are becoming very conscious of this vulnerability and strive ever more to out-produce everyone else. They eye with growing concern, horror even, the emergence of China. The two countries mutually loathe each other.

GLOBILISATION

The emergence of Third World countries as manufacturers has naturally led to the creeping unemployment within the White countries. For how can one compete with the sweat-shop conditions of India and Bangladesh? How can one expect Europids to work sixteen hours a day for a bowl of rice?

For an overview of this problem read my *Threat of Globilisation*.

GEOPOLITICS

Our main priorities as a Race are:

The creation of an *Imperium Europa*, with borders sealed to all non Europids.

The repatriation of all aliens from within the Imperium.

Straight and fair competition amongst Europids only, within the protection of the frontiers.

The barter of our food surpluses alone in return for whatever we need from outside the Imperium.

The enfeeblement of all those outside the Imperium through the instigation, by whatever means, of wars amongst wogs.

The seizing of ever more additional, suitable territory at every opportunity.

In short, a policy of Racial Exclusiveness, aggressive aggrandisement.

In practice, a total war by whatever means for finite resources.

Only an *Imperium Europa* can ensure the survival of the White Race. Only the unified strength of this 5% minority of Biological Aristocrats can stem the burgeoning billions from overrunning and, ultimately, exterminating us. *We must return to the Way of Nature.*

IMPERIUM

0505

YORKSHIRE MOORS

XVII

DANGEROUS ADOPTIONS

A BELIEF, A RELIGION CAN BE pro-life or anti-life. A religion can act as the philosophical underpinning for the survival of a race or civilisation. As discussed earlier, monotheistic religions are synthetic, man-made, artificial, anti-nature and anti-life. They negate the here and now and instead fixate on the after life, the pie-in-the-sky. Certainly the most dangerous of the monotheistic, synthetic religions is Christianity. With its pandering to everything that is weak, pathetic, handicapped, bungled and botched it has brought our Western Civilisation to the brink of destruction. Two thousand Christmases have led us to the end of our survival as a species on this planet. The dosage of masochism, the suicidal poison that this perversity propagates, increases every year. The latest fad amongst the Christian do-gooders is adoption — of Africans!

Brainwashed couples are adopting Kenyan, Nigerian and Burundian babies, thinking they are performing some holy good deed. Lunatic missionaries in Africa urge White couples to adopt these Blacks and, if they could, would help send them over by the container-load. These Christian zealots are simply aiding in the destruction of our race through the miscegenation that these adoptions inevitably promote.

Christian couples, ignorant of the harsh facts, adopt Black children without even wanting to see them beforehand! God will provide! What stupidity! What utter lunacy! And local do-gooders, especially the pernicious-priests, urge them on, encourage them and promote them on TV, so that other lemmings may follow.

Earlier this year, on BBC Prime, there was a discussion programme precisely about child adoption. Five leading London child psychologists emphasised how ill-advised, dangerous even, it is for Whites to adopt Blacks, especially males. A child-psychiatrist, who was most adamant about this, was himself a Jamaican Black. He said, and I quote: 'I will never, under any circumstances, advise White couples to adopt Black children. It is highly dangerous, both for the adoptive parents as well as the child.'

Now why is this? Of course those of us who have been to Africa and observed Blacks closely in their element, know exactly why! Without the White Man's constraints, the White Man's ability to inflict instant punishment, the Black man reverts to the primitive savagery his genetic make-up forces him to. Leave the Black man alone and within six months, he will happily don his loincloth once more.

Moreover, there is the US experience during the sixties and the ruinous influence of Martin Luther King. This debauched reverend, this pervert, child molester and rapist used to bed White prostitutes in motels, two at a time — every day.

However his oratory (his speeches were written by his mentor, the communist Jew, Levinson) changed the attitudes of Whites towards the Blacks. After each inflammatory speech, guilt-ridden White parents introduced their daughters for the reverend's *Spiritual* advice. He invariably raped them. On one occasion, a fourteen-year-old resisted his persistent advances for hours. MLK then threatened to jump from the twelve-story hotel window, actually putting one foot outside, unless she did what he demanded. She finally relented.

Hoover, the FBI director, dutifully recorded these bedroom seductions and rapes. He used to send copies of the conversation tapes to King's wife, Coretta. As Hoover's assistant Sullivan commented: 'One had to admire the woman's resilience — enduring the constant creaking of the bed springs.'

Sullivan later wrote: 'MLK was one of the seven most debased and degenerate men the FBI ever had to put under surveillance.'

CONSEQUENCES

During those days, adoptions of Black children by White couples in the USA invariably turned sour. Two typical examples will suffice. A Baptist couple (unlike Catholics, Baptists actually believe the Christian tripe!), adopted a black male baby, two years older than their beautiful monozygotic twins. Two lovely girls whose pictures remind one of Barbie, the platinum-blonde doll. At twelve years of age, their adopted brother, in a fit of savage rage, knifed them to death after they had refused his molestations. The police counted over ninety stab-wounds.

In another case, an affluent couple, advanced in age, adopted a young six-year-old Black child. Neighbours commented how the adoptive parents showered their love and care over him. They sent him to the best private school in the area and bought him the best of anything he wanted. At twelve years of age, the boy poured petrol over them as they slept and burned them alive. The father was killed, while the mother suffered serious burns that left her handicapped for life. No wonder there are no longer any adoptions of Black children by White couples in America today.

Why does nobody speak about such realities? Why don't child psychologists explain the stark truth to these would-be adoptive parents? Is it fear of being branded racist which keeps them silent? Is it possible one can compromise his professional knowledge for fear of the media outcry? Where has our moral fibre gone?

The truth must be told—whatever the cost. In the coming Imperium couples who have adopted, or who cohabit with Blacks, will be expelled from the Imperium. With them will have to go their mixed-breed offspring, the innocent victims of racial treason. All will become outcasts—as in India of old with the laws of *Manu*. They will live the rest of their lives in Africa, where they can then enjoy a truly Black life. Not one single non-Europid will be tolerated within the coming, inevitable, unstoppable *IMPERIUM EUROPA*.

IMPERIUM

0105

CHAPTER XVIII

MENS SANA
IN
CORPORE SANO

'A HEALTHY MIND IN A HEALTHY body' — so said the Romans and the Spartans before them. An ethos, an ethical concept of life based on health and strength. A time when the White Race dominated the known world. We were indeed strong: Spiritually, Mentally and Physically.

Two thousand years of fetid Christianity have enfeebled us to the point of racial suicide. We have been disarmed by the enemy within: the enemies of Europe and their lackeys. Obnoxious TV hosts, media bosses, editors, columnists and journalists all propagating multi-racialism and the destruction of Europe. All squealing, shrieking and snarling that we must let inassimilable aliens within our midst, to contaminate our women.

Our armed forces held in check while savages attack them at detention centres with chicken-leg bones straight into their eyes. Oranges, with razor blades embedded, hurled at their faces. Scalding hot food graciously served to the immigrants, flung contemptuously in the face of Maltese cooks.

And if our boys had to react, to defend themselves?

Then the entire weight and viciousness of our traitor-politicians falls on top of them. Recently, after a particularly violent riot, our army and police had to perforce quell the rioters. Two politicians, or better *zewg pulcinelli* (two clowns), representing the opposition, initiated an inquiry — not on the rioters, but on their fellow citizens, our Maltese brothers. The result: four police officers are undergoing investigations and could lose their jobs. I want to make it clear that we of *Imperium Europa* will not forget these two traitors.

A generation of children raised pampered and spoilt. A diet of garbage fast-food and lack of exercise have produced armies of weak willed, fat little brats. A race of *figli di mamma* (mummy's children)!

EUGENICS AND EUTHENICS

It is clear that we have to take on a New Way. Within the coming Imperium, 'Men will be trained for war — and women for the recreation of the warrior'. — Throughout the Imperium, schools will raise new generations of men and women that do not continue to be an embarrassment to Nature.

Firstly, we will adopt a Eugenics programme throughout the Imperium. By this I mean the breeding of strong, intelligent men and women. Severely handicapped or mentally defective persons would either be aborted or terminated through humane euthanasia within the first hour of birth. That alone would save untold misery to parents and billions of euros in wasted public funds.

We will encourage the breeding of super-babies that will attain the level of present-day professors — but at twelve years of age. A breeding upwards rather than the dysgenic disaster we are heading for. China has already started such a programme, unhampered as it is with that debilitating disease, that virus of Christianity: pestering priests and busy-bodies that have painted our genetic scientists as criminals.

At the same time the Imperium will promote Euthenics. The strengthening of the Race through Sport, Outdoor Life, Environment, Education and Diet.

Sport: We will return to the Spartan Tradition in European Thought. Schools where discipline and a rigid regimen for both mind and body will turn out lads and young ladies with stacks of character, will and fortitude.

Outdoor Life: Everyday sport as part of the curriculum. Travel throughout the Imperium, especially to the more impervious, remote regions. Exploration, mountaineering, long treks across the countryside: always with an element of roughness and danger.

Environment: Huge open spaces, vast forests surrounding Sky-Cities. Clean mountains, clean seas, clean countryside. No pollution anywhere — back to Nature!

Education: Good, solid Racial Consciousness — a pride in one's Race, ethnicity. A whole Race proud to belong to that Biological Aristocracy that is the Europid Race. Racialists all, who would never dream of defiling the *Sacred Gene Pool*.

Diet: Healthy food, Nature's blessing. The best food from every Region within the Imperium. *Mens sana in corpore sano.*

IMPERIUM

0402

XIX
THE
FAR RIGHT

THREE YEARS AGO, A LEARNED friend of mine, a true Libertarian, remarked to me: 'Norman, I fear that the Far Right is taking over the world.' Since then a lot has happened in international politics. Right-wing parties are steadily gaining influence all over Europe. The farther the EU expands eastwards, the stronger these parties seem to get.

Italy has had the National Alliance elected as the third strongest party. It is an invaluable ally to the government coalition of the 'centre-right'. Just ten years ago this would have been unthinkable. *Alleanza Nazionale* was ostracised, boycotted, ignored by the establishment parties and its votes practically counted for nothing.

Again in Italy we had the rise of the Lega, with its outright anti-immigration policy. Its leader, Umberto Bossi, openly called for shooting at boats carrying illegals. When asked how he could push for the drowning of humans he replied: 'Well, I didn't call for the shooting of illegal immigrants, just at the boats! — Just don't be in them!'

In Belgium, the Vlaams Blok (now the Vlaams Belang) has garnered 30 percent of the vote in some areas. Likewise the Danish People's Party. Haider's FPÖ is still strong, while in Germany the NPD simply refuses to go away. Notwithstanding a sustained effort, employing every dirty trick in the book in order to stamp it out, it keeps winning local parliament seats.

But it is in France that the Right is winning big. There, Le Pen garnered six million votes in the presidential elections. Most of his voters were real Frenchmen, many of whom pluri-decorated in wars across the globe on behalf of France. The mainstream candidate benefited from the immigrant vote, as well as a system stacked against the outsider. All Le Pen's votes did not muster a single seat in the Paris parliament — and yet, the coming European elections in May 2004 will transform Le Pen's party into the largest French group of Euro-Parliamentarians in Brussels. It could be like this, all over the rest of Europe with other 'Far-Right' parties.

But let us define our terms. What is the Far-Right? Is it quasi-Fascist or Nazi? The media screams that it is and labels such parties 'extreme, Fascist or Nazi'. Therefore, are 30 percent of the Belgians, the Danes and six million Frenchmen Nazis? Ridiculous!

These millions of voters all over Europe are nothing but ordinary citizens. Average men and women who are opening their eyes to this Moloch that is engulfing them. People who are recoiling in horror at the multi-racial mess drowning their countries. Citizens who are tired of seeing Africans in their midst, rioting at the drop of handkerchief. People afraid to go out after nightfall for fear of being mugged, raped, if not brutally murdered by savages.

This is not the Far-Right. This is not the manifestation of some 'extreme' form of political ideology. This is simply nations waking up and starting, just starting, to defend themselves.

COMMUNISTS

We have had almost a century of communism. A cruel, despotic, anti-nature philosophy that left eighty million people murdered in cold blood with a bullet at the back of the head. Yet when communism fell, we never had a Nuremberg trial of leading communists. We never had Wiesenthal Centers hunting communist criminals around the world. On the contrary, communists simply donned smart business suits and carried on as normal. Now, why is this?

Is it because communism was never the White Man's creation? Is it because many of the most important founders and leaders of this movement, were all members of that tiny tribe that has always been hostile to Europe? That tribe of untouchables, those chosen ones, those mischief-makers who control the world's media? Perhaps — just perhaps!

MALTA

In Malta it is no different. Our Movement, *Imperium Europa*, is labeled 'Fascist, Nazi, extreme, loony right, mad minority' and such like by the local papers — those puppets in the hands of obscure forces orchestrating the whole media-melody. I myself have faced constant lies and a character-assassination campaign that goes on every day in the papers, TV and radio. However, 'That which does not kill me makes me stronger.'

I was banned by the local media for over four years. While every piglet in the farm dug his little hoof in me, I was gagged by snarling ex-communists, posing as Liberals. Communists and priests, both controlling the local media here, led a campaign of lies about me and our Movement. But it was to no avail — they have not broken us, let alone stopped us in our fight to regain our country.

Those who control the media here say that they ban us because we 'spread hate'. Now, hate and love are a question of perception, depending on a particular society at a particular time in history. Christ was crucified because he 'spread hate'. A jealous Sicilian who stabs the girl he wants because she loves another, proclaims it is love that pushes him to murder. And just who do these media hosts think they are to judge others, to be the value-givers of love and hate? These so-called liberals are nothing more than pocket dictators, ex-communists, Marxists, collectivists.

We spread love. Love for our Race, our Civilisation, our various European Nations, our Country, our People. We love all these more than anything else since they make us what we are. We spread a message of love, just as we did on Valentine's Day with the National Alliance card: 'Love Your Race', or in Maltese: *IMĦABBTEK LEJN RAZZTEK*.

I have declared time after time that we are neither Fascists nor Nazis. That we are of the Radical Racialist Right, Revolutionary Reactionaries. That we come from a long line of Revolutionary Conservative thought that includes Guénon, Evola and Ortega y Gasset. However, since enemy slander has not stopped, why bother? We are what we are and we will continue doing what we are doing now: nothing will stop us until our goal is achieved.

But lately the censorship has started to develop cracks. As Leader of our Movement, *Imperium Europa*, I am being invited to TV debates, interviews, radio talk shows etc. We are now in a position to pick and choose amongst the squabbling, competing mass media. We will always honour our commitments to those that honour theirs. We are intrinsically fair-minded and all we ask is a minimum of fair play. Too much to ask from media 'experts'. For we all know what is the definition of an 'expert': X unknown quantity, SPURT drops of liquid under pressure!

We who have endured. We who have taken it on the chin. We who have survived and simply refused to throw in the towel, are now too strong for our enemies. In fact, we get stronger by the day. We can no longer be ignored, laughed out of existence. So now, the music has changed: we are now considered 'dangerous'.

And we are! We are dangerous to all enemies of Europe, those who work day and night for the destruction of our race. Dangerous to the lackeys who serve them and thereby commit treason against their own people. Dangerous to those pernicious priests who urge the assimilation of African savages in our midst. We are dangerous to all these traitors.

Yes, we are mortally dangerous to our numerous enemies. Those media bosses, TV hosts, columnists, plying their message of multi-racialism and lies. Yes indeed — we are dangerous!

And one day, soon, they will come to realise just how dangerous we can be. As soon as we, of the International Right, consolidate political power all over Europe: *faremo i conti, con tutti gli interessi!*

XX

HIGH CLASS - LOW CLASS

Up until the beginning of the First World War, Nobility and Money were synonymous — they came together. Upper Class (UC) people had wealth. They also had the privilege, the choice, of keeping apart from the Lower Classes (LC). It was easy for them to do so — money was a great divide.

All this came to an end after that great conflagration which pitted European against European and left the continent bled white. The Nobility and Upper Classes were decimated during that Great War since they led 'up front'. Casualties were proportionately higher for the Upper Classes than for the Lower ones.

Today, money is no barrier to the Lower Classes. In fact, these earn as much as, if not more, than the UC. With two or more jobs, a greater number of children working as soon as they leave school, the LC have greater earning power than ever before.

This money power gives the LC the ability to follow and swarm around the UC — much to the annoyance of the latter. Try as they might, the UC find it extremely hard to shake off the LC nuisance. These follow the UC with the unshakable determination of a bloodhound.

Changing meeting places is no good. The LC have an uncanny ability to sniff out the latest haunts of the UC. Within a week or two, you will find them there — with a smirk on their stupid faces, as if to say: 'We're here — and you thought you could get rid of us!'

DEFINITION OF TERMS

But what, one may ask, makes a person UC or LC? Since it is no longer a question of money, then the terms follow a cultural connotation. Today, UC stands for cultured people — cultured in every sense of the word. LC stands for the opposite: the crude, loud-mouthed, poor-tasted insufferable mob.

One can observe the difference between the two types by their taste: from music, to the arts, to sport, to the choice of TV programs they follow.

For example, some weeks ago, TVM, the national station, featured Puccini's *Tosca*. It was a great performance: strong, passionate, with a superb tragic ending. At the same time, NET TV, a party station pandering to the greatest number of voters, regaled us with the usual *Porċina* (pig sty), that most boring program showing some village feast: *San Bubollu!*

A tiny minority of Maltese viewers, naturally UC, watched Tosca while the great mob wallowed in the inanity of *Porċina*.

So far, so good — but what happens when the two classes meet? How can the UC avoid the *Porċina* fans? This is the problem! For it is no use setting up money as a barrier. It is no use hiding in some five-star hotel to enjoy a well-earned holiday, a good quiet lunch with Vivaldi as background music; you are sure to find that LC family, with their young brat howling at the top of his voice: *Ma, ara ħadli il-ġobon!* (Mummy, he took my cheese!)

CULTURAL BARRIERS

The UC can only separate themselves from the LC through the cultural divide. They have to set up cultural barriers, cultural constraints and not monetary ones. The choice is vast and it is just a question of, as the Italians put it, *l'imbarazzo della scelta* (being spoiled for choice).

In the seventies young UC people started going out late: 11pm, midnight, 1am, 2am and even 3am — just to keep away from the LC. It did not work for long: LC youngsters followed the pattern.

Jacket and tie, Black Tie, formal dinners, strict no-smoking areas, a whole array of barriers and constraints act as a cultural Berlin Wall to keep the LC away. Even table manners continually adapt and become more complex and subtle, just to keep the LC confused, unsure, uncomfortable and ill at ease. One must remember that in the old days Kings ate with just a dagger. Table manners and an ever-increasing armoury of cutlery, evolved as a means to keep cultured people in blissful apartheid from the LC. Upper Class and Low Class are still very much with us today. The battle between them is a Cultural battle and not a monetary one. One can be UC and be moderately poor — one can be filthy rich and still very much LC.

The battle between UC and LC is today more subtle, more lethal. The outcome, or more precisely, the survival of the UC minority means the survival of our civilisation — since UC are the bearers of our Culture.

If the UC minority loses this battle of survival, if those ten percent who watched *Tosca* should switch channel and join the *Porčina* crowd — then Western civilisation will end up as one warm mud bath.

IMPERIUM

0104

XXI

ARM
THE
PEOPLE!

THE CLASSIC EXAMPLE OF A Military State is Sparta. There, the Dorians under the guidance of Lycurgus directed the whole attention of the State toward military prowess. Infants were publicly examined and if found physically defective, left abandoned in the hills to perish. The Spartans ate frugally at public mess halls, under strict supervision, so that luxury and indulgence would be curbed. Both boys and girls underwent military training and the Spartan army was known throughout the classical world as the toughest and most disciplined of its time.

The Spartan Tradition in European thought influenced whole countries, right up to this day. France, Sweden, Prussia, Austria and National Socialist Germany were all, at one time or another, great admirers of the Spartan way of life.

And yet Athens, the centre of culture and high living, of great drama, tragedies, philosophy, music, sculpture and ceramic art, finally won the Peloponnesian War against its great rival, Sparta! This proved that high culture and the joy of living may be combined with fitness and the readiness for war. Eventually however, Athens declined and degenerated through the importation and miscegenation with non-Doric, non-White peoples. As a direct consequence, Athens succumbed to the might of Rome! *Roma Imperialis!*

Rome started as a small tribe in the marshlands of Lazio. Through negotiations or war, more surrounding tribes were merged with the original core of three, till they became twenty-nine tribes. These then smashed the more evolved Etruscans. Rome became a world power, and its basic policy was always: 'If you want peace — then prepare for war.' Eventually however, as with Athens, softness and decadence crept in. Material well-being became the only goal for the people and the immigration of Egyptians and Jews finally killed Rome.

Throughout history, healthy armed nations prevailed over decadent, unprepared ones. Barbaric hordes swept from afar, over the ill-manned gates, and vanquished the 'civilised' peoples. These had become too soft and therefore deserved, as per Nature's law, to go under.

Up to fifty years ago, the White Man towered over the rest of humanity. When he was virile, warlike, expansionist and lived according to Nature's laws, he was unbeatable. The enemy within however, undermined the European and through the abject religion of Christianity, a veritable virus, brought about our decline. Not only that, the international-manipulators with their control on our media, set us up against each other in one fratricidal folly after another. Today, we are on the brink of extinction as a sub-species.

WAKE UP OR DIE!

Germany under National Socialism had a vigorous and healthy youth. Sport in schools was given high priority. Recreation was really *re-creation!* The time to regenerate oneself and become a better, stronger individual. The weak, the genetically defective, were prevented from breeding, a policy copied from socialist Sweden which was the first, in 1929, to adopt such a eugenics programme. Few today remember the fact that it was democratic, socialist Sweden to first sterilise thirteen thousand genetically defective Swedes. A good and sound investment, and today one can still see the result: Sweden has a completely healthy, non-defective popula-tion — the healthiest nation in the world.

Outside of the United States, National Socialist Germany also had the most liberal gun laws in the world. Yet crime was minimal since the nation was strong. The citizenry protected themselves from criminal el-ements, which were immediately identified and neutralised. National So-cialist Germany was one of the happiest, healthiest and safest countries in the whole world.

Times have changed since then. The decline and decadence decreed by the democracies has reached a nadir. In England, just one homosexual paedophile who murdered nine children left in his care single-handedly brought about the abolishment of gun ownership, thus depriving millions of law-abiding, gun owners of their sport and ability to protect their fam-ilies. Instead of ensuring that no homosexuals would ever be given charge of minors (teachers, scout-leaders, girl-guide-leaders etc.), brutal legisla-tion was quickly passed outlawing guns. As the Duke of Edinburgh aptly put it, amidst the shock and furore the murders provoked: 'He could have used a cricket-bat!'

The whole scope of the traitor politicians, perennial puppets of the international-manipulators — the Mendellsons and the Jack Straws — was of course, the disarming of the British people. Since the child-murders, crime in Britain has soared. Armed criminals seized their chance as they swooped on a disarmed citizenry. Police in England are so inundated with burglary alarm-calls and hold-ups that the answer, 'Sorry, we have no one to send at the moment!' has become their normal response.

Recently, one British householder who spotted two coloured men burglarising his garden shed, phoned the police and received the stan-dard reply. Thereupon he waited a few minutes and rang the police sta-tion again, calmly saying, 'No need to send anybody — I just shot both of them!' Within minutes all hell broke loose: helicopters, armoured cars, police cars with sirens wailing, the whole works! Naturally, the object of the whole exercise being the arrest of the householder.

The decline of democratic Europe progresses each year. European cities have become jungles of concrete, infested with trousered apes. Our women get mugged, beaten and raped. Reverse discrimination goes on unabated, cruelly punishing Whites while encouraging Blacks. Our traitor politicians offer only platitudes and Christian cant.

The White Man is finally waking up from his stupor. Patriots in the Low Countries, France, Germany and Eastern Europe are recognising who is the real, hidden enemy within. As Europe unites, the crucial, fundamental political battle is what kind of Europe will emerge: an Aryan or Judaised Europe.

The only solution for the old continent is the triumph of the Imperium *IDEA*. Within the coming *IMPERIUM EUROPA*, 'Man would be trained for war — and women, for the recreation of the warrior'! — All else is folly!

Self-defence in unarmed combat (grappling and striking) would become compulsory at all schools. One remembers the sissy socialists moaning over the sale of toy guns! While our racial enemies train their young to hate us, train them to fight and bear arms at the age of four, our Christian Democratic-Socialist wimps wail for our disarmament. They would rather leave our children disarmed and defenceless, to be sacrificed like lambs, to have their throats slit. All in the name of 'world peace'.

Within the Imperium all citizens would have to bear arms for self-defence. Every household would have to own at least one gun, similar to current Swiss Home Defence Corps. All drivers would be obliged to carry a handgun in every car. Every able-bodied citizen would be expected to defend himself in case of unprovoked attack or robbery. If he does not, then *prima facie* that would be construed as a show of cowardice, or worse, as aiding and abetting crime.

The Elite guiding the Imperium will, like the Spartans, the ancient Athenians and the old Romans, forge *A New Consciousness — A New Order — A new People!*

IMPERIUM

0307

XXII

THE
DEATH PENALTY

A FEW WEEKS AGO I GAVE an interview to Police Supt. Raymond G. Zammit. He has a diploma in criminology and is doing his last year for an MA in the same subject. The Supt. is a lecturer at the Police Academy.

Supt. Zammit is the author of a very informative book entitled *Meta Tibki il Korp* (Tears of the Corps), a history of policemen who died during the course of their duties. He is now preparing his second book, regarding the Death Penalty; and this was the reason he sought me.

The Supt. was astounded to learn that Norman Lowell, a Radical Racialist Rightist, is dead against the Death Penalty.

Retribution in the courts is nothing but a sublimated sense of revenge. 'An eye for an eye' is ingrained in our subconscious. Since earliest times man has sought 'justice' through penalties, often increasing their harshness in proportion to their ineffectiveness. We must remember that in Medieval Britain, boys used to be hanged for stealing a knife or a fork, for pick-pocketing — while pick-pockets deftly went about their business during the hangings.

In the White World, crime by Whites against Whites was always relatively low in comparison with, for example, Black on Black crime. South Africa today, an independent nation, is a glaring example of rampant Black crime.

Thus, while the need for the Death Penalty subsided in most of the civilised White world, especially in Western Europe after WWII, the clamour for it in America has increased from year to year. States that had abolished it are under increasing pressure to reintroduce it. And the reason is obvious. Two completely different races, one sophisticated and the other most primitive, live cheek by jowl. Black on White crime in the USA is fourteen times greater than White on Black crime — and the Blacks constitute only 12% of the population.

Faced by this jungle creeping into their suburbs, from which the Whites flee as the 'black ink' spreads, the cry for the Death Penalty echoes throughout America. President Bush, possibly the stupidest President in the entire history of the USA, has understood this simple, basic truth.

In Holland the murder of Pym Fortuyn and van Gogh, the latter by a Moroccan turned Dutchman through the simple expedient of a bureaucratic rubber stamp, has revamped the Death Penalty debate. Short shrift for murderers seems a fast, effective solution. But is it?

WHITES UNDER SIEGE

The White race is a dwindling minority of 5 percent of the world's population. In fifteen years it will be 4 percent. We are under siege. Blacks and others are breeding within our midst and soon, very soon, our capital cities will be overrun. We will become minorities in our own heartland.

In this scenario the Death Penalty is certainly to be encouraged. For the chances are that it will be used predominantly against murderous minorities in our midst. In plain language, it would help, albeit in a very small way, in cleaning up the stables. But for us of *Imperium Europa*, the Death Penalty can never be the final solution.

SERIAL KILLERS

Serial killers have always been the object of abhorrence and revulsion. The cry for the Death Penalty for these murderers comes naturally. But is this the solution to this particular problem? When one executes a serial killer one kills with him the genetic key to solving the problem. His children carry in their very genes their father's inclinations. This tendency to snap from a perfectly normal person to a murderous machine may lie dormant for generations — but it is there, lurking, ready to manifest itself again.

Serial killers in the USA are hardly ever executed. Lucas murdered over 400 people, of whom over 300 corpses have been found. Geneticists study him. In his DNA may lie the secret for the ultimate cure for serial killings.

The Russian Rostov murderer caused outrage and fear. He used to gauge the eyes out of his victims, before castrating them and sodomising them. When he was finally caught President Yeltsin promised swift execution, but, after the trial no more was heard. No photo of the mass murderer was ever exhibited, in order to placate the victims' families. Not only that, it is a strongly held view that he was sold for two million dollars to a Canadian institute specialising in genetics.

Years ago the study of phrenology, the linking of crime to morphology and the shape of one's head, was becoming a science. Now, we can move beyond phrenology to genetics. With the discovery of DNA and the continuous growth of genetics as a major study underlying most human problems, including crime, it is time to revalue the efficacy of the Death Penalty.

IMPERIUM EUROPA

In our future, inevitable, unstoppable *Imperium Europa*, there will be no place for the Death Penalty. Once established, the Imperium will cleanse itself of all non-Europids. They will be forcefully repatriated to their respective continents. Those non-Europids serving either jail-terms for murder or, as in the USA, are in death-row for crimes against Whites, will all be summarily executed in a matter of days.

As for Whites serving for the crime of murder, these will be transferred from prisons to specialised clinics. There, they will spend the rest of their lives being studied. They will serve as human guinea pigs in the service of the Imperium. They will help us solve, once and for all, the genetic problem of serious crimes like murder, rape, paedophilia and others. Eventually, as the culling continues over generations, such crimes will certainly decrease.

We need to revert to science, not superstition — to genetics, not gallows — to eugenics, not electrocution. The days of the Death Penalty are rapidly coming to an end.

IMPERIUM

0502

XXIII

MURDER
MOST FOUL!

As I HAVE DISCUSSED ABOVE, Rudolf Hess was an expert on World Masonry. He knew every single lodge in the world and kept records on them. He was also in close contact with Scottish Masonry. In 1939 Hess flew all the way to Scotland in a final, desperate attempt to prevent war amongst racial cousins. He could easily have flown to Dover, Cornwall or Margate, but instead chose the hazardous, long solitary flight to the north of Scotland. His aim was to meet Scottish Masons and urge them to convince the British fraternity to avert the slaughter.

Churchill, an English Lodge Mason, killed the Hess peace attempt. He even refused to meet him — or so we are officially told! The Hess Papers, due to have been made public years ago, were again wrapped up till 2037. Upon their release, Churchill would come out as he truly was!

After the war Rudolf Hess, a true hero of Europe, the man who could have saved millions of slaughtered Whites in that great, senseless fratricide, languished in solitary confinement for nearly half a century — a sentence not even fit for a murderer. We were led to believe that it was the Russians who had objected to his release throughout these long years. However, when Gorbachev assumed power, one of his first acts was to publicly call for the release of Hess. *Guarda caso*, the British resolutely refused — and finally, Hess died mysteriously at Spandau prison during the British term of custodianship.

One autopsy hurriedly concluded that he had died of strangulation with a telephone wire, after jumping off a table. The second autopsy, commissioned by the Hess family and carried out by the world's foremost forensic expert, agreed that, yes, death was by strangulation — but Hess had been throttled from behind. There was no evidence of the telltale jerk produced by a fall.

A Scottish lady, married to a Maltese and now living in Hamburg, was the nurse at Spandau. She was the first who saw Hess dead in his cell. Perhaps, one day, she may decide to tell us what she knows.

Hess died just as world opinion was pressing for his release. A re-united Germany, just a year away, would surely have released him. Hess had to die. Why?

Hess had to die because on his release Europeans would have been told who were the real schemers, perpetrators and victors of World War II. We would have been told that Britain knew, conclusively and without a shadow of doubt — that it had the proof, in writing and endorsed by a former monarch — that Germany would never have attacked her if left alone to crush Bolshevism. We would have known that World War II was nothing more than a struggle for the soul of Europe — won by the international-manipulators.

CARMELO BORG PISANI

I was a very young bank clerk at the National Bank of Malta when I met CBP's brother — a serious, sad Monsignor whom I never saw smiling. He effected a bank transaction every three months, and I took these opportunities, over a few years, to talk to him in dead earnest. He once told me *'it-tragedja ta hija ghad trid tinkiteb kollha'* ('my brother's tragedy has yet to be fully written') implying that the whole sad story about his brother's final days had yet to be uncovered. These words compelled in me a burning desire to find out the whole truth regarding CBP.

Years later, discussing Hess with a very informed Englishman of undoubted integrity, I asked why the Hess papers had been sealed, yet again, for another fifty years. He casually remarked that CBP's papers had suffered the same fate. Now, why would a relatively obscure Maltese fascist merit the Hess treatment? What was this secret that the Foreign Office was guarding so jealously?

My informant, a 33rd degree Mason, revealed to me that the answer lies in a Memo of Discussion raised by the then Governor, Lord John Gort. In it, he noted a meeting he had with the leading Maltese personality on the island at the time, hereinafter called X.

Now, the Monsignor, on behalf of the whole Pisani family, had pleaded repeatedly with X that he may intervene with the Governor to save CBP's life. X always reassured the Most Reverend that he would do his best.

In actual fact, the Memo reveals that X urged the British to execute CBP without further delay, as otherwise an enraged populace, suffering daily bombardment, would turn against the British. As the Memo notes, this Judas was only safeguarding his position, knowing only too well that, upon a fascist victory, he would have found himself tending a flock somewhere in Ethiopia.

The British never wanted to hang CBP. Put into the position of Pontius Pilate, they washed their hands. As the Iscariot had killed Jesus with a kiss, so did X sentence CBP to death.

One day, the CBP papers and Memo will see the light of day: and this perfidious betrayal, this murder most foul, will become official history.

And — who was X?

IMPERIUM

0602

XXIV

THE
ACTIVIST

Dedicated to all those *Adherents*, who fight bravely against incredible odds, for the survival of our Great White Race:
ENDURE!
For Victory shall be OURS!
AVE!
Ave! Mi Fratres in Spiritu!

THE ACTIVIST

THE POLITICAL-SOLDIER, THE ACTIVIST, IS the one who rises above the silent majority. It is he who fights every day, wherever he may be, office, shop-floor, clubs to spread the *IDEA* he believes in. His unstinting efforts and dedication may make him eligible to enter CORE, the leading nucleus in the country or region. An Activist is not chosen — he chooses himself. These are the rules that govern him:

1. You will find obstacles of all kinds: family, 'friends', funds.

2. You will never again live 'a normal life'.

3. You will however, live a 'meaningful' one!

4. Don't worry about what other people say about you: they should respect you for *who* you are, not *what* you are.

5.   Do not waste time on stupid people.

6.   Seek comradeship amongst the worthy.

7.   Our enemies have no valid arguments against us. Their only weapon is fear. Must I fear what others fear? — Nonsense!

8.   Be brave! Never crawl.

9.   People admire bravery and respect a man of principles.

10.   Some of us can achieve more under anonymity.

11.   Apparent quitters are a dormant asset.

12.   Contacts in high places are never wrong. Cultivate them: police, army, judges, journalists, successful businessmen.

13.   Put all your energy and skills into the involvement.

14.   Seek your drug for your relaxation.

15.   Keep improving your website: attractive, interesting.

16.   Keep your business dealings clear, clean and fair.

17.   A hostile press keeps an eye on us. Play it with a relish!

18.   No random attacks on immigrants — counter-productive.

19.   Keep the spotlight on our internal enemies and the international-manipulators.

20.   Never deny your own views. This is worse than anything the enemy can do. Never apologise!

21.   There is no greater satisfaction in life than to save the future of our children.

22.   The struggle is a mission fought by the Shining Knighthood of our Sacred Blood.

AVE ATQUE VALE!
Imperium
0401

CORE

The best of the Activists. It is CORE (Command, Organisation, Revolutionary Elite) that imparts general strategy and ideology. It leaves tactics and operations in the hands of the Activists. CORE groupings in the various countries and regions are the precursors of the Elite.

FOR:

1. Supremacy of Culture over Politics

2. Beyond Fascism and Parliamentary Democracy

3. Beyond out-dated dichotomy of Left and Right

4. Differentialism

5. Revival of the Sacred

6. Return to Indo-European pre-Christian values

7. Substratum of primordial pagan wisdom for the Elite

8. A nature-oriented, cosmological belief

9. A Spherical, nonlinear view of history

10. We are living in an interregnum of final duration

11. Revival can happen at any time, suddenly

12. Organic Culture as against mechanistic civilisation

13. Culture as an Organic Life-Form

14. Organic Imperium

15. A Spiritual not Economic Imperialism

AGAINST:

1. Decadence of Socialism, Liberalism, mechanistic Democracy

2. Egalitarianism — lowering down, social and cultural atrophy

3. Universal human rights

4. Technocracy

5. Materialism

6. Modernity

7. Globalisation

8. Americanisation — *Homo dollaris uniformis*

9. Judeo-Christianity

DUALISM:

1. Faith - Reason

2. Body - Soul

3. Past - Future

4. Time - Space

5. Individual - *Volk*

6. Myth - Reality

> Fight!
> Search for: Leaderless Resistance Louis Beam
> And carry on from there:
> Build your cell of four — no more.
> Do what you think is right!
> *Ave atque vale!*
> THINK! — ACT! — BE!

If you feel there is something wrong with this modern world.

If you can see the disastrous effects all round, in every sphere of life, but cannot somehow pinpoint the fundamental cause.

If you recognise the fact that the White Race is disappearing off the face of the planet. — And: if you want to do something about it —

Then: Help our Movement.

Our PayPal account: imperium.europae@gmail.com

The Elite

This is the realm of The Elite, the masculine side of *Imperium Europa*.

The Elite jealously guards its five attributes :

Radical — Racialist — Right — Revolutionary — Reactionaries

RADICAL

We are not of the pusillanimous, moderate, centre parties, tip-toeing cautiously on the centre strip. They have their ears to the ground, always on the lookout to gauge what majority-mediocrity is bleating about, at any given time. These parties of both the Left and the so-called Right, lead from behind.

We lead up front. We are light-years ahead in the realm of IDEAS — and we proclaim what we believe in, openly, without fear. Indeed, we are *Radical*.

RACIALIST

And proud of it! We are not racists, in that we do not place a moral or value judgement on the races. We observe them all — and come to the natural conclusion that races are different. In consequence, we intend to safeguard this difference, this biological aristocracy that is the White Race. That race that gave humanity and the world everything. We intend to protect our genes, ourselves and our progeny, within the non-porous borders of our coming, inevitable, unstoppable: *IMPERIUM EUROPA*. Indeed, we are *Racialists*.

RIGHT

We are not the collectivists, the socialist slaves of the Left. We believe in the supreme integrity of the Individual. We will place all responsibility, in all spheres of life, on the *person* and not on society. We will give maximum liberty and responsibility onto the Individual, in the Dominium sphere of politics.

In the Imperium sphere, we believe that government should be in the hands of qualified persons. In fact, the most qualified: the Elite. Bred to lead, trained to endure hardship and stress, above all in mundane vicissitudes, this group of Super Men will ideologically, disdainfully discard the socialist, equalitarian dogma of death. Indeed, we are of the *Right*.

REVOLUTIONARY

We are not the conservatives of the old school, fossilised in the past, timorous of the future. We are not monarchists, aristocrats of titles, of dukedoms, baronets, bishops and bishoprics! We are not knights of the Catholic Church, organising pilgrimages to the polluted waters of Lourdes. We are not Liberals, advocating the dissolution of the last vestiges of the fabric that holds our struggling society together. If anything, we are Libertarians in the pure sense of the word: in the Dominium sphere.

We are always ahead of the rest, in whatever counts for the survival of our Race. Never contenting ourselves with the flat monotony of the plateau of IDEAS. We will never cease to Think, to Act, to *BE!* Indeed, we are *Revolutionary*.

REACTIONARIES

In the purest sense of the word. Yes, we are Reactionaries! Like an antibiotic that attacks what is alien, noxious and deadly, so do we, *Adherents* of *IMPERIUM EUROPA*, react to all attacks on our Spirit, Race, and People.

We will never tire. We will be ceaseless, incessant in our attacks, by all means at our disposal, on all our numerous enemies: those within and those outside. The internal enemies, those international mischief-makers, are the most deadly. It is with them that our final battle has to be fought and won. It will be a pitiless war, with mercy neither given nor asked. We will go after them and attack them again and again till we vanquish them all.

Then we will square things up with their lackeys: obnoxious TV hosts, columnists and journalists, media bosses, traitor politicians and pernicious priests. — There are not enough lampposts! Yes, indeed, we are *Reactionaries!*

We, of the Radical — Racialist — Right — Revolutionary — Reactionaries!

XXV

THE WAY FORWARD

W E HAVE COME A LONG way since our very first meeting at the *Fra Ben* when we launched our Movement. That was February earlier this year. A modest beginning but, as I stressed in my after-dinner speech, one of great portent. For on that day, the *IDEA* of IMPERIUM was publicly launched. There was no going back. The seed was sown.

We were not many — we were the precious few. But within each of us, within our souls and hearts, was that innermost yearning, desire to change our country, nay the whole Western world. We all felt that there was something wrong with the way things were going in Malta and the White World — and we were determined to fight this malaise and save our Country, our great Race and Civilisation.

Yes, we have come far since our modest beginnings. We have contested an election on a national scale — and emerged stronger. 1,600 core votes and thousands more as second preferences. Yes, our work and our efforts were rewarded. We expected better — but our enemies trembled!

Now what? Which is *the Way Forward?* Should we form a party and have party members pay a yearly fee, as the others do? Should we hold general conferences and public meetings and what not? Should we organise outdoor festivities, banalities and circuses for the party faithful?

None of all that! This is the year 2004, the age of TV, the media, the Internet. We already have two excellent websites. They draw new visitors every day. We are beginning to appear in somewhat better light on mainstream media, with a few columnists occasionally breaking a lance or two in our defence. We are winning the battle of ideas on the shop floor, in the factory, the offices, the pubs, schools, the university.

Yes, we are impinging our stamp and view of life on the nation. We are forcing issues, real issues above the economic level, to be discussed. We are imposing our tempo, choosing our field of battle — and winning. Our priorities are becoming the nation's prime preoccupation.

THE ELITE

We must not follow the other parties. We do not need to have thousands of party faithful, sheepishly paying their yearly dues and expecting we push their issues up front. The voters, those masticating bisons, must be kept firmly away from the decision-making cadre, the Leaders, the Elite. These alone are the ones that matter — nobody else!

As I wrote in my book *CREDO*:

'What nonsense! The herd, living in bovine contentment watching TV, pirouetting through the banality of fashion, fads and fantasies, should serve only as a resource pool for selecting the best of the Europid: a privileged class that, in turn, strives for ever higher forms of existence.'

The problem today is to find out whether there are such individuals still living — to discover them, give them a bearing, organise them, imbue them with a doctrine founded on Eternal Values. Values transcending economics. The values of Imperium, *Auctoritas* — Inequality, Hierarchy, Justice, Distinction and most of all: Race.

Today's Individualist, alone or with a chosen few, must strive, fight, to wrest control from this democratic mess. He has to direct the Europid towards a new beginning — a revolution towards a re-valuation of all present values.

An utmost contempt for a view of life based on materialism, economics, welfare — or, the other side of the same coin, the altruistic whimpering of Christianity. For the Individualist it is not a question of 'turning the other cheek', but of 'doing unto others what they would like to do to me: but to do it before — and better!'

The small shopkeeper, the civil servant, the man on the production line, the salesman is incapable of this revolution. It takes another type of man: the Inhuman.

This time the masses should not be enrolled in the political movement of the revolution, but held at the outside, as auxiliaries, to the Individualists. A Leadership must be formed to work on furthering its creed, taking great care to keep itself separate from the masses. Above all, there should be *no compromise* on fundamental principles.

The Individualist today has an unbounded freedom to communicate through the Internet. The international-manipulators have not yet found a way to control this fountain of diffusion, as they have done so well with the press and the TV. This is the Achilles heel of the whole decrepit system and it is here that the attack should be directed.

A total cultural war waged by the Individualist, every Free Spirit, every Thought-Action Man, on the present system: War in the arts, music, theatre, universities; war against hypocrisy and democracy, a fragile form of government founded on mediocrity, equality and fear.

War; shunning the useless vote and distraction of ordinary politics. A total war to topple that tottering totem. And always, *Memento Audere Semper*.

A destruction coming as a great liberation to us, who feel alienated, strangers in this mad, modern world. Us: who have no country. Us: the anti-modern! Us: anti-proletarian and anti-bourgeoisie. Us: *Reactionary Revolutionaries!*

For the victory of international subversion, promoting the collectivist ethos of both communism and liberal capitalism, was neither the inevitable tide of history, nor is it permanent. Man, depending on who and especially what kind he is, has the ability to 'do and undo'. It all depends on an iron will and a sound, philosophical underpinning. For the course of history is spherical, not linear. A spherical ball moves in any direction. So the course of our Race can change dramatically. The *umsclag*, *la svolta*, which we Absolute Individualists work for, hope for, believe in, can happen tomorrow.

The political world is at present in an interregnum: *Anno Zero*. The Satanic force of egalitarianism, unleashed in 1789, peaked with the

Jewish-Bolshevist revolution. It is now a spent force, moribund. The only political forces remaining are the mushy centre — the detritus of the various democratic-socialisms aided by a decadent, decrepit Christianity. We, the inhuman minority, must grasp the reins of that herd of bison which seems awesome, but in effect is a giant without a head of its own, ready to acquiesce, to serve.

We have to present a credible Elite to replace that democratic minority: those posturing poltroons, perennial political puppets, picayunes, pathetically pandering to their pathogenic masters; the international-manipulators.

One has to target the best, artists, writers, soldiers: '*Bisogna scavare nei più provondi abbissi, per trovare dei fondamenti, per ereggere nuovi edifici, alti e belli*' ('One has to dig to the foundations, to build afresh, upwards, tall and beautiful buildings').

Such intrepid individuals can be found in all classes. From 'errant' nobility, to the most humble folk. An inherent, anarchic, savage, nomadic instinct sublimated into an organised, coagulated, liberating action against the whole, rotten structure.

A new race of ascetics, breathing Inequality, Hierarchy, Class, Distinction, Discrimination, Distance. For there can be no liberty within equality — it is self-evident! True Liberty can only be within a system based on Inequality.

A Third Way: avoiding the communistic bureaucracy of today's parliamentary system, while rediscovering the person, as opposed to the atomised individual in this cybernetic age.

The Absolute Individualist must discover the power that is in him, confident of quality over numbers. An anarchist, a survivor, holding within him the jewel of an inner, Spiritual fortitude, resisting the degenerate world he is constrained to live in.

The greatest force is the power of the will residing in the excellence of the few. A minority of elitist Individualists which is good enough, dedicated enough, knowledgeable enough, trained enough, organised enough — can move mountains.

Self-education in all the basic knowledge of a mentally equipped Elitist. An insight into the historical context of the struggle. Appreciation of
all the major facets of the correlated and universally prevalent degeneration: cultural, social, biological and above all, *Spiritual*.

All this is necessary for that wholeness of view, fullness and readiness
of combat, of the complete belligerent. Adequate knowledge of all relevant law, police procedure, methods of hostile infiltration, provocation,
corruption and intimidation. Increasing specialisation of the Elitist as he
joins other Elitists in the common struggle. Living on a higher plane. A
purpose of life; loyalty and courage in the service of the Eternal Values of
Race. The Eternal Laws of Life. A Credo transcending geography, countries, states, nationalities.

And the end justifies the means — so long as these are in harmony and
in fulfilment of the basic principles. In fact, the end prescribes the means
and these, in turn, determine the result.

An ability to retain flexibility, to discard that which is traditional but
no longer serves a purpose. A calm discerning of what can serve best,
what to make use of in today's modern culture, without becoming its
slave — conserving the essential, fundamental principles. An unerring inner guide, a *egemonikon* for the Individualist.

Such an Individualist must overcome himself at all times to his
limit. Brooking no opposition or restraint, every moment of his life is
a splendour, a work of Art in itself. All that does not kill me makes me
stronger!

He is never a criminal. He is Beyond Good and Evil. Whatever his
'evil' deed — it is a thousand times nobler than the miserable 'good' deed
of the common man. As Ernst Jünger so aptly put it: 'Better to be a delin-
quent, than a petty-bourgeois!'

A minority of less than a quarter of a million, spread over the White
World, representing the best of this biological aristocracy which is the
Europid race. A minority of High-Culture Bearers.

A minority of Supermen who are the prime target of the international-manipulators. These last are always on the lookout for these Absolute

Individualists, ready to vilify them through the controlled press. Ready to go to all lengths to crucify them — if need be, to exterminate them.

The Inhuman, sublimated into the Absolute Individualist in the Nietzschean sense, disciplined, inured to solitude, formed into the Philosopher-Soldier, the Statesman, the Elite, the Superman of the Future. A new Heroic Aristocracy; an Aristocracy of the Spirit, of Character, of a Total View of Life — an innate, unerring *Weltanschauung*.

A Periclean Age — an age that re-discovers those Aryan, Eternal Values and Spiritual ideals which come to us from time immemorial — pre-dating the Romans — from the arch Minoan-Achaean 'Battle-Axe-Race', founders of both Rome and Sparta.

An Elite Order, at the top of which stands a Rex, beholder of an *IDEA* embodying that mysterious, indefinable, charismatic, Spiritual authority bestowed 'from above'.

THE MASSES

Granted, we need voters to get elected when we contest elections. Yes, we need the vote, but nothing else! The masses will be made to understand that we, the Elite of *Imperium Europa*, are the ones who lead, take decisions and bear responsibility. *Non pensare, c'è chi pensa per te!* (Don't think, others are thinking for you!) The masses are craving strong Leadership. They are crying out loud for it — and they shall get it!

The CORE group must at this stage remain anonymous. Only myself, as Leader, will be exposed to ridicule and attack. I am inured to that anyway. This CORE group must work quietly and incognito towards the propagation of our ideology. This is paramount.

The CORE group influences the Adherents, those who visit our sites and join us in our reunions and other activities. Adherents, in turn, will spread the message on chat lines. They will debate and demolish our adversaries, by opening appropriate threads on our enemies own discussion forums. Adherents must grasp every opportunity to debate our opponents at the place of work, school or university. They must be self-motivated: write letters to the press, phone-in on radio and TV programmes. Gradually, our world-view, our *Weltanschauung* will seep into the nation's consciousness.

Of course, we must be physically visible. We are not going to leave the market place to those two lesbic prostitutes: the squalid socialists and the Christian hypocrites! Some of our activities:

Monday Club dinner — every first Monday of the Month.

This is for those who would like to know more about us, in the comfortable and posh surroundings of a well-appointed restaurant.

Club Invites — where various clubs invite us, specifically the Leader, to dinner at their premises and then, for him to deliver an after-dinner speech. We have already had numerous such invitations, all of them hugely successful, with tremendous enthusiasm and spontaneity greeting our ideas. Dining halls, seating over a hundred, were overbooked weeks ahead of the appointed date. Extra tables were squeezed in and unseated guests stood at the bars throughout the evenings.

Mass Indoor Rallies — these are being organised. Basketball courts, gymnasiums, large halls will be ideal for us to meet hundreds of those who want to listen to our message. Of course, these have to be professionally choreographed with background music, sound system and our Lightning and Sun banners prominently displayed. All this to give a feeling of belonging. A realisation that one is not alone. That one is not a lone madman, as the enemy tries to portray us. A feeling of growing strength, uniting the Individual with the whole Movement.

Promising speakers will address the crowds. Again here, one must overcome oneself and speak publicly whenever an opportunity presents itself. One may start with small groups of listeners, gradually gaining confidence till one will be able to face a packed hall. The art of Public Speaking can be mastered. Every speaker will develop his own style, pathos, tone. The Leader will speak last.

CDs and DVDs — I am informed that such recordings of my interviews, speeches and TV appearances are being passed from hand to hand. This is to be encouraged. The message must get out there: whatever, whichever way!

Radio and TV — the mediums that reach most. As the media-mediocrity-monopoly ends, as it is bound to, once those pernicious-priests are kicked out of the way, we will be given more Radio and TV time. We will become increasingly strong, picking and choosing our programmes, our interviewers, our debating adversaries. We will run circles around them all! Of course, we will never forget Smash TV! Of course, we will never forget those who supported us.

What is *Imperium Europa*?

Imperium Europa is not the Leader. It is not the CORE group. It is not the hundreds of Adherents who are close to the Leadership. Neither is it those anonymous Activists, those cells of four, working in their own special way (see *The Activist*). Nor is it the thousands of voters who gave our Movement their trust.

Imperium Europa is bigger than all this. Bigger than its founder and his followers. Far, far bigger than all of us put together. *Imperium Europa* is an *IDEA*! It encapsulates everything! It is this *IDEA* that will save the White Race from certain extinction through racial suicide. This *IDEA* born in Malta, the Sacred Island in the Mediterranean, will yet grip the White World and place our Race once again, at the summit of humanity. We, of *Imperium Europa* are the bearers, propagators, the spearhead of this *IDEA*.

One way or the other, this *IDEA* will prevail in Malta. We, the Elite, must achieve political power on the island. Only thus can we turn this bankrupt island around. We will revalue all present, decrepit values.

ELECTIONS

These will come, sooner rather than later! Should we decide to contest, we already have individuals of quality, ready to represent our Movement in every electoral district. Now, with the EU law stipulating proportional representation with a threshold of 5%, we could elect one or more candidates to parliament. This would mean the breaking of that political duopoly by those two lesbic prostitutes! How they fear this!

We will poke hot-irons on the pants of both. We will compel the party in government to do as we say, or else! We would have our agenda implemented as a priority, in order to save this once beautiful Island and its people. We would put first things first. We, of *Imperium Europa* will save this island.

We will set an example to the rest of Europe. We will make them emulate us — and not vice versa. We will not go the way of Bradford, Brixton and Birmingham, Liege or Paris, Milan or Rome. We will lead Europe out of this multiracial mess it is in. We, of *Imperium Europa*, will lead the fight to save Europe.

Only we can do it. *Noi, soltanto Noi!* Only we, privileged and powered by the Spiritual Force permeating this Sacred Island. Great Malta, the Sacred Island of *Melitae* can help save Europe and the White Man.

We have a job to do. It is up to each and every one of us to do his part, to be pro-active, to initiate ideas followed by direct action. We will achieve our goal. *The Way Forward* is clear.

IMPERIUM

0408

XXVI

REVOLUTIONARY CONSERVATISM

Conservatism is not mere inertia, but principled behaviour. Nor is Conservatism in favour of the status quo. Were this the case, Stalin in the Soviet Union would have been a conservative, since he was all for the status quo: keeping himself in power.

One has to distinguish between conservative behaviour and conservative principles. Simply being in favour of the status quo, whatever that may be, is at best conservative behaviour, but this need not be based on conservative principles. For Conservatism is not ideological, but principled. Conservatism, as different from an Ideology, differs from place to place, from time to time. It is not uniform — it is not ideological.

This diversity does not mean incoherence at the level of principle. Throughout Conservative thought there are these bedrocks:

(1)   Belief in a Transcendent Order, or body of natural law, which rules society as well as conscience. Political problems, at bottom, are religious and moral problems.

(2)   Affection for the proliferating variety and mystery of human existence, as opposed to the narrowing uniformity, egalitarianism, and utilitarian aims of most modern, communist as well as liberal systems...

(3)   Conviction that civilised society requires order and classes, as

against the notion of a 'classless society'. Conservatives have often been called 'the party of order'. If natural distinctions are effaced among men, oligarchs fill the vacuum.

(4)   Freedom and property are closely linked. Once one separates property from private possession, Leviathan becomes master of all.

(5)   Faith in prescription and distrust of 'sophisters, calculators and economists' who construct society upon abstract designs. Custom, convention and old prescription are checks both upon man's anarchic impulse as well as the innovator's lust for power.

(6)   Recognition that change may not be salutary reform: hasty innovation may be a devouring conflagration, rather than a torch of progress. Prudent change is the means of social preservation. According to Plato, prudence is the mark of a statesman.

TRANSCENDENCE

Conservatism believes there is a metaphysical order, supra-individual, non-human. It stands over and above the physical order of things and is the source of the physical order. This Transcendent Order is mysterious: one can have knowledge of this dimension of Being, but one can never fully grasp it.

Knowledge of Transcendence comes to us through Tradition. The Tradition that Conservatism embraces is not only the activity of handing something down from earlier to later generations; it is also and primarily the activity wherein the Transcendent Order passes itself down to us. By living traditionally, human beings allow this metaphysical order of the 'Cosmic Force' to infuse our fundamental understandings, attitudes and practices. Human life is thereby informed and ordered by Transcendence. Life is given a unity whereby one may attain to the 'good or natural order' that Transcendence has determined for us.

The anti-conservative and anti-traditional person, the 'liberal', is one who denies the existence of Transcendence. He claims that the only order that human life may have is that specified by wants-and-desires; to discover empirically what these are, and to find the most efficient means of satisfying them. The liberal thereby posits an order that is uniform, since it is equally applicable whenever and wherever.

In contrast, the Transcendent Order affirmed by the conservative is manifold. It can be and has been realised in the temporal order in a variety of ways that are equivalent, but not reducible, to one another. It is mysterious — the Transcendent Order is not known, apart from, and only through, the various traditions in which it has manifested itself to us. For while humans may act to preserve a particular tradition, it is beyond their power to create a uniform one-size-fits-all traditional ideology.

The reactionary, in the sense of one who resists any change at all, is a poor conservative. Time and circumstances bring with them the necessity for change. The Conservative must resolutely discard the husk of Tradition and admit change when necessary — not at all costs and certainly not hastily. The Conservative will take pains to ensure that change will take place as a reform of the historical institutions that incarnate the principles on which he acts, not as a revision that overturns those very principles.

CONSERVATISM AND CAPITALISM

The conservative has a healthy distrust of capitalism, especially its tendency to usurp the place of other institutions in society. Capitalism tends to elevate itself, its merely economic considerations, to primacy of place within a community. This entails not only an implicit denial of a Transcendent Order, but also an explicit denial of the diversity of human existence. Such a denial is shared by present-day 'multiculturalism' which, far from affirming the distinctiveness of cultures, denies to any culture the authority to conserve its distinctiveness.

Conservatives do to some extent defend capitalism, since they defend property rights. Private property allows each person effective ownership and control of the means of providing for himself and for his family. It allows a person to be, to some extent or other, independent of others and responsible for himself. However, Conservatives keep Capitalism at an arm's length. They tend to defend it as the lesser evil, recognising that there are other aspects to society, Spiritual aspects however imperfectly understood, that have priority over merely economic considerations. Conservatives defend property rights for other than economic reasons.

Economic concerns should not become all and everything. Life is not a matter of getting and spending, merely horizontal interactions. The Conservative recognises the political and cultural dangers of such a situation. Everything becomes selling and buying. All would be gauged on money values alone. Hence, the Conservative defends private property primarily as a bulwark against these dangers, not because of its economic efficiency.

THE THREE FOES OF CONSERVATISM

Conservatism as an actual political force in present-day society has been defeated by the 'Managerial Revolution'.

Essential to capitalism is the notion that ownership and control go together. In capitalism, control of the company one owns is secured by legal ownership. One who legally owns a company is typically the one who controls it. The individual capitalist, legal owner of his company and direct administrator of it, is the typical and principal agent in the capitalist economy. In principle, there seems to be no significant difference between the corporation and the individually owned company, save for the number of owners holding legal title.

In actual fact, this is not so. As the size and complexity of the corporation grows, so does the distance between legal ownership and administrative control. It becomes increasingly necessary to hire Corporate Managers: those whose profession it is to administer the running of the corporation and who have the technical, managerial education to do so. In time, these managers, professional engineers and administrators who are the product of specialised academic training, gradually took over effective control from the legal owners of the large corporations. These latter, the stockholders, increasingly had no understanding of how to run the companies they legally owned.

The managers effected a revolution in which control of a company became separated from its legal ownership. Managers became the new dominant economic class. The replacement of the individually owned company by the corporation as the dominant force in the economy, along with the takeover of de facto ownership from the stockholders by the managers, resulted in the replacement of capitalism by a new economic form that is neither capitalist (because legal ownership no longer entails economic control), nor socialist (because there is no expropriation of capital by the state or by the people).

As stated earlier, Communism and Financial Capitalism meet at their highest point. The highest point of Communism today is nothing else than the multinationals. Huge conglomerates, with a multi-racial, unseen board of directors, more often than not manipulated by one or two of the usual tribe, operating from some unreachable, hidden headquarters. And below them, far, far below them, millions of shareholders, blind as to the operations, the machinations, the goals of their all-powerful, mysterious Moloch. Today's multinationals are nothing else but the meeting point, the convergence, the apex of both Communism and Capitalism! This apex is Liberalism.

At the same time, a parallel development occurred within government, in the emergence of a professional civil service. These Governmental Managers had become necessary in an executive branch where there was an increasing distance between 'legal ownership' (by the voters and their representatives in parliament) and 'administrative control' (by the new civil service, the product of the efforts of 'reformers' who sought to eliminate graft and patronage). Just as the Corporate Managers assumed control from the stockholders and were no longer responsible to them, so the Governmental Managers assumed control from the voters and their representatives, and were no longer responsible to them.

These two groups of managers became allies and together, eventually formed the new ruling class of managerial society. After all, they fulfilled similar functions in their respective spheres. Many were capable of moving back and forth between the two camps. They shared a common background of training and culture. This similarity of background has been reinforced by the emergence and evolvement of a third, distinct group in the managerial ruling class. Alongside Corporate Managers and Governmental Managers have arisen Cultural Managers. Those who administer mass cultural institutions such as the universities, the mass media and the realm of law.

Historically, the Cultural Managers were the last managerial group to emerge. However, they are the most important of the three branches of the ruling class. This is because Cultural Managers are the ones who establish the terms of 'acceptable' political and social discussion. They control the institutions wherein the ruling class receives its training and credentials. They ensure that new recruits to the ruling elite will have their same understanding and attitude. That they are all members of the same 'clique'. Cultural Managers control the institutions of public discourse: the media. They disseminate propaganda designed to legitimate the new ruling managerial class and to denigrate its opponents.

The most important reason for the alliance of the business corporations, the government bureaucracies and the institutions of mass culture, is that their Managers are all usurpers. They share the same enemies. All three types of Managers are opposed to the authentic capitalist society: one in which ownership and control are vested in the same people.

The Corporate Managers seized power from the individual company owners.

The Governmental Managers seized power from the constitutionally elected representatives.

The Cultural Managers seized power from those institutions helping towards the understanding and evolvement of society.

The Managerial Class seeks to destroy 'bourgeois society' by replacing:

- The individual capitalist with the transnational corporation.

- The 'rule of law' with the mass state.

- The variety of social and cultural institutions (the family, the church, regional and ethnic groups and so on), with a uniform and centralised 'culture' bent on consumerism.

What is today called 'Liberalism' is in effect the ideology of the Managerial Classes — it is the dominant ideology today.

NEEDED: A NEW ELITE

With the defeat of 'bourgeois culture' by the new Managerial Class of the corporations, the state and the media, Conservatism lost power as a social and political force. Some conservative institutions still survive: the family, religion and the larger part of everyday social life: these are in their nature conservative. There is still much in present-day society that is traditional. This remnant has received and continues to receive fearsome blows from the Managerial Class. These know that the most effective way of undermining and destroying a tradition, is to undermine and destroy its institutions and guardians.

For the traditional society to safeguard itself, it requires an institution, itself traditionally rooted, whose special role is to recognise and defend the knowledge of the Transcendent Order. We require a New Elite: an Elite of the future: an Elite as were the Templars and Teutonic Knights: an Elite of Supermen. We are in desperate need of New Guardians.

This New Elite Order must be above the Three Managerial Classes. A New Elite above economic considerations. An Elite that will spearhead the coming Conservative Revolution. An Elite that will instil a New Middle Class, replacing the disorientated middle class of today, that in effect has subrogated the proletarians of yesterday — for today's middle class has much in common with the traditional proletariat.

The present day middle class glories in its affluence and consumes whatever managerial capitalism sets before it. However, it conspicuously lacks the material independence, security and liberty of the old middle class, the one before World War One.

We of the RRRRR must appeal to a new Middle Class formed on Conservative Principles. A New Middle Class formed on Regional, rather than National character. A class conscious of being protected by an Elite: guardians of the Imperium.

This New Middle Class should be the political target of the RRRRR: the Radical, Racialist Right, Revolutionary Reactionaries. This New Middle Class is our vertical niche market. One that will enable us to bring about political and social revolution when the right moment arrives.

A 'revolution from the middle' — a revolution, a counter-culture in mortal opposition to managerial society of today's Liberalism. A revolution that will place the Guardians, the Elite, the 'Inhumans' over and above the Three Managerial Classes of today.

Up to now, we of the Right have been 'beautiful losers'. We have often focused on the truth of our positions, as against the 'liberal' ideology of the managerial class. This, at the expense of devising means for making our RRRRR position an effective force in society. No more! From now on, we of *Imperium Europa* will formulate policies that will win us political power. *Poi ne vedremo!* (Later, we shall see!)

THE REVOLUTIONARY CONSERVATIVE

The RRRRR must seize control of the managerial structures of power from its current tenants. This seizure would leave these structures of power largely unaffected. We must therefore go further: we must overturn managerial society, since it is the epitome of all that is against our beliefs. Of the Five Rs the Revolutionary is the most important. For in the present situation, one is a Revolutionary precisely to the extent that one is a Conservative!

The Conservative Revolution certainly cannot take place simply by destroying the managerial society. We have to nurture all that is Conservative in the New Middle Class. The local councils, small businesses, social clubs, customs and folklore, the Regions, etc. The Revolutionary Conservative must cherish these; encourage them to flourish and to recover them from the usurpation by the three Managerial Classes. These last have nothing but contempt for them.

These efforts at conservative change will inevitably bring the conservative forces into conflict with the managerial class. To resist, conservatives must have some means of coordinating themselves, so that they can constitute a common front against their formidable foes. What is needed is not another mass political party, but a Movement led by a New Elite, capable of inspiring resistance. The Movement's Leaders must be the stuff of statesmen.

Above all, the Conservative Counter-Revolution will come to nothing if it dispenses with its first and most basic principle: the affirmation of a Transcendent Order. There will be no liberation from the tyranny of the managers, and their anti-traditional principles, without a Spiritual Vision. Transcendence must break in upon us, as it had broken in upon our ancestors, so we may live in accordance and attuned with it. The Conservative Counter-Revolution is in need of the gift 'from above'. With this gift, traditional life may be renewed and restored. Tradition is lifeless, a husk, unless the knowledge of the Transcendent Order upon which it is founded is woven into the most basic understanding of the world and the universe as a whole. This understanding, which is mysterious, can never be fully grasped and mastered, let alone abstractly formulated and inculcated.

We of the RRRRR can never ally ourselves with the religious lunatics of the Christian-Catholic-cretins. They have no idea of true Spirituality, of true Transcendence. They blindly adhere to an anti-nature religion, a suicidal religion fit for children and slaves. A non-Europid religion based on lies, damned lies and nothing but lies — a religion created and propagated by those masters of the lie!

The Counter-Revolutionary-Conservative must rather look to the re-appearance of Spiritual life that is genuinely Traditional, pre-Christian, harking back to the earliest ages. And how do we recognise an authentically traditional form of Spirituality? It can be recognised because we have knowledge of what it is and what it involves. The researches of the Traditionalist School of comparative religion, to which belong such people as René Guénon, Ananda Coomaraswamy, Julius Evola, and Mircea Eliade, have recovered for the Counter-Revolutionary an awareness of the world of Tradition and of the metaphysical principles towards which it was oriented.

We must seek out and return to our authentic, Traditional roots through the revelation of Tradition in Cosmotheist form. Revolutionary Conservatism will recover as a dominant force in Aryan life when Spirituality again becomes the apex above culture, politics and the rest.

This is the battle that the RRRRR must be aware of, fight for and win!

IMPERIUM

0409

XXVII

OPERATION TAKE OVER EUROPA!

FRIENDS OF MINE, OF CONSIDERABLE intellectual reach, who agree with most of my political ideas, who sincerely believe that an *Imperium Europa* would be the best possible solution to the malaise affecting the Europid Race, stall, stammer and stutter their scepticism as to how this could ever be fulfilled. They also ask specific questions about the actual policies of the Imperium.

A common question is how it will be possible for the Individualist to be himself in such an Imperium. What happens to the Free Thinker, the Artist, the Buddhist or Muslim living within the non-porous borders of the Imperium? And just who would be the High Culture Bearers? The political Elite? Who elects them? And who is to define High Culture and High Politics?

Good questions — questions that deserve an articulate reply. We have to go back to the origin of all our present problems.

The Two World Wars were the greatest fratricidal follies that left the Old Continent bled white. Everyone emerged as loser, including and especially: Britain and France. Alone, Britain could never win a war against Germany — but it could certainly lose one! Thus Britain by necessity had to call America into both conflicts. This it did, in WWII, with the help of people like Brandeis and Morgenthau, who were instrumental in persuading Roosevelt to enter the war, notwithstanding that the vast majority of the American people were against intervention.

Britain went to war ostensibly in the defence of Poland. Now, a nine-year old child with an atlas would have realised that Britain could not help Poland, in any tangible way, by giving it a banal guarantee of protection. Not only that, but Britain also had to forge an unholy alliance with communism. Hence, the reason Britian did not attack Soviet Russia, when it invaded Poland from the East, two weeks after the Germans. This ultimately ensured the dismemberment of the British Empire at the hands of Russian communism and American finance-capitalism. Roosevelt too, had secretly urged the Poles to resist the reasonable German demands for a corridor to Danzig, thereby stiffening the Poles' obdurate stance and making war inevitable.

Millions of Europeans were offered as cannon fodder in the interests of international communism and international finance — two sides of the same coin — ostensible enemies but both controlled by the same international-manipulators. These latter were the only victors that emerged after that great conflagration came to a destructive end.

Then followed half a century of pseudo-war between communism and American liberalism, both in perfect synchrony in their maniacal obsession to destroy all vestiges of national, ethnic identities and the aristocratic view of life. NATO and the Warsaw Pact, spiritual twins and both controlled by internationalists, kept Europe prostrate and divided. And the White Man paid the bill for every cold-war confrontation, each bush-war — none of which was ever conclusive of course.

For the Warsaw Pact army was never a threat to NATO. How could primitive Russian troops who got a sound licking from the fuzzy-wuzzies in Afghanistan — how could these same troops and their demoralised East European allies, ever conquer Western Europe? That part of Europe inhabited by two hundred million of the most intelligent humans on earth, armed with the most sophisticated weapons?

It was perfect perfidy. A continuous psychosis and fear of war. A hatefulness inflamed among fellow Europeans — kept aflame on both sides of the Iron Curtain by those past masters of propaganda, treachery and deceit.

Stalin in 1952 had offered to withdraw his troops back to the Russian border, if the Americans would agree to withdraw theirs across the Atlantic — and the USA refused, despite the fact that the vast majority of the German people and those of Eastern Europe were ready for this re-alignment.

During the Cold War the two Thalassocratic (rulers of the seas) powers, the United States and Britain, strangulated the central Tellurocratic (ruler of the land) powers, Germany and Russia. For historically, the interest of those in power in the USA was always to keep Europe prostrate and divided. To separate Germany from its natural ally: Russia.

Bismarck and the Prussian Army General Staff had always believed that Germany and Russia should and would never go to war. Later, that was precisely the whole object of the Tripartite Pact, whose architect General Haushofer, firmly believed would liberate Europe from the Thalassocratic stranglehold.

The USA and Britain, arch enemies of Europe, persevered, as they do to this day, so that Germany and Russia, leaders in a great Eurasian block, would never become the centre of world power. That a *political* Eurasian landmass of 400 million Europeans would not become a reality. For the US government, controlled by corporatists-internationalists, is the most dangerous enemy of all Europeans, with their traditional culture, regions, ethnicity and identities stretching from the Channel to the Pacific.

However, Communism, a creation of the international-manipulators, Marx, Lenin, Trotsky, Zinioviev, Beria, Sverdlov, Kamanieff, Kaganovich, Suslov, Grishin, Andropov and the rest of them — not one of them a Russian — could not be made to work. No amount of effort, sacrifice, blood, sweat and tears could make this Oriental system fit the White Man. The billions in soft loans by international finance, the mountains of butter, eggs, meat and cheese hauled over the Iron Curtain, could not prop up communism indefinitely. Finally, the international-manipulators decided to let it go and the poor Che Guevaras around the world were butchered within a few months. They had served their purpose.

Fortune Magazine of 29th June 1981 revealed that there were seventeen thousand multi-millionaires in dollars or diamonds, mostly Jewish, in the Soviet Union during Brezniev's time. His Jewish wife Victoria, according to daughter Galina, used to swim regularly in her private swimming pool — full of champagne! The metamorphosis was complete: the Naked Communist had become the Naked Capitalist.

No EU Foreign Policy

After World War Two, all European powers ceased to have a foreign policy of their own. Britain became an appendage to the USA, while Germany and France emerged as industrial giants, but passive, political pygmies. Europe for all intents and purposes stood as the Eastern appendix of the Atlantic, that US lake.

The EU has tried timidly to fill this political vacuum. Yet only recently we witnessed the pathetic spectacle of European countries, former world powers, haggling amongst themselves as to who would accept just thirteen Palestinian fighters. These had been encircled at the nativity site in Jerusalem, and were seeking refuge. Each European country did its best to wiggle out of the problem. A sorry spectacle indeed, baring the stark reality that Europe today is an economic giant, but still in disarray when it comes to a common foreign policy. (In this context, it is noteworthy that it was mostly Mediterranean countries that took most of the Palestinians, the Nordics preferring a disdainful distance and benign neglect.)

This lack of political unity is understandable. For how can one have unity of thought, purpose and action amongst a myriad of official languages and governments, all parading their petty nationalism? Only oversized bureaucrats in Brussels can sprout such an economic colossus, timidly tip-toeing behind America, while hanging on to its apron strings.

WHY?

As noted in my earlier writings, The French Revolution, that demonic cataclysm, wrenched the feeble last vestiges of the Aristocratic view of life. It replaced the landed aristocratic gentry, an organic aristocracy, with plutocracy, an aristocracy of money. In fact, finance today utterly dominates and controls production, and determines all its factors: location, machinery, workforce, etc. Collaboration among humans now rested, not on common heritage, but solely on economic exchange and profit. Society became a fight for survival amongst isolated, egoistic individuals with no sense of kinship — a war of all against all. A system of simple horizontal exchanges and interactions.

Paradoxically, both the Marxist and Liberal view of life coincide perfectly. In both systems, at their extreme forms, mankind is reduced to a vast, faceless proletariat and middle-class-morons, instead of a rich diversity of nations, peoples and boroughs. Both Marxism and Liberalism destroy historical memories, eradicating man from his past and placing him on the production line. Their goal is the same: material well-being. There is no place for any communal myth, which gives that mystical union to kindred peoples.

At this point the politician serves as a puppet for big business. Politics become a delivery service, accommodating the strongest lobby within the melee. Government is reduced to a servicing tool for special interest groups.

We have now reached the stage where consumerism is the only survival mechanism left that keeps afloat the financial capitalist system — a system that depends upon a never-ending cycle of increased production, waste, and spending in order to survive — all the while existing only with the concomitant despoliation of nature. Financial Capitalism has rapaciously raped Mother Earth.

A Financial Capitalism that has now reached its highest stage: Globalisation. A world market where labour is treated just as any other commodity — where the multinational conglomerate has become the apex, the highest stage of both Financial Capitalism and Communism.

Finance Capitalism has coerced productive capitalism, through the total competition that Globalisation brings, into accepting the suicidal policy of importing millions of aliens into White heartlands. These migrant workers take over White jobs through a gradual lowering of wages and standards. More ominously, these invaders are outbreeding the Europids in our own countries.

Globalisation: an ever-increasing race for the optimum production (anything), location (anywhere), optimum labour (anybody) and lowest wages (rock-bottom). The utter dependence of the White Man on others for his very survival and defence. A strangulation process that can only mean the disappearance of the White Man, that biological aristocracy constituting just 5% of the world's population.

This is the tragedy unfolding before our eyes. This is what our hidden enemies and internationalists have in store for us. Their aim is a world dictatorship by a tiny homogeneous group with a burning sense of mission: an implacable thirst for world power, vengeance and hatred for the rest of humanity: a world human-mass of rootless, raceless, coffee-coloured zombies.

DEMOCRACY

Mass Democracy, barely a hundred years old, has proved to be an expensive experiment.

It is an anti-noble, anti-merit system where the counting of heads, like sheep, is standard procedure — levelling everyone and everything to the lowest common denominator. A fragile form of government based on mediocrity, equality and fear. A system that has had its innings and which, fortunately in our view, is rapidly coming to an end.

Honest Liberals recognise these contradictions and dangers posed by Democracy and speak of 'a balancing act at two levels of recognition. At one level one finds the important recognition of the dignity and freedom of the individual immigrant and the citizen alike, and on the other level one finds the need to recognise the freedom of individuals to preserve the societies they willingly form in virtue of self-rule, self-preservation and cultural diversity. And whether this contradictory state of affairs "ought to" or "ought not to" exist is simply irrelevant.'

Well put — and let the devil take the logical hind-part!

Honest Libertarians realise that leaders like Pim Fortuyn and Le Pen are not, as Arjen Nijeboer states 'a crisis of the representative system'. They are indeed the natural progression of the Democratic process after fifty years of hypocrisy, inertia and confusion on the part of Europe.

And yet, a Liberal wants to eat his cake and have it too. He wants un-fettered individual freedom together with the security, the cohesion and ethnic identity that Democracy and Liberalism simply cannot provide, due to their inherent adversity to such concepts.

DOMINIUM AND IMPERIUM

The EU nation-states are a progression of the city-states of Athens, Sparta and Corinth. And yet, The Roman Empire superseded these and conquered them with ease since they were divided and politically fossilised. Such states perforce have to become satellites of continental states or Empire. The EU today is a classic example of nation-states that in effect are vassals under the imperial ambitions of the USA.

In my view, there is no other way except for Western Man to unite within a new Empire — on a planetary basis. Such an Empire will be divided broadly into two main parts: Dominium *and* Imperium.

Dominium is the female side of politics, and refers to all that pertains to the Individual: His freedom of choice, religion, language. His preference and pertaining to an ethnic group, with a common elan, common memories, frustrations, fears, modes of recreation. In short, all that which is anarchist, all that falls within the framework of private life: be it addiction to drugs, alcohol, preference to music, literature, etc. The Individual is free! The Dominium is Diogenes.

In our Imperium everything, but everything will be allowed: polygamy, drugs (not dealers since all drugs will be freely available, as are cigarettes and alcohol), freedom of religion, free debate, art, the sciences taken to their logical conclusion in genetic engineering, cloning, space exploration, whatever the Will wills! — All will be allowed, so long as the freedom of the individual does not impinge on that of others, or on society.

In our world, we will transfer the *responsibility* of one's actions onto the *person* — not on society. The Individual will bear the full consequences of his actions. This means that there will be no welfarism, no free hospitals, no free drug-rehabilitation centres, no free syringes, no free schools, no free meals, no nothing within our Imperium. Whatever one does, one pays for it!

Nothing, but nothing within the Imperium will be free — except the minds of men!

Indeed, the Individual within the Dominium will be allowed unlimited freedom of choice, inside the confines of the Imperium borders — unfettered freedom both in the economic and social fields. However, nothing will be tolerated which harms the Imperium.

IMPERIUM: this is male, dominant, powerful, dynamic, merciless. It sets itself no limits. It grasps every opportunity for expansion, penetration and domination. Its prerogatives are mainly Race, Territory and High Politics.

- Race will be protected from miscegenation.

- Territory will never be ceded.

- High Politics will be the realm of The Elite.

RACE

A simple genetic test would be undertaken by everyone within the Imperium. This is an inexpensive, quick genetic scan that determines precisely the genetic affiliation of the individual. An EID (Europid ID) card, storing all information about the person, would be issued solely to Europids — no one else!

This EID card will serve as both money and as a key to everything. Without the Europid ID card, one will not be able to buy or sell. Ours will be a cashless society. Without the EID, one will not be able to travel, find employment, procure food, drive, whatever. In short, without the Europid ID, one becomes a non-person — one starves!

Lacking the Europid ID card, every single alien within our borders will be starved and forced to leave. Non-Europids will be forcefully expelled from within the Imperium. With them will have to go their Europid spouses and mixed offspring, the innocent victims of racial treason. Couples who have adopted non-Europid children will also have to leave — they will be classed as outcastes and exiled. We will return to the old laws of *Manu* — and we will be inflexible in their draconian application.

TERRITORY

The Amur and Ussuri will forever be the demarcation line between Europids and Mongolids. Opportunities, like the financial collapse of Argentina, will be taken advantage of in order to wrench more and more territory from the yoke of the financial imperialism of the USA, thus bringing the White parts of Latin America within the fold of the Imperium.

In Africa, a 4,000 mile-cut-line from Bangui to Djibouti, fifty miles wide, will forever separate the Negrids, swept to the North through our coercive weapon of food, away from the All-White-South.

HIGH POLITICS

Both Race and Territory are safeguarded by High Politics. This is the realm of the High Culture Bearers: the Elite — not millions of minions casting their useless votes every five years. The masses, those masticating bison, can carry on living their lives of miserable ease! They can continue enjoying their 'freedom'. Their only 'duty' to the Imperium will be to act as a genetic source-pool from where the Elite of the future can be drawn.

For Freedom is inextricably woven with Power! The source of Freedom is Power! That which wants to be free, must also be powerful. One can not have Freedom without Power: economic, political, cultural, *Spiritual* power! The power to preserve what one has, as well as the power to prevent encroachment by others — and when survival dictates — the political will and military might to seize every opportunity to gain from weaker neighbours.

An Elite beyond parliaments, parties, politicians, prostitutes and pernicious political priests. A new Aristocracy of the Spirit — an Aristocracy based on meritocracy. An Elite of a quarter of a million, spread over the Imperium, High Culture Bearers: an Order of Men as were the Templars and Teutonic Knights. They would be the guardians of the Imperium. Their sole concern would be Spirituality, Race and High Politics. This Elite will forge a new Science of the Spirit.

And where is the Individual in such an Elite body, one might well ask? Well, any group of persons, whatever their number and reciprocal similarity, whichever the degree of their firmness in assessing their opinion and their convergence of ideas — that group ends with breaking into smaller groups, adhering to different variants of the same opinion. Within these subgroups in turn, there emerge other, smaller under-subgroups, and further on, down to the last limit of such division — that of the single Individual!

And who elects the Elite? They elect themselves! For history is nothing but the eternal struggle amongst competing Elites, with their concern with the secrets of nature, as they seek to positively impact and alter the entire culture, structure and direction of society. The Imperium is the exclusive domain of the Elite.

Yes! *Capitalism within a Racial Context in an IMPERIUM EUROPA!*

THE ONLY SOLUTION — BUT HOW?

The only solution for the future of Europe and indeed, Western Civilisation is an *IMPERIUM EUROPA* — a European Empire. A Europe not of bankers and bureaucrats, but a Europe of High Planetary Politics and Peoples. An Imperium of *Regions* against artificially constructed petty nation-states. An Imperium based on the Holy Roman Empire, with a central authority embodying both the Political and the *Spiritual*. A centre to which all Europids will refer and relate. A hub, whereby all parts of the Empire would feel organically whole, while retaining the specific peculiarity of each region. Retaining initiative, diversity, interaction, castes, classes, character, personality, hierarchy; all converging to a superior *IDEA*. A common language steeped in European tradition, erudition, and Imperium will bind us all: Latin!

But how do we get there? There is only one way; simple and effective: *We must take over Brussels!* We must place our best members in the EU parliament and wrest a majority. We must beat the dotty-democrats at their own game. This is possible since voting for candidates on a national scale favours us, unlike normal elections.

To cite an example: Le Pen garnered six million votes in the presidential elections. Most of his voters were real Frenchmen, many of whom were decorated multiple times in wars across the globe on behalf of France. The mainstream candidate benefited from the immigrant vote, as well as a system stacked against the outsider. All Le Pen's votes did not muster a single seat in the Paris parliament — and yet, the coming European elections in May 2004, could transform Le Pen's party into the largest French group of Euro-Parliamentarians in Brussels. It could be like this, all over the rest of Europe.

Elitists, solitaries, visionaries, revolutionaries, High Culture Bearers, high-quality individuals must emerge, must come out of their desolation, despondency and despair. Let them stride out into the open, *viso al sol* and do battle in that dung-heap democratic political arena. *Basta con il passato — basta con le memorie di gloria! È ora di agire! Vincere!* (Stop with past dreams, memories of past glories! It is time to act! To win!)

These Men should contest every single European Parliamentary Election either as independents, or within Right-Wing parties and even through other popular parties. Once in Brussels, they will then naturally seek each other out and converge within a new grouping that will carry their common beliefs and ideals.

Individuals of the highest calibre hailing from every country in Europe, agreeing in substance, on the need to stop the rot, to work for the survival of the Europid race — disagreeing over details and dates — must band together within a new Parliamentary Group in Brussels. A group to be called: *Nova Europa*.

This was Jörg Haider's idea and it is the only way.

We have to take over Europe! — It can be done!

Once there, we will launch an onslaught to convince other individuals in other groupings to join us, or at least vote for our motions. We will turn around that big, overbloated, overblown, bursting bureaucracy buzzing with babbling, bungling bureaucrats and busybodies! *Un colpo di timone* (a grip on the rudder). We will impinge, imprint our way of thinking on the rest — and eventually, take over political control of the old continent.

This should not be all that difficult. All that is needed is an iron will to succeed and a total commitment to the task in hand.

The precursors of the Elite, soon to be grouped in *Nova Europa* in the Brussels Parliament, would convince the Populists, the former Christian Democrats, that their ideals of a Christian-Catholic Europe would eventually vanish, if things had to be left as they are. Not one single crucifix would remain in a single schoolroom in the whole of Europe. The Muslims and the international-manipulators, who side with them on this issue, would soon see to that.

We would convince the Federalists, who are close to us but who still naively believe in the Nation-State, that these very Nation-States carry within themselves the seeds of fratricidal strife. One should remember how the tribe has always used petty Nationalism to foment war amongst racial cousins. How Mad Albright almost succeeded in setting up and getting British and Russian soldiers to shoot at each other in Pristina. Her malicious intent was to induce the Russians into the defensive, fomenting their suspicions regarding Western Europe and to erect, again, a new Iron Curtain. In conformity to the traditional US Thalassocratic policy versus the Telluric giants, Albright's intention was to divide Europe in half again. That was the whole scope of the war against Serbia.

And who cares about the Kosovars' human rights! In Tadjikistan, where the Americans have a military base, the puppet government is literally boiling opponents in scalding water — and not a peep of indignation from Boobus Bush! Our *Nova Europa* group would also convince the Liberals that their much-vaunted free-market policies have no chance of working against the sweatshop competition of the Far East. That already, Europe is straining to keep up a competitive stance against a free-economy China, whose labour force will work eighteen hours a day, with a low, basic-wage and no social benefits.

The Liberals will be made to realise that, yes, their free-market ideas will work, and work very well — within the non-porous borders of a *Nova Europa*. Where competition will be straight and fair, amongst Europids. That a captive market of one billion Europids, the most intelligent and sophisticated humans on the planet, is quite enough to satisfy even the most ambitious of Liberal-entrepreneurs.

The Greens are our natural allies. We will remind them of their Right-wing origins and help them find themselves again. We will point out their inconsistencies; saving the white shark while slaving the White Man with their fretting about immigration, Third World plight and other inanities. The more intelligent and honest of them are beginning to realise and admit such incoherencies already.

As for the Socialists, these have their hearts in the right place. Their only flaw is their lunatic equality-dogma. We could coax them to our point of view, on one hand demonstrating the hard facts of what immigration is doing to White working people. We would remind them that in the old days in South Africa, British Unions backed their South African counterparts in defence of the White work force. Socialists will be made to see what their equality-dogma has done to South Africa — for both black and White workers. On the other hand, we could explain to the Socialists what a clean, fair and safe world we intend to build for Europids. That good honest competition never did anybody, least of all Socialists, any harm. That their ideals of a fair deal and a fair wage will only be achieved within our *Nova Europa* — where the financial speculator, impervious to the declining working conditions and increasing sufferings of a Europid workforce, will be firmly put in his place.

And lastly, as for the Communists, these will be the easiest to win over to our side. Since the fall of the wall, they have been like headless chickens — they lack an ideology. And their types are idealists, who cannot live without an ideology, guiding them in every facet of life. That is why in Russia and in every ex-communist state, Right-wing parties are so strong, as ex-Communists join the New Right in droves.

We will offer Communists our alternative. One that, unlike theirs, has not failed — has not even been tried! And even if they do not join us, their voting patterns will converge with ours — for the wrong reasons!

Ironically, the hardest to win over will be the petty nationalists, the little Englanders and their like: Fog over the channel? The continent must be isolated! They are the hardest nuts to crack. But as they watch us breaking new ground, getting stronger, they will see reason. They will have no choice but to join us. We will welcome them with open arms, as our friends, political brothers — and give them positions of importance and authority within our emerging *Nova Europa*.

Then we will go about setting *our* priorities! Planetary priorities that will take into account first and foremost the survival of the Europid. All else follows from that.

Simply put, our priorities in order of importance will be:

Spirituality closely followed by *Race*, nurtured through *High Culture*, protected by *High Politics* enforced by the *the Elite*.

And then all the rest: finance, the economy, sociology...

By the year 2012: *Anno Zero*, our New Europe or *Nova Europa* will burst out of its cocoon into an *IMPERIUM EUROPA*!

MAGNA EUROPA EST PATRIA NOSTRA!!
IMPERIUM
0311

XXVIII

COMING
CATACLYSMIC CRISES

In my analysis 'Operation Take over Europa!' as to how we, of the Radical-Racialist-Right-Revolutionary-Reactionaries can take over power on a planetary scale, I had elucidated, in broad terms, that the key to our final success is the takeover of the Brussels Parliament.

Again, I must acknowledge the paternity of this simple and brilliant *IDEA* to Jörg Haider. Obviously, the clean air and high altitudes of Carinthia must have had something to do with it!

But why is this takeover needed? Why now? Why the urgency? Why is it imperative for us, the precursors of the Elite of the future, to act immediately, decisively and wrest power from the '*ammuchiata*', the doodling-democrats, the establishment ensconced in Brussels? Indeed what, if any, are the dangers looming in front of us?

Good questions that demand a detailed reply. This, in order that every one of us becomes conscious of the spectral scenario that lies just ahead. For the world political scene is about to precipitate: suddenly, cataclysmically. As with the disappearances of whole civilisations, the fall or radical change will be abrupt: not a gradual sliding down beneath the waves. The Mayas in Mexico are a classic example.

In our case, that of Western Civilisation, all will precipitate and crystallise before *2012: Anno Zero!* — That singular and special date in the history of our planet: our beloved *Gaia*.

Imminent Collapse

After the two fratricidal wars, WWI and II, planned, perpetrated and prosecuted by our internal enemies — those international-manipulators scattered throughout the globe — Europe gradually emerged as an economic giant and a political pygmy. We have had fifty years of EU bureaucracy, half a century of abject servitude to Financial Capitalism based in Washington and Bolshevist Communism centred in Moscow — both controlled by the same tribe.

The fall of communism presented the tribe with the most serious threat to their existence since the Hero took them on, in the 1930s. Never had they been so vulnerable, so exposed. Anti-Semitic, or more precisely anti-Jewish movements sprang up everywhere: Pamyat in Russia, in Hungary, Poland everywhere. Suddenly the mask of the hidden enemy was torn off and we could see who was behind it — who had led us to bleed ourselves white for nearly a century. Suddenly the spotlight focused.

As a distraction, their cousins in the West set up an orchestrated squealing and howling campaign against 'racists and Nazis'. Suddenly their cemeteries became the objects of vandalism, their synagogues and houses were sprayed with swastikas. Sick octogenarians in America, Chile, Brazil or Argentina were 'discovered' and hauled to show-trials. Anything would do to take the heat off.

And they succeeded — for a time. They then gave us the first Iraq war, when Saddam, a former staunch friend of the USA, was tricked by the US Ambassador to Kuwait into believing that America would turn the blind eye, attempted to re-take what is rightly Iraqi territory: that artificial, corrupt operetta state called Kuwait.

Then they provoked the war in Serbia. Sharon, then defence minister of the rogue state of Israel, was spotted by journalists in Macedonia, just a month before the opening of hostilities, when Albanian and Serbian cafes started blowing up with weekly intervals. When asked what a war-horse like him was doing on this powder-keg, he had replied he was 'on a peace mission'!

Then came September 11th. The attacks were a boon to the international-manipulators. Now, they had an enemy to point their fingers at. They could now easily convince *Boobus Americanus* that they had been right all along, after all. The Arabs are our enemies! International terrorism is the foe to ferret out. The tribe suddenly became America's staunchest ally again. They were safe again — for a time.

And so we had Afghanistan, where the most powerful air-force in the world ridiculously bombed fuzzy-wuzzies in sandals and turbans. The latest technology was used, with bombs costing thousands of times their targets.

And after Afghanistan we had Iraq II. This war on Iraq was initiated solely because the country, situated only a few miles away from the bandit, terrorist state, could pose a potential, future threat.

And now, the same mischief makers are screaming for more bombs against Syria (because that is where Saddam hid his WMD!). Bombs against Iran (because they are building them). Bombs against Libya and Algeria (because they intend on having them) and so on. The state of Shylock can never, ever be satisfied.

But this second war against Iraq is, as I had predicted in my book, *CREDO*, 'America's last war before its dissolution'. America is no longer a nation but a polyglot people all squabbling among themselves. History has shown that no multi-racial country can survive for long. That fences make good neighbours. That without the separation of different, incompatible races, dissolution and disaster inevitably follow. Spengler, Pareto, Lukas and Polin, to mention just a few, amply and emphatically demonstrate this, with numerous examples.

Within a short time, anytime now, there will be an implosion in America. Anything could set it off: like blacks rioting during another blackout in a major city. Or even a small nuclear device, set off by any one of the numerous enemies America has diligently fostered, through its servitude to the tribe — a nuclear explosion in the vicinity of the White

House or a nuclear station, or in the middle of one of those multi-ethnic paradise-cities on the East Coast. Panic would certainly degenerate into a racial conflict, nationwide, due to the smouldering animosity amongst the races. White pent-up anger would turn into cold fury.

The Whites would be cornered and constrained to regroup and fight a second civil war, where the colour of the skin will be the uniform. A short, sharp cruel war with no Geneva rules, no quarter given or asked. Europids will have to resolutely expel all aliens from their territories, confining them to the cesspool cities like New York, Philadelphia, San Francisco and Los Angeles. Europids will defend and maintain the farmlands of central USA, starving out all the rest. Within six months, America can be cleaned up and regained for the European. Our enemies will be surprised to what lengths we are ready to go, to recover our nations.

SIX CRUCIAL MONTHS

During those crucial six months, when the Whites in America would be fighting for their survival, for the recovery of their land, there will be an awesome, planetary-power-vacuum.

Our racial enemies, the Asians, would see their opportunity and seize it. China and Japan are both very vulnerable countries, cornered by the Pacific Lake, exclusive property of the Thalassocratic USA.

China is presently infiltrating hundreds of its nationals across the Amur, every month. These illegal immigrants are cohabiting with Russian women. Presently, a weak, impoverished Russia cannot effectively police such a long border. The Chinese eagerly eye the vast riches of Siberia, the raw materials for their newly unleashed free economy. They will surely step up this infiltration Northwards upon the disintegration of the USA.

Likewise the Japanese, a predatory, Imperial race, would seize their chance for expansion. Japan is an overpopulated, bottled-up little country, with no raw materials or agricultural land. Japan would have two options:

A.   Strike at their Chinese neighbours in order to re-occupy Manchuria and predate Siberia themselves or, more likely, reach an agreement with the

Chinese for the partitioning of all that lies east of the Urals. China's nuclear capacity, though small in comparison to Russia's, is enough to impose parity of terror.

or

B.   Japan would use hundreds of available sea craft and make a dash for Papua New Guinea, re-group there and then invade Australia. Once on shore, nothing could stop them. Japan would thus achieve its dream: that of dominating a continent laden with the raw materials and food resources it now lacks.

At this point, the EU, an economic bureaucracy lacking political will, a cluster of quibbling and quivering nation-states, would pose no threat, no fear to either China or Japan. Time would favour the aggressors in their *Blitzkrieg* into the Urals and towards Australia. A democratic, divided and dithering Europe would be useless — worse than useless.

At this point Russia and Germany, the two Tellurocratic giants would inevitably be drawn together. What Bismarck and later, General Karl Haushofer dreamed of, would be imposed by force of necessity upon the two great peoples: the Teutons and the Slavs. They would both turn their backs on the Anglo-Saxons and the Latins, and go it alone. At that point, Germany and Russia would become masters of the world.

With the political and military support of Germany, Russia would not hesitate to pre-empt China with a first, knock-out nuclear strike. China, whose billions depend on the great river and its tributaries for life, would be no problem to the Russians. One nuclear bomb at the source of the Yellow River would finish China — Russia would only have to drop one every five years, on the anniversary of Hiroshima preferably, in the Gobi Desert, to remind the Orientals to keep their place.

With Siberia secured, the now-strengthened Russians would feel safe. The Japanese with their ingrained, age-old envy and hatred for us would pose no problem. They are indeed a paper tiger. Japan is the weakest country in the world; an overpopulated island with no resources or food growing areas. It is totally dependent on imports and value-added manufacturing and exports. Just one nuclear aircraft-carrier circling it for a few weeks, impeding access of vital resources and food, would send the Japanese back to feudal times.

THE MIDDLE EAST

Meanwhile in the Middle East, the paranoid, terrorist state would seize the opportunity to expand its borders. With their two hundred or more nuclear weapons trained on the Heartland of Europe, they would feel unbridled. They would probably invade the tin-pot nation of Saudi Arabia, a vast, underpopulated country with just a few cities on the coast. It would be easy for the tribe to occupy these cities and divest the huge, petroleum reserves from such a weak adversary.

They would do as they please: massacre the Palestinians, occupy Lebanon, link up with Turkey, cut off Syria and Iraq from the Mediterranean. The international schemers would have a field day!

AFRICA

During these six months of world instability, conflict and chaos, India would finally implement its dream of disgorging its surplus population onto Africa. Hundreds of ships of all sorts, laden with millions of famished Indians would cross the Indian Ocean and swarm, like locusts onto Africa, from Zanzibar to the Cape. With their relatively superior weapons, they would massacre the blacks and colonise the continent.

In conclusion, the overall result of all this scenario would be the loss of Australia and Africa for the White Man, together with the enfeeblement and isolation of the English and the Latins. Germany and Russia would emerge as the only world powers. America, a regained White country, would turn inwards, to isolationism, and fend for itself.

Israel would be master of the Mediterranean — and still remain a nuclear, psychotic world menace, threatening the Telluric-titans.

THE IDEAL SOLUTION

The ideal solution to this frightening scenario of course, would be that Russia and Germany would be convinced, roped in with the British and the Latins into a strong, united Eurasian landmass.

That is why we, of the Radical-Racialist-Right-Revolutionary-Reactionaries have to act *now!* That is why we have to wrest power in Brussels and create a *Nova Europa*. A grouping of patriots from every single EU member country. Only such a strong, solid, political block, imbued with a *Spiritual IDEA* could draw and keep within the White fold, the two Telluric giants and cousin peoples: the Teutons and the Slavs.

We must pre-empt and prevent the partitioning of Europe and the cousin, Europid peoples. Such a separation, with the Germans and Russians going their own way together, would mean the eventual loss of the Mediterranean Northern Littoral to the Muslims. For Israel would promote, aid the illegal immigration and infiltration of North Africans into the now debilitated, Latin countries. It would even manipulate Arab terrorism there, especially in Italy. — They have already done this before.

One remembers how Italy was always the chief target for that sinister force of prime evil. It has now become increasingly clear that the *Brigate Rosse*, the communist Red Brigades and FAR (*Fronte Azione Rivoluzionario*), the far right terrorist group, were both manipulated, led, financed by the same obscure mentors — operating from a super-secret NATO base outside Udine.

While it took months of fruitless efforts to locate kidnapped Prime Minister Moro — even though the Italian police knew from day one, the exact block of apartments he was being kept imprisoned in — it took just a few days to locate and liberate US general Dozier!

For it is of paramount importance for the international-manipulators to keep Italy destabilised — on a permanent basis. Only in this way can the Imperium be stalled. Only in this way will Israel survive. Anything would do for the international hidden enemy to further de-stabilise and weaken the White Race.

That is why project *Nova Europa* is the most urgent priority now. A grouping, a majority in the Brussels parliament composed of patriots from all member countries. A *Nova Europa* that, during the imminent emergency scenario, would rapidly metamorphose into an IMPERIUM EUROPA, holding Germany and Russia firmly within the Europid family of peoples. Only the *IDEA* of Imperium can do this — nothing else!

Only an IMPERIUM EUROPA will have the intrinsic *Spiritual* power, translated into a *Racial* bond uniting the four Europid cousins: the Anglo-Saxons, the Teutons, the Slavs and the Latins. A bond manifested through *High Politics* under the iron leadership of *The Elite*. Only the Imperium could save the White Race in the coming, planetary struggle.

The Imperium will embrace all the Aryans, wherever they are, whatever their present religious beliefs. The Kurds, an Aryan people speaking an Indo-European tongue, would be protected from the mixed-Mongolid Turks. We will welcome some of the Persians, the ancient Aryans. We will protect every single Europid, wherever he may be — whatever his present circumstances. We will welcome within our fold every White minority, scattered amidst the billions of the Third World. The Imperium will serve as a planetary chalice, holding the *Sacred Gene Pool*.

We will again Hellenise all the Mediterranean islands and push the mixed-Mongolid Turks over the Bosphorus. An obdurate, obstinate and obtuse people, not one single Turk, except those of Europid genes, must remain in Europe. Turkey should never be part of the Imperium. Thrust deep into Europe's underbelly, Turkey poses an awesome genetic threat.

Zbigniew Brzezinksi (not a Zulu), former Secretary and Advisor to the US president, put it brazenly: 'The world power-position of the USA could best be secured by the ethnic destabilisation of Europe as a possible competitor. This multiracial Europe will consequently be too busied by these circumstances to concern itself with global politics. A certain player in this game would be the Turks, considering their sheer population force. Thirty percent of the Turks are under fifteen years old. One can only imagine what would happen, if the aging German population were to absorb still another two to three million Asians incapable of being integrated. It seems this can be only prevented by the collapse of the European Union "Molochs" (Hebrew for "kings"). One can only hope that this is done through our efforts as soon as possible!'

And only today, the 21st Nov. 03, just a day after the devastating attack by Al-Qaeda on British interests in Istanbul—attacks that killed the British Consul and gutted the HSBC—the British Foreign Minister Jack Straw (also not a Zulu), solemnly proclaimed that 'it is now evident and imperative that Turkey joins the European Union'!

Australia will revert to being a last bastion for the White family—a continent reserved for Whites only. A short, sharp repatriation programme will return the Asians and other non-Europids back to their continent.

In Africa, a 4,000-mile cut-line from Bangui to Djibouti, fifty miles wide, will forever separate the Negrids from the All-White-South. An electronic cut-line, where not even a lizard could cross undetected. We will organise huge, free food depots and millions of biogradable, 5-litre gin bottles—and gradually move these centres northwards, fifty miles at a time. Those of us who have been in Africa, know very well that the Kaffir will walk hundreds of miles for a free meal. Of course, the gin would help the Negrids settle their internecine squabbles amicably!

Once most of the blacks are over the cut-line, we will sever their food supply and leave them to the tender mercies of the Arabs. For the Arab knows very well how to deal with the Negrid: the Arab can explain things better—in the only way the Kaffir understands.

South America must become part of the Imperium. Opportunities, like the financial collapse of Argentina will be grasped, in order to wrench more and more territory from the yoke of the financial imperialism of the USA, thus bringing the White parts of Latin America within the fold of the Imperium. Chile would join us readily. In Brazil, a firm policy of separation would soon deplete the black population through famine and aids.

The whole sub-Amazonian White-cone, as well as the Panama Isthmus and its adjacent territories, will be the White Man's sole preserve.

THE ARABS

The Arabs have always been our friends since World War I. They resented the Turkish Ottoman Empire and, as everyone knows, felt betrayed by the British when this collapsed at the end of the war.

The Mufti of Jerusalem, the great Haj Amin al-Husayni — he was the only person whom the Hero offered hospitality at the Imperial Palace in Berlin — with the Palestinian flag flying higher than that of the Third Reich. The Mufti was an unashamed admirer and loyal ally till the end. The Hero also greatly admired al-Husayni for his 'noble bearing and superior intelligence'.

The great Mufti certainly knew who the 'world enemy' was! He gave his life, right up to his death in 1971, for Palestine. He tried, unsuccessfully, to liberate Iraq from British colonialism. During the war, he recruited 60,000 Muslims and formed them into the SS Division *Handshar*, in the fight against Bolshevism.

Over six powerful radio stations in Berlin, al-Husayni thundered his message to all Muslims across the globe, from Morocco to Indonesia, and urging them to join Germany for the liberation of both Palestine, and mankind, from the international-manipulators: 'plutocracy and international-finance and communism' — the three-headed Hydra.

He often repeated, 'The Arabs are to be considered the natural friends of Germany and Italy and their allies'. The Mufti planned a Unitary-Arab-State comprising Palestine, Syria, Lebanon, Jordan and Iraq. An embryonic Arabic Imperium — at peace with the European peoples.

Both Nasser and Anwar Sadat were pro-Axis during WWII. The Mufti was right — up to the creation of the terrorist state, the Arabs were our natural allies. All the present resentment and hostility between the Arabs and ourselves has been sparked by the creation of that abomination called Israel — and stoked, fomented, provoked ever since.

The Arabs have nothing but oil — we have everything, except oil. It should be the perfect symbiotic relationship! We must allow no one, I mean no one, to instigate us against the Arab world, to sour our relations with them. We should adopt a policy of good neighbourliness.

The festering wound of Palestine has now reached a stage where 'Israel will fight till the last American', as is presently happening with Iraq II. This must not be so for Europe. Europe must not follow *Boobus Americanus* in this folly. We have nothing to gain from Israel, except trouble. We have to leave Israel well alone to sink or swim on its own.

The Mediterranean is a natural ditch dividing the Arab world from ours. The two cultures can go their own separate ways. We must not interfere with the Arabs, with their way of life — we should let them pursue their Islamic culture. It is of no concern of ours. Indeed, we should encourage them to revert back to type: chador, bourka, beards, sandals, turbans and all.

An Islamic Imperium stretching from Morocco to Kashmir, an evolution of al-Husayni's dream, uniting the divers Islamic nations and sects, is now not only feasible, but desirable. We should encourage this development. Europeans have nothing to fear from it. We will control Islam simply through our genius for food production.

The only trade between these two Imperiums will be the barter of our food with their oil. The Muslims cannot hope to feed their burgeoning billions — they simply do not have enough food producing areas. They will have to sell their oil to the Europid. It is useless to them anyway, more so once they revert back to their true, cultural way of life.

As for the so-called 'war on terrorism' — we should start asking WHY? Why did it happen? Why the Twin Towers? What caused it? Once we answer that fundamental question, once we go to the root cause of it all, once an IMPERIUM EUROPA takes the lead in solving, once and for all, that festering wound in the Middle East — then the 'war on terrorism' will simply evaporate.

Again: the Arab world is no enemy of ours. Someone, somebody turned it so. We should leave the Arabs well alone to their way of life, and instead concentrate on turning the vision of IMPERIUM EUROPA into a reality.

For the Arabs would present no problem to the coming Imperium.

In actual fact, they would be invaluable to us for two reasons: the food-for-oil bartering system and also, the whole Maghreb would serve as a *cordon sanitaire* against the Negrid. We could easily reach a political and economic agreement with the Arab world.

The Imperium would liberate Palestine in exchange for:

A.   The Mediterranean — this would become *Mare Nostrum*. Arabs would only be permitted to sail up to twelve miles from their shores. If they overstep, we will bomb them mercilessly. They would have to use their turbans for bandages!

B.   Their Religious Leaders, their Mullahs, their Madras and Mahdis would recall all Muslims of non-Europid origins to return to North Africa, under penalty of their equivalent of 'mortal sin'. This would considerably ease the pain of the repatriation programme we have in mind, once the Imperium is installed.

C.   We will barter oil for all the food they need — under fair terms.

THE TRIBE

That would leave that fundamental, central problem, that viper's den in the Middle East — that refuge, where every international rodent retires to, rests and recuperates after each destructive mission is accomplished within the host country. A radical new approach to Israel has to be found; otherwise we shall never, ever have peace within the Imperium. As the Italians, in their inimitable style, put it, '*Pace in tutto il mondo, con Israele sotto terra!*'

Jews still have that huge territory, many times the size of Israel: the Jewish Autonomous State of Birobidjan, in Siberia. It was given to them by the founding Bolshevists, in gratitude for Jewish finance and leadership of the communist revolution. A Jewish autonomous state with its own independent radio (in Yiddish), independent press, private schools, an autonomous tax-system collected by, from and for Jews — within a free-market economy! All this throughout the bleak Soviet years, while millions of Russian Europids lived as slaves.

Jews could have stayed there, out of sight and out of mind in the backwoods of Siberia, with no chance of provoking any more mischief — with the concomitant anti-Jewish feelings, as they elicit wherever they go. But no, they have to be in the limelight, they have to be the central subject of every conversation, world-wide. They have to be centre-stage all the time — always them!

National Geographic Magazine of February 2000, in an article on remote Siberia, claimed that Jews were leaving Birobijan at the rate of 500 a month and that only 8,000 were left at the time. This means that by now, Birobijan is finished as a Jewish homeland. They scuppered it themselves.

But now Madagascar is also gone — or better, the island is now ours! We will never offer it again to them. It forms part of our planned All-White-South-Africa. It is destined to be a Nature Reserve.

The Imperium will immediately adopt a hostile attitude to the bandit state. We cannot allow a psychotic, nuclear-powered nation on our doorstep, a constant threat to us. We will impose total economic sanctions, an embargo enforced by a maritime and aerial blockade. Economic collapse should follow within a few days, and here we will be in dire danger. The Masada complex could take over — they could bomb Rome and Berlin in a fit of Talmudic vengeance.

The Imperium must be ready for such a nuclear attack. We have to be alert, ready to parry and counter-attack, unleash nuclear devastation on their major cities, preventing, as much as possible, damage to neighbouring Arab states.

Should the tribe wish to come to an agreement, we could offer them New Caledonia (like Madagascar, it happens to be French!). A huge island in the sun, endowed with raw materials and vast, food growing potential. They will have to go disarmed, and will never be allowed to re-arm. A constant air and naval surveillance programme will ensure this. They will not be allowed to export or import. They will be made to learn to just live and let live.

The tribe will be tested to prove their real, nation-building capabilities, this time without holocaust handouts and American largesse. We shall see whether the parasite can live without a host. The international-manipulators would probably go to pieces within two years, tearing each other to bits.

A PLANETARY IMPERIUM

Thus the White Man, the Europid, the envy of the rest of humanity, could live in peace with himself within the vast borders of a planetary Imperium.

Two White rings will encircle the globe, North and South of the Equator. To the North, the Imperium will stretch from Ireland to Vladivostock. Across the Bering Strait it will join a Nova America, comprising Alaska, Canada and a re-dimensioned White USA or Vinland, as White Americans will probably choose to call their regained territories.

In the South, we will have an All-White-South-Africa, as well as Australia and an All-White-South-America. Of paramount importance, the Europid will control the food growing areas of the planet. This is our ultimate weapon: the White Man's ability to grow a food surplus. No other race is capable of this. The Imperium will trade food for all it needs from the rest of humanity. We will barter enough food to keep them from starving — nothing else!

ECONOMY & FINANCE

We will again adopt the Gold Standard — this time on a planetary basis. All Euro issuance will have to be backed by Gold — mined from within the confines of the Imperium, or bartered for food from without. All-White-South-Africa mines and the Urals are more than enough to keep pace with the volume of currency in circulation. The price of gold will be directly related to the currency and velocity of circulation — inflation would finally cease to plague the European Man.

The Euro will be the standard currency throughout the Imperium.

All the *Regions* would choose their respective, optimum economic niche. No regional protective barriers would be allowed. Total, free, complete competition would be straight and fair — amongst Europids. The vast free market will itself regulate production, price and profit. Unions will evaporate on their own: dodos.

Yes! Capitalism in a racial context within an IMPERIUM EUROPA.

ARISTOCRATIC VIEW

The Elite will inculcate an Aristocratic view of life throughout the Imperium. They will promote a culture of an *Aristocracy of the Spirit*, of *Character*. An Aristocracy that will combine the best of both Race and The Individual — and that vital link between the two.

Within the Imperium the military will enjoy a superior status to the bourgeois. A professional all-Europid army, composed of the best from the four Europid cousins, will guard the vast borders and stamp out mercilessly any attempt to infiltration. Non-Europids caught within our borders, after a stipulated deadline, would be shot on sight.

Democracy, a female concept of politics, has rendered the warrior, in the traditional (*Spiritual* rather than historical) sense of the word, into a soldier. Now, etymologically the word soldier is derived from *soldare*, *soldi*, meaning money. This in effect means that the modern soldier is nothing more than a mercenary employed by the bourgeois, whose values prevail over those traditional, *Spiritual* ones formerly held by the warrior caste.

The bourgeois does not have to fight himself, but engages the 'soldier', the mercenary, more often than not in squalid wars of mercantilism, in the interests of plutocratic capitalism.

Behind the high-sounding words like 'peace-keeping force' or 'defending freedom' or 'liberating the Iraqi people' or 'a war to end all wars', there is usually nothing more than the interests of the multinationals.

Lacking a *Spiritual* ideal, today's soldier, the conscript, weaned throughout his civilian life on a diet of anti-militarism, is then expected to fight and lay down his life so that others like him can carry on living their own lives of miserable ease!

No wonder the debacle of Vietnam, where the most modern, best-equipped army, lost a war to a tin-pot nation with soldiers in sandals, beads of rice as rations and bicycles for transport. The difference was that those Orientals had a belief, a vision — albeit a communist paradise.

In the final analysis however, whenever threatened, the bourgeoisie depend on the military for their survival, be it physical or economic. Now this is a paradoxical state of affairs since the dependant class, is master over the guarantor! Hence, the military caste should not only be distinct, separate and elitist, but also above civilians in status.

The ingrained anti-militarism of democracy is the natural expression, the antithesis, of that *Union of Men*, of which the military caste is the highest expression. For the warrior, in the true sense of the word, is not a brute, as defined and depicted by the bourgeois, but the embodiment of an interior calm, a *Spiritual* plane.

The warrior, unlike the soldier, is not animated by hatred towards the enemy. Since he is fighting for a belief and an *IDEA*, the warrior respects the enemy warrior holding a different aim. On the other hand the soldier, fighting for an economic issue, a mercantile war, as in the case of the Allies during the two World Wars, needs a strong dose of hate for him to fight.

Millions were inebriated by hateful propaganda against all that was German. The hate spewed over the radio and in the press — controlled by the international-manipulators, the real schemers behind those two great, fratricidal conflagrations — reached a nadir, a bottom, an evil, never surpassed since.

On the other hand, the Prussian military caste, ascetic warriors in a modern age, direct descendants of the Teutonic Knights, as well as the German army in general, never needed hate in order to fight — and fight very well. For the Germans were not fighting a mercantile war, but a total war for an *IDEA*; an embryonic IMPERIUM EUROPA!

Even in today's enfeebled military, there sometimes emerges that no-ble warrior spirit of old. Whenever the nation is in extreme danger, close to total collapse, there have been instances when, at the very last moment, the military took matters into their own hands and saved the situation.

Heroes all of them, including the ones that failed, not because they did not try, but because they were betrayed by a decadent Monarchy, as happened in Spain with Tejero.

Heroes: Pinochet in Chile, Videla in Argentina, Papadopoulos in Greece, the junta in Turkey, *Principe* Borghese in Italy — all moved by the same warrior spirit: values of loyalty, hierarchy, command, obedience, frankness in the rapport between Men — honesty, courage and a Spartan spirit of sacrifice.

WAR is LIFE!

War as a constant metaphysical battle, both internal within each individual, as well as external, in the case of Nation, Organic State, Race. For war is for warriors not soldiers, for castes not conscripts. Not for mercantilism but for a great *IDEA*: that of Imperium!

Wars, giant struggles, great conflicts, have been mostly between Whites. They have been fratricidal and always toward the object of economic gains or to generate business. Battles of rich versus poor, petty nationalism always manipulated by the Judas goats.

No more! If anything, we should promote wars amongst wogs. We could induce and encourage non-Whites to kill their kind in ever more decent numbers. We should instigate famine and disease wherever the White Man has not set foot. War should be for the sole benefit and final planetary victory of the Europid.

War is life! War is a self-overcoming! A liberating wind. War, as innovator. War as a hygienic exercise for the White world, together with a eugenics program, eliminating the weak within the Race. War as a final clean-up of the planet from the superfluous billions, the pullulating, non-creative, inferior masses.

COLLECTIVISM

Socialism as a frame of mind will be extirpated from our Imperium. Nothing will be free. The very word 'equality' will be expunged from our dictionary. Young generations will be weaned on a High Culture promoting Aryan values.

The forty-hour week, that socialist-capitalist sacred cow, will be abolished. Mussolini established it in the 1920s, two years after New Zealand, and since then, whilst everything has changed, it has remained. Instead of constant wage increases, extracted by the massed battalions of organised labour, inducing inflation, there will be a progressive reduction of working hours, giving the Europid time to develop himself: to change from *Homo oeconomicus* into the complete *person*.

We will reduce our income tax to a 10% flat rate for everybody — without distinction as to his wealth, as in Roman times. No tax should be more than this.

Tax collection will be used to operate the Imperium: the army, the police, the Regional Authority. It is for these purposes and for very little else, that the Imperium will collect the 10% tax from all. We will reduce government to a minimum in the Dominium sphere.

All trade with those outside the Imperium will have to be approved by the Central Economic Policy Staff, under the authority of the Elite. Foreign trade will consist solely of barter: our food surpluses in exchange for their oil, gold and other rare metals we may need. Foreign aid will be a thing of the past.

We will again respect, revere our *Gaia*. The environment will always have precedence, priority, over economic matters. Any industrialist or industry that infringes this rule will be regarded as having committed a 'crime against the Imperium'. The board members, and management themselves, will be harshly punished with long prison terms and hard labour.

High Politics will determine all these matters — not vice-versa.

THE ELITE

The highest authority within the Imperium will be the Elite. A body of Men, a quarter of a million: guardians of the Imperium. These leaders, veritable SuperMen, are all Male, imbued with a Sacred High Dominance quite apart, distinct, distanced from the Nation. A Perfect example of such an Elite was the Prussian State where, at the apex, the Teutonic Order stood as guardian of the Eternal Values.

Authority vested in the Elite must be absolute or it is no authority at all. It is unconditional, not subject to any other power or right. It is not subject to the law but above it. — *Princeps legibus solutus est.*

The Elite is not and should never be a representation of society — it is above it. For the political sphere is separate and above the social, purely economic and social aspect of the Nation. The Elite represent the State. The State: the Imperium is *form* — Nation is *matter.*

And it is a false notion of today's degenerate world that the family is portrayed as the basis of the nation. This is a Female concept in tune with Democracy.

Apart from the fact that families are now disintegrating, (divorce, single parents, etc.) it is not through the family that the basis of High Politics and the Imperium must be found — but elsewhere; in the *Union of MEN.*

This is the basis of the political sphere, i.e. the Imperium. In most societies, primitive or evolved, in every civilisation and culture, young men make a *passing through* at maturity. From their adolescent, maternally dominated life, they pass to the masculine sphere, often enduring rites involving pain, anguish and trial — and become truly Men!

It is within such *Union of Men* that the Imperium must be based. A leadership above the Nation. The *auctoritas*: the Imperium. The Apex, the Soul, the *IDEA* of Eternal Values is safeguarded by this Elite; *Union of Men.* A divine mystery of High Dominance — a Divine Right of Kings.

PROJECT GENESIS

A top priority for the Imperium will be space exploration. Not only material considerations impel us to colonise space. There is also the all-important factor of racial survival. For too long has our race kept all its eggs in one basket. Now that we have the means to do so, we must spread out. A meteorite could wipe out all life on earth. A nuclear catastrophe would do the same. Therefore we have to send our best sons out into space, safe to procreate and carry on the great mission of European civilisation. However, we must ensure that space remains a White Man's preserve.

We will send orbiting spaceships, carrying incubators with our best genes: our best future sons and daughters. These embryonic containers would be automatically activated through a command from Earth and hurled into outer space, towards pre-destined, distant planets. Thus the White Race would be able to re-generate itself, safe, millions of miles away from earth, in case of a planetary catastrophe.

Beyond even our immediate racial survival, space exploration is an imperative need for the White Race. Our Promethian spirit demands that we go out, that we seek the new — and master it. Without this spirit our civilisation would never have been — without it, it will die.

One of the pioneers of rocket technology, the Russian Konstantin Tsiolkovsky, once said, 'Earth is the cradle of mankind, but one does not stay in a cradle forever.'

The White Race is a pioneering race. It must always have new frontiers, new challenges or else it will turn its abundant energies inwards in self-destruction. We must carry on the struggle, ever striving, out there in the infinity of time and space.

And if there is a God out there, somewhere in the outermost reaches or innermost recesses of the universe, *we will find Him!* We will turn the spotlight of our Aryan intellect upon Him and hold Him in its full glare.

We will stand proud, naked, square in body and mind before Him — and we will hold his gaze.

IMPERIUM

0311

XXIX
OUR
DESTINY

TOWARDS A NEW CONSCIOUSNESS —
A NEW ORDER — A NEW PEOPLE

Dedicated to the memory of:
DR WILLIAM PIERCE
Founder and Chairman of
THE NATIONAL ALLIANCE
Inspired by Dr Pierce's memorable lecture: Our Cause.

WHEN PRIMORDIAL MAN STARTED TO evolve up the evolutionary scale he began comprehending the world around him. He became conscious of his feebleness, of his vulnerability. Nature in all its manifestations was dangerous to *Homo erectus* and later *Homo sapiens*. Life was truly ugly, brutal and short — and man needed a palliative to it. He invented God.

Like art, traces of which have been found in the Dordogne dating back to BC 15,000, religion made life bearable, tolerable. While art acts as a seductress, transporting us to a different level of perception, a flight from reality — religion gives man the excuse to renounce the self-overcoming, the daily struggle in search of 'worldly achievements' that reality demands, and to bear his tribulations — for the promise of a pie in the sky.

Religion can take two forms: passive or assertive. Buddhism is the best example of the former while Christianity, in the Middle Ages and right up to the eighteenth century, was certainly assertive, non-compromising, and underpinned the White Man's conquests across the globe. It gradually lost this drive and today is indistinguishable from atheistic communism. Not surprisingly, communist leaders in the West quote the Bible and the Pope in their efforts to woo majority-mediocrity.

Today, Islam is the prime example of an assertive religion. It is contemptuous of Christianity, which it regards as a religion fit for women only. Mohammedanism underpins the political aspirations of the Arab World. What the Palestinians could not achieve in the name of Nasser, they will certainly gain in the name of Allah.

Ayatollah Khomeini toppled the shah from his peacock-throne through Islam, while Saddam Hussein defied the whole world and prayed on TV at the height of the Gulf War.

CHRISTIANITY

As we noted earlier, Christianity evolved in the ghettos of Rome and proliferated largely amongst the lowest strata of society throughout the Roman Empire. To the Roman nobility it was a detestable religion with its appeal for humility, forgiveness, tolerance and resignation to any situation.

Within a few centuries, like a virus infecting the whole body of Europe, it managed to supplant the old gods, who had become worn out. By the second century even the emperor had converted (after all, the concept of 'Divine Right' appealed greatly to the emperors for maintaining their grip on power). The cross triumphed and stood on the Roman hills, where formerly the imperial eagle had surveyed the Empire.

The true Christian actually turns the other cheek to his tormentor. Thus, Christianity is anti-survival, anti-life. It is the greatest aberration of the instincts. If really taken seriously and adhered to, if followed to its logical conclusion, Christianity would kill its true believers.

Two thousand Christmases later, this disease has debilitated us to the extent that the White Man has come to carry a guilt complex for his very existence. Examples are too many to enumerate. Suffice it to mention one: White girls, healthy, of child-bearing age, forsake motherhood and follow an emaciated Albanian 'sister of the poor' to the pest holes of Asia, tendering to the festering wounds of starving Hindus. — Christianity is a *Chandala* religion.

Young men and women, bereft of a vision, of a philosophy of life, embrace Christianity and as missionaries part to Africa, saving Black babies from being devoured by fellow Blacks. They scream at us and demand that we admit these inassimilable aliens within our midst.

All this would not be a real problem if our young people had to have a vision of an *IMPERIUM EUROPA*, underpinned by an authentic belief, fit for the White Race. A vision that would not leave that vacuum which Christianity now fills. The unfortunate thing is that the most honest, the most idealistic of our youth — it is they who take Christianity seriously.

The Will of the Universe

As I have elucidated in my *Coming Cataclysmic Crisis*, we are living in dangerous times. The whole planetary, political scene is in flux. Anything could happen, anytime. And the White World is unprepared. Actually we are weak, very weak. We are weak in *Spirit*, in political will — we are divided amongst ourselves. We lack real leadership. We are like a ship without a compass, having lost our sense of direction. We have no bearing, no distant, fixed star to guide us.

In short, we are like a nation, like a race without a soul. And this is why we are in such a predicament today. Yes, we have enormously difficult problems, and it is imperative that we prepare ourselves mentally and *Spiritually* for the final battle ahead. We need a philosophical and *Spiritual* underpinning — an all-encompassing worldview.

We must rediscover ourselves, our inner nature. We need to listen, heed that divine spark within us and base all our decisions on a clear, comprehensive philosophy illuminated by that spark. We need to understand that deep inner source from which our feelings and intuition about Race and High Politics, and all concomitant issues, arise.

We have to find that link between Individual and Race. The knowledge that the former does not exist as an end in himself, but for something greater, a continuity, an eternity. On the other hand, Race can only flower through the perpetual self-overcoming and self-improvement of the Individual. *Individual and Race — Race and Individual*: a symbiotic relationship.

We must be attuned to the Race-Mind, the Race-Soul — that source of divine wisdom, as old as the universe itself. For now, for the first time in the history of our Race, we are on the threshold of understanding clearly and precisely the mystery of Life itself.

The universe is continually changing, evolving. With its more than 120,000 surveyed galaxies, Creation is moving towards ever more complex, ever higher forms of existence. And not only that: *the Universe is evolving as a Conscious Whole.*

Yes, we as a Race are a manifestation of the Creator. Our planet Earth, our living *Gaia* is itself a manifestation of the Universe. For the *Universe has a consciousness, a will of its own.* We are part of, a manifestation of the Creative Will, the *Cosmic Force* of the Universe.

We must become the conscious manifestation of the Universal Will!

This realisation shoulders us with a tremendous responsibility. A mantle of authority, the moral authority to do whatever is necessary. Brooking no opposition or restraint, we must be diamond pure and diamond hard in carrying out that responsibility. That of serving as a willing, conscious tool: the manifestation for the Realisation of the Creator's purpose: *the Will of the Universe.*

Ever improving ourselves, ever moving forward, ever ascending, unveering on the steep path towards self-perfection, towards the Superman and beyond:

Breeding amongst ourselves — Holding ourselves apart from the submen all around us — Harnessing lightning and cosmic energy — Ever more sophisticated observatories, as were Stonehenge and Mnajdra — An

Aristocratic view of Life — Discerning, discriminating the beautiful and noble to the ugly and perverse — An agonising path upwards rather than the easy, downward slide.

A quest for the Grail. A galactic quest for the understanding of the Creator's purpose: the path to Divine Consciousness. *For the Universe has a Divine Consciousness* — and we must become an integral part of it. We must strive towards Divinity — *we must become Divine!*

COSMOTHEISM

It is high time to adopt this new belief in *THE SACRED GENE POOL.*

A belief that *The Universe is evolving as a Conscious Whole.*

That the *Universe has a consciousness, a will of its own* — *a Divine Consciousness.*

That *We must become the conscious manifestation of the Universal Will!*

That *We must become Divine!*

We must become ONE with the Divine Essence!

In short: a *COSMOTHEIST* belief!

Only thus can we be assured of the continued survival and strengthening of the White Man — and the accomplishment of his *Sacred Mission within the Cosmos.*

NATIONAL ALLIANCE

NATIONALVANGUARD.ORG

A Unique, Personal and Strange Experience
by Norman Lowell

On Tuesday 23rd July 2002 at about 11pm Malta time, I was watching TV, alone in my bedroom. Suddenly the green TV lamp glowed to a strong orange and then turned to brilliant white, before bursting with a loud bang. Glass shattered and scattered around the room. A strange happening — a heightened feeling, tension gripped me.

Next day the news that Dr. William Pierce, one of the great fighters for the White Race, had passed away at about that same time.

Three days later, Saturday 27th: Natvan.com broadcast *OUR CAUSE*.

Homage — Honour — to Dr William Pierce! — *Onore!*

Imperium

0311

XXX

RACE CRIMES

WHY DENY HATE-MOTIVATED CRIME?

LATELY I WAS INVITED BY Rev. Mark Montebello to a full-day, international seminar at a four star hotel in Malta. The subject: Why Deny Hate Motivated Crime? Various guests, some from Eastern European countries, were invited, as well as a plethora of the usual do-gooders along with some mainstream MEPs.

When, after all preparations had been finalised, and, just a month before the actual date, it transpired that Norman Lowell of *Imperium Europa* was to participate — the champions of Democracy took to flight and scampered away. They resembled a bunch of Salvation Army girls, taking to their heels on judgement day!

To his great credit, Rev. Montebello stuck to his guns. He insisted that since Lowell was invited and the main hosts were in agreement to his presence, he would rather cancel the seminar than buckle under this squalid blackmail. We of IE may not agree with most of the good Rev.'s ideas and opinions, but one has to respect him on his stand. We will never forget this.

DEFINE TERMS

But let us define our terms. What is hate? Well, like love, it is a natural feeling. A defence mechanism, ordained by nature in the pursuit of self-preservation — of all species. A professional boxer hates his adversary with a passion during those crucial fifteen rounds. Boxing is the sublimation of a life-or-death combat. Hate is essential.

In war, armies are incited by propaganda to hate the enemy. Millions were inebriated by hateful propaganda during WWII against anything German. The Talmudic hate spewed out reached a nadir, a bottom, never equalled since.

WHAT IS A HATE CRIME?

This is a modern invention by international multi-racialists in their quest to deracinate Whites. Hate Crimes are whatever the Media, the present culture bearers, define as such. A few examples:

Rhodesia was declared a 'Threat to World Peace' by the United Nations some years ago. It was the most peaceful, serene, prosperous country in Africa... with an abundant food surplus. It was brought down simply and solely because it was considered racist (which it was not). The real reason of course, was that it was ruled by civilised Whites.

Today Zimbabwe, formerly Rhodesia, is in shambles. The people are famished and the government, a black government, is run by thugs — as everywhere else in Africa. Mugabe, who studied to become a Jesuit, is a bloodthirsty murderer who has incited his tribal people to murder White farmers and take over their land. In some particularly horrible cases Whites were cannibalised and Blacks celebrated the murders by drinking their blood. To the media, Mugabe has not committed a single Hate Crime.

The same in South Africa. A few years ago, it was one of the strongest countries in the world, with a vibrant economy. Today, the SA Air Force is grounded for lack of fuel! The Kaffir!

South African farmers are brutally murdered in the Transvaal. Again, the primitive Blacks who commit such murders are let off lightly. In the eyes of the world's media, they have not committed a Hate Crime.

Black violence on Whites in Europe and especially the USA is endemic. Mugging, rape, murder is overwhelmingly Black on White, even though the Black population is only a fraction, some 12% of the population in the USA. Of course, all this is not a Hate Crime.

Black gangs intimidate peaceful, law-abiding Whites, especially women. Lately, a pack of savage Blacks beat up and nearly killed four Catholic girls playing tennis in Marine Park, Brooklyn. The Blacks could not wait their turn to play. The media was quick to assure us that, naturally, this was not a Hate Crime.

Mexicans are now routinely beating solitary Whites all across America. Shouting anti-White slurs, these maniacs mercilessly beat defenceless Whites in orgies of pure hate. Again, no Hate Crime according to the controlled media.

In Malta

We have had our fair share too. One remembers the particularly gory murder when a Black brute of primitive, if not primordial features, cut up in pieces his Maltese girlfriend who had decided to end the relationship. Her deracinated, degenerate father quickly appeared on TV forgiving the monster — you see, it was not a Hate Crime.

Some years ago two Arabs cut up a lad in pieces, with a broken bottle. They dumped the body slices in Valletta harbour. Not a hate crime.

BUT! When Norman Lowell spoke at Safi, aha! The Police summoned legal experts to go over the speech in order to determine whether a Hate Crime had been committed. Whether our sacred race-laws had been infringed. These anti-freedom laws were enacted by our pusillanimous politicians when egged on by the internationalists who made them adopt, almost to the letter, British legislation on the subject.

As the internationally renowned lawyer and authority on Race Hate

Laws, Lee John Barnes, wrote regarding my case:

> I was interested in your article regarding the case of Norman Lowell and the charge of 'Inciting racial hatred' that he has been charged with under Maltese law. This section of the Maltese legal code is stated here:
>
> 82A. (1) Whosoever uses any threatening, abusive or insulting words or behaviour, or displays any written or printed material which is threatening, abusive or insulting, or otherwise conducts himself in such a manner, with intent thereby to stir up racial hatred or whereby racial hatred is likely, having regard to all the circumstances, to be stirred up shall, on conviction, be liable to imprisonment for a term from six to eighteen months.
>
> As you can see from the section of the British equivalent, section 5 of the Race Relations Act of 1976 (below), the wording of the offense is virtually identical.
>
> This shows that the laws on racial hatred that have flourished across Europe since the 1970s have been enacted as part of a European-wide plan to criminalize nationalist dissenters to the 'master plans' of our political elites. It also shows the inherent political nature of the offenses, rather than any apolitical motivation for enacting such criminal laws.
>
> The recent flood of European Directives from the European Union on racial hatred can potentially become law in every European nation if they are derived from Directives. The entire scope of free speech is being restricted across the whole of the European continent.
>
> The 'Enlightenment' was defined by the rise of the methodology of modern science and by the aftermath of the prolonged religious conflicts that followed the Reformation. Thinkers were horrified at the slaughter that took place over minor religious doctrinal differences across Europe and sought a new unifying language based on the principles of science and logic rather than the intolerant teachings of religious faith. The thinkers of the Enlightenment (called *philosophes* in France) were committed to promoting secular views based on reason or human understanding only, which they hoped would provide a basis for beneficial changes affecting every area of life and thought, and that would allow a bridge to be built between the people of Europe that transcended the artificial differences of religion, and allowed European racial re-unification around science and logic. These new languages were reason

and liberty, though once again they became Urizenic as they degenerated into the political dogma of the French Revolution rather than racial unity of all the European folk nations.

The European Enlightenment allowed individuals the intellectual (if not the legal) right to criticize the Monarchies and the Churches of Europe. The modern era of Europe is characterized by a return to the primitivism of intellectual intolerance and the hatred of the Nationalist heretic who criticizes the new Urizenic monstrosity of the European Union, which is nothing but liberal fascism. The era of the 'European Enlightenment' has ended and a new 'Liberal Fascist Dark Age' begins.

This is the hypocrisy we are living in: a system of double standards. And who is imposing such a tyrannical system on our people, muzzling them, their liberties in their own lands? Who is behind all this? Who is this Moloch that wants to destroy the White Race, that 5% of the world's population, that race of Biological Aristocrats that gave humanity everything? Who is behind all this?

It is the world's media of course. It is the media that determine present-day cultural values, worldwide. And WHO controls the world's media? Them! That tribe of international vipers that threw the gauntlet two thousand years ago and vowed to destroy us. Those, whom one who knew them well once defined as Satan's spawn. It is They that bribe and pressure our politicians to impose these hateful Race Laws. Laws that go against our long tradition of freedom of thought, expression and association. Laws that throw us back to the Dark Ages.

Laws that place White people as second class citizens in their own lands. Thus, while Blacks, Arabs and what not say what they want, act how they feel in our own territories and heartlands — while these aliens impose their culture upon us, contemptuously elbowing us aside: we have to pussyfoot around them.

Take the Vlaams Blok, the biggest single party in Belgium, which was banned. That is democracy! Take Britain, the media similarly screaming for the banning of the BNP: a party catering for the British people. A party that garnered one million votes. Banning one million native Britains! That is present-day democracy, as dictated by the international manipulators.

In the USA, White Student Unions are highly discouraged. The media screams racism at the first tentative efforts by Euro-American students to protect themselves, their identity, in a Student Union that caters to Whites. At the same time, Hispanics, Blacks, Mexicans reinforce their identity and hatefulness against Whites, by freely banding in their own, exclusive groups funded by White tax payers.

Affirmative Action is directed solely against Whites. No White can claim unfair dismissal because of his race. No White can push himself into a job, claiming racial quotas. All these are reserved solely for the benefit of all non-Whites.

What is 'Racism'?

What, then, is 'racism'? It is more than just a dictionary definition. In effect, it is any opposition by Whites to official policies of racial preference for non-whites in their own lands. It is any preference by Whites for their own people and culture. Any resistance by Whites to becoming a minority people in their own lands. Any indication of an unwillingness to be pushed aside, stomped on and spat upon. Racism is: any normal aspiration of nationhood and self-determination by Europids.

We in Malta are not prepared to go that way. We will not tolerate it. We of *Imperium Europa* will always speak openly and without fear. For this is our country! This is not Rhodesia, SA, the Netherlands, America or Britain — this is our country and our people. And we will do everything in our power to save both!

We will continue to proclaim our message of truth, come what may, race laws or no race laws — Jews or no Jews. Our website: www.vivamalta.org, is a fountain of information for those interested in learning more about us. Getting to know what the real struggle is all about. Vivamalta.net is a focal point for those without a bearing — for those yearning for a message of hope.

RACIALISM not RACISM

Let me make myself clear: We are Racialists, not Racists. We do not hate others. We simply love our own kind — like all the rest do: Blacks, Arabs, Chinese, Mexicans and what not. We love our own kind: Kindness, Kindred, *Kinder* — one's own kind. This is Racialism.

We will fight those instigators of Hate. That tribe of international manipulators who led us into fratricidal wars, wars against our own kind. Perpetual wars right till the present time: Madeleine Albright and William Cohen made us bomb our Serbian cousins.

Stupid wars like the first Iraq war. Afghanistan, where the latest technology was used against fuzzy-wuzzies in sandals and turbans. Bombs that cost thousands, if not millions of times the worth of their targets.

Then came *Boobus Bush*, the stupidest President in America's history. A second Iraq War based on lies, nothing but lies (CNN) by those great masters of the lie. And now the same mischief-makers are screaming for war against Syria and Iran. Wars, perpetual wars all on behalf of a bandit state, a viper's nest in the Middle East.

This is the problem, the fundamental problem: The World Problem! Unless we solve it, once and for all, unless we find a cure to this worldwide malady, we will never have peace. We will have eternal hate and hatefulness.

INDIVIDUAL RIGHTS

We of *Imperium Europa* stand for Liberty, true liberty of each Individual, Region and People. We stand for Individual Rights, not human rights — for these last do not exist. They are a figment of the imagination. They are the latest invention of those manipulators in order to ensnare us.

We stand for the right of every race to live according to its wishes, its culture, pursuing its destiny. We do not want to interfere in the affairs of others: hence our vision of an Imperium uniting the four cousin sub-races: Anglo-Saxons, Teutons, Slavs and Latins.

We will not tolerate others to interfere in our own racial affairs. We will go our own way — and bid the rest do the same. To each their own. Only then, with the grand separation of the races, can this planet have that peace that we all, Whites and non-whites alike, have always yearned for.

IMPERIUM

0504

XXXI
SKY-HIGH CITIES
(ARCOLOGY)

W HEN, IN MY BOOK *CREDO: A Book for the Very Few*, I had written about a future city in the middle of Malta, housing most of our population, many were incredulous. Today, five years later, there are those who still cannot visualise such an edifice.

The skyscraper race, the race for the tallest building in the world, is far from over. There are more than fifty proposed buildings that would break the current record. Some of the more conservative structures are already in construction. The more ambitious buildings in the group are only theoretical at this time.

Are these buildings possible? According to some engineering experts, the real limitation is money, not technology. Super-tall buildings require extremely sturdy materials and deep, fortified bases. Construction crews need elaborate cranes and pumping systems to get materials and concrete up to the top levels. All told, putting one of these buildings up would easily cost tens of billions of euros.

Experts are divided about how high we can really go in the near future. Some say we could build a mile-high (5,280 ft/1,609 m) building with existing technology. Others say we would need to develop lighter, stronger

materials, faster elevators and advanced sway dampers before these buildings are feasible. (Sway dampers are 400 ton concrete blocks that circle
the upper storey to counteract high winds.) Speaking only hypothetically,
most engineers won't impose an upper limit. Future technological advances could conceivably lead to buildings that are Sky-High Cities, many
experts say, housing a million people or more, and, what's more, new ar-
cologies are currently being designed and proposed, where earthquakes
are the real engineering feat to overcome, not height.

   We on this Sacred Island of *Melita*, are compelled to build further up-
ward in the future, simply to conserve our precious land — this humus
that is so unique. When one builds upwards, one concentrates living
space, instead of spreading out and destroying unspoilt, natural beauty.
Our Skyscraper City would also be very convenient and practical, cluster-
ing niche businesses thus reducing commuting time.

GRADUAL TRANSFORMATION

Of course, Rome wasn't built in a day. The gradual transformation of our
Island back to its pristine glory will take years. A process of education,
una battaglia di cultura, weaning our upcoming generations on aesthetics
and respect for their motherland.

   We would start clearing up our coastline, pushing buildings back a
healthy two miles all around the island. Narrow bicycle and horse tracks
would fan out from the centre towards the coast, much like spokes in a
wheel. For the elderly, covered, futuristic electric 'people movers' similar
to escalators and treadmills would open up the countryside.

   At the same time we will start clearing the obnoxious flats and garish
villas ruining our skylines. After that, those hideous blocks choking our
valleys. Step by step, year by year, we will heal this Island.

MELITA — SPIRITUAL CENTRE

Malta, this jewel in the centre of the Mediterranean — *Mare Nostrum* — will

become the Spiritual, mystical Mecca for the Aryan. Our pre-historic sacred sites, Neolithic temples, Medieval bastions, at once awesome and inspiring, will be the destination for millions of discerning Aryans, yearning
to discover their genetic and Spiritual roots. Yes, we Maltese will be the
guardians and curators of these unique, sacred sites on behalf of the Imperium. — We will defend them with our lives.

Of course, the population would need to be drastically reduced. This
island was never meant to accommodate 400,000 people. The maximum
ideal number would be 200,000 — a high-quality people sieved through a
eugenics programme. Those with very low IQs would be dissuaded from
breeding, while high-IQ persons would be encouraged to sire at least
three children.

Of course, with total mobility within the Imperium, our youths
would be free to choose to travel and live anywhere they wish. Older
folk may retire elsewhere, in exotic places within the White World. So,
keeping the population around a quarter of a million would not be a
problem.

Euthanasia, as practised by the pre-Dorics, the Athenians, the Spartans and the Romans, would again become a natural and normal process
in eliminating the weak, the bungled and the botched. These would get
progressively fewer as the genetically defective are bred out, over a few
generations. We have to move on, beyond two thousand years of morbid,
Christian-Catholic cretinism.

One Arcology where Mosta now stands would house most of our
population. Every single building on the island post-dating 1800 will be
gradually razed to the ground. Olives and rubble walls will again cover the
island. The Three Cities, Mdina and Valletta and one revolving, Sky-High
City will be quite enough to comfortably house our population. Solar and
wind energy will ensure our needs, while an underground transport system will girdle the island. Not one single vehicle will be allowed to pollute
this Sacred Island.

The manufacturing base, except for the most specialised and sophisticated of niches, would be gradually eliminated. Our quality population

would move up the notch to a culture-oriented way of life. This would include both work-place and leisure time.

Endemic fauna and flora will again thrive: giant owls, ferrets, the wild rabbit — the unique and exceedingly rare Maltese ox and the wild boar will again be introduced in the wild.

Only tourists of the highest quality would be permitted to set foot on our Sacred Soil. The whole island would be listed as an Imperium heritage area.

One huge university, drawing students from all over the Imperium, would serve as an intellectual magnet for the Elite, High Culture Bearers, specialising solely in the Spiritual origins of the Europids. Their field work would be all around them! They would study the scores of temples, buried under the tons of concrete that forty years of 'progress' have dumped on our tremendous past. Special submarines would serve as moving observatories of the other, numerous temples, submerged offshore around our beaches and cliffs. Indeed, Malta would become the focal point, the Spiritual apex of the coming *IMPERIUM EUROPA*.

Tarxien Temples, Malta, the original world centre of The Cult of Great Mother, the progenitors of whom are the two virgins, both from Ephesus: Diana and Mary. The huge, Mother Goddess statue, representing the central role of the all-powerful Mother-Earth — *Yin*.

Mnajdra, Skorba, Xamxija (Shem-sh-sunny), and our other magnificent temples, all facing South-East — so precisely aligned to the penetrating rays of the rising sun at the winter solstice — bear testimony to the previous 'Solar' veneration of our Aryan forefathers — *Yan*.

Melita — The future centre for an authentic, nature-oriented belief for the Europid.

Melita — Linking the Aryan back to his *Oneness* with the Cosmos.

Melita — Spiritual centre of the Imperium — *Cosmotheism!*

XXXII

ARCHITECTURE

ITS RELATION AND RELEVANCE TO HIGH POLITICS

A TRULY INTERESTING AND IMPORTANT QUESTION that relates directly to our *Imperium Europa*. In answering, I will not revert to a purely political reply — *un discorso puramente politico* — but I will try to elucidate the strong relationship between Architecture, real Architecture and not copy-cat architecture, to High Politics.

Architecture has been with us since primordial man. He had to create a habitat, be it atop a tree, inside a cave, anything that could serve him in the battle for survival. Serve him as shelter from the elements and as defence against wild animals and hostile tribes.

In the Dordonne, the Lascaux Caves present paintings that seem as fresh and dynamic as any Picasso. This prehistoric art is sixteen thousand years old. This reveals that primitive man sought to embellish his surroundings, to improve and edify his ambience, please his gods, fortify his consciousness amidst his brutally rugged environment.

Here in Malta, the hewn niches within our world-renowned Hypogeum, cannot fail to arouse the sense of the Spiritual. Our ancestors created that vital Sacred Space without which Man is void.

ARCHITECTURE: FOUR MAIN CATEGORIES

UTILITARIAN

A factory is utilitarian. So is the kitchen in a house. A bathroom or spare toilet.

LEISURE

A football pitch is a place of leisure. It lies empty for a whole week, yet on a Sunday, it spins millions of euros in turnover and draws crowds by the thousands. A basketball court, a tennis lawn again provide that leisure space, so essential for the enactment or sublimation of the hunt, or of war.

POWER

Cathedrals, palaces, castles, churches, skyscrapers are all expressions of Power. Religious power (the Vatican, St. Peter's), Political power (Palazzo Sforza), Economic power (Twin Towers) and so on. One is filled with awe on entering St. Paul's Cathedral in London. The enormity, the Spartan simplicity, the power!

SACRED SPACE

Stonehenge immediately comes to mind. Monoliths in a circle with the empty countryside all around. A mysticism, a sacredness that never fails to strike home to anyone with a sensitive predisposition and a perceptive eye. Our Mnajdra, here in Malta, perfectly aligned to the rising solstice sun. Man attuned to the Cosmic Spirit, the Cosmic Force. In truth, Cosmotheism has been with us since the beginning of time.

MAN AND HIS ARCHITECTURE

Sumerians: Between the Euphrates and Tigris. They had two kinds of buildings: the flimsy mud-huts near the river delta and solid, massive edifices further into the hinterland. This was early man's response for survival during the yearly inundations. Flimsy huts can be rebuilt quickly — while the hanging gardens of Babylon and the imposing *Ziggurat* were built to withstand centuries. Incidentally these last, the *Ziggurat*, were the progenitor of the skyscraper, though their function was Spiritual rather than purely utilitarian.

Persians: Their capital Persiopolis. An open city with no outer walls. So confident were the Persians of their power, that it never occurred to them to erect defences around the city. A capital city, the centre of a vast Empire with a complex infrastructure. Roads linking the East to the West. An efficient postal service. High Culture and High Art — Alexander, the Macedonian barbarian, simply walked in and burnt everything to the ground. Persian architectural remains are a testimony to the high level of Persian civilisation.

Spartans: Again, a capital city with no defensive walls. So confident were the Spartans in their army, that they dispensed with walls. Spartan discipline and endurance guaranteed Sparta's security. Unlike the Persians, the Spartans left no architectural remains, no Art of any consequence. What they left was *A Spartan Tradition in European Thought* that to this day still fascinates youth in every European country.

Prussia was a legacy of Sparta. Sweden with its conquering Vikings right down to the Black Sea was likewise. Eton and Harrow, present day Gordonstoun in Scotland is Spartan. HRH Philip, Duke of Edinburgh was educated there.

It is indeed ironic that the Persians and Spartans, both disdaining walls, had to fight such bitter battles such as Thermopylae.

Athens: A Walled City. A city proclaiming Reason, Order, Calm Composure, Rationality. Athenian Apollonian Architecture! The Parthenon symbolises all this. Eventually, the Peloponnesian Wars depleted Athens and Sparta emerged as the victor: the city walls were demolished.

BRING DOWN THE WALL

Pink Floyd, with their song, evoked the age-old dilemma. Wall or no wall? Shall we have a *Festung Europa* or open borders?

Romans: conquered the Hellenes militarily but not culturally. In effect they became the students, imitators of the Greeks. They copied them assiduously. The Roman phalanx was re-organised into Maniples which was a more maneuverable formation: with each cohort working independently of each other, it was the ancient form of Blitzkrieg and won over both Sparta and Athens, crushing all resistance. Romans did the same against the Gaels (*bello gallico*). Order prevailed against disorder and improvisation. Discipline and efficiency saw the day against the fierce Celts. Then came Hadrian's Wall: the symbol of rest, of 'enough is enough'. The Celts sailed around the wall in their boats.

Later, much later, came the Maginot Line. The same signs of fatigue, weariness, *voglia di riposare* (desire to rest). Then the Siegfried Line — and we hung our washing on it!

The only exception, the only city walls that endured and were not breached, are in Malta. After the epic Great Siege of Malta, the Knights built our awesome, majestic walls around Valletta. The only reason these walls endured was because as soon as they were built, they became redundant! The siege became a thing of the past.

In the seventies, the film *Zardoz* staring Sean Connery placed this dilemma of wall or no wall as the central theme. A highly civilised race insulated itself from the barbarian hordes behind an electronic wall. Eventually, the protected species became tired of their leisurely life and committed racial suicide. They themselves opened the gates — they desired death.

The Dark Ages: The era of sieges, of castles. Of unimaginable cruelties by a hideous Catholic religion. Massacres in Provence, Wald-Aosta, the Cathars. Castles and towers proved futile against the burning hatred, blind ignorance of Catholic zealots.

Rinascimento: Petty family feuds, low walls with watchtowers furtively eyeing neighbours. But also, the Glory of Architecture: Palaces projecting power, hosting great works of Art, offering leisure and pleasure. Palaces as places signalling Sacredness.

Sombre palaces, where the Doge and patrician families were the focal point, the reference point for the people. Architecture as a symbol of Power.

Modern times: Skyscrapers serving the utilitarian, housing thousands. Skyscrapers serving as symbols of Corporate, Financial Power.

Fascism in the 30s. Similar but less austere than the Roman buildings of old. Fascism projecting Roman Order fused with modernity. Functional and stylised, straight lines racing towards the future. *Futurismo* with its obsession with speed. A solar vision of life: *una Vision Solare!*

ARCHITECTURE: ETHOS OF THE TIMES

Like the Romans, the British projected an Imperial Order. Buildings on crests but never on the skyline. Doric columns projecting power and order — the Male Imperium side. But once through those solemn columns the subject, both native Briton or colonial, would find libraries, scholarships, education and etiquette, a way of life. The Female side, Dominium.

Today we live in an era of dialectic materialism. An era that is rapidly coming to an end. *Homo oeconomicus* has had his innings, but his world is about to collapse. A functional, ugly world where money and speculation rule. Speculation of property, leading to ever more hideous buildings, built solely as a hedge against inflation — and to hell with aesthetics and the environment!

A DIGRESSION

We had the tsunami and the moaning and groaning, the woes and wails. In the Andaman Islands, inhabited by primitive cannibals, where the highest mountains range from one to three meters, there were no casualties. The islanders sensed the incoming wave and quickly scrambled up coconut trees. After the surge, they shinned down and continued with their simple, nature-oriented lifestyle.

On the other hand, at Pu Che, a hideous conglomeration of concrete, piled on the coast, the greedy islanders and fat tourists got what was coming to them! Thousands were trapped as nature took its revenge. And was the lesson learnt? Of course not! The Thais are quickly rebuilding their concrete tourist villages exactly where they stood before. For Thailand is swept by a more devastating wave, the tsunami of greed. It is engulfing, destroying their culture.

However, there is always a silver lining. A turtle, previously considered extinct, has resurfaced at Pu Che. The tsunami was well worth it!

BEAUTIFUL or USEFUL

It was Ouspensky who said: 'It is beautiful because it is not useful'. And it is true. For usefulness or utility, aesthetics are not a priority, but cold efficiency certainly is. In Architecture it is much the same. In the thirties and forties Corbusier in his *Towards an Architecture* and Gropius with his *Bauhaus in Germany* both insisted 'The house is a generator', or 'A house is a machine for living in'. Usefulness!

Today, we have tried to move away from the ugly. And, to a certain extent we have succeeded. In the process we are omitting a most important element: the significance!

John Ruskin, the famous educator at Oxford once said, 'Good architecture displays Firmness, Commodity and Delight'. Quite true — but what about *the significance* of the building?

Let us take the Sydney Opera House in Australia: sails of a yacht. And we all know that yachts denote success in life! But where is *the significance* of the building? There is no national message. What have yachts got to do with parliaments? What do yachts have to do with Operas?

Likewise Scotland's Parliament, by the Spanish Miralles. He was inspired by overturned boats at Holy Island, off Northumberland. A truly inspiring and creative idea but again, where is *the significance* to parliament? Actually, the edifice is fragmented, scattered, non-orthogonal, non-hierarchical — an exact representation of the confused, modern, fragmented society we are living in.

Instead of a building portraying an aura for calm debate, order and hierarchy, we have huge wide apertures with distracting views. Glaring lights and enormous, intruding anvil beams that add to the confusion.

Where is the significance of our buildings? In Valletta we had our petty politicians proposing that our bombed Theatre site a site embedded in the nation's sub consciousness — *l'Opera House, il Teatro* would be rebuilt into a modern Parliament. The architect designated, a man renowned for his profusion of books professing the Sacredness of Space, did not care two hoots — you see, one does anything for a fee! *Where is the significance, the sacredness, the sacred spaces?*

OUR VISION!

We of *Imperium Europa* have boldly proclaimed our Vision for our Sacred Island. One Arcology housing some 100,000 — pyramidical and symbolical, or conical and revolving, where Mosta now stands. Money is the only constraint, for we already have the technology.

All buildings post-dating 1800 will be razed to the ground. Solely Valletta, Mdina and The Three Cities with the countryside all around.

> From one of my writings while in a somewhat intoxicated mood:
> The masses, the Aryan masses gladly acknowledge their place.
> This they do, only when they perceive real Leaders.
> The masses bow to them and let them Lead.
> This reminds me of the *Upanishads*.
> The *Veda (Wedhah)* and *the Rig Veda*.
> The oldest texts of wisdom known to man.
> Put into writing some 3,000 BC.
> They have been there since the beginning.
> They encapsulate everything about everything.
> We can never understand them intuitively.
> Since they are in Sanskrit — the perfect language for the mysteries.
> One thousand essays and more in the tongue of the Gods.

Not even English can capture their full meaning.
Not even a better language than that — ancient Greek —
can fully convey their full message.
In the *Veda* is the rigid rule of Class:
The *Brahmin*: the Spiritual Men.
The *Kshatriya*: the warrior class.
The *Vaisyas*: the merchant class.
The *Sudras*: those always willing to serve and work.
In the *Veda* the land is not private property:
It belongs to Brahman.
In the Old Testament: 'The land belongs to the Lord.'
Man works the land — but it can neither be bought nor sold.
A scheme were the whole nation becomes a tenant:
on this *Sacred Island of Melitae*.
Communism into National Socialism into National Futurism!
We in Malta: the Region of *Melitae*:
within the coming National Futurism of the Imperium:
can be the role-model for this.
All buildings post-dating 1800 razed to the ground:
just one Arcology where Mosta stands today.
The Three Cities, Valletta and Mdina.
Countryside all around:
farmland specialising in esoteric herbs.
Fields of wholesome, nutrient filled crops, vegetables and fruit.
Countryside belonging to all Maltese:
the fat of the land belonging to us all.
Us: landlords in the true sense of the word!
Tilling the soil: at leisure with pleasure.
Tiring hands, receiving the fruits from an abundant Nature.
Laden, bulging breasts: she feeds us all, to surfeit.
Malta! O Malta!
We will place you at the pinnacle of the pyramid.
Malta! — Paradise Lost and Found!

Our *Imperium Europa IDEA* is thousands of years old! The Countryside belonging to the people, enjoying the fat of the Land. A return to the Voice of the Gods: *Cosmotheism*.

ARCHITECTURE, ARISTOCRACY, ARYANISM

We will truly restore Valletta, our capital city, back to its former glory. As a matter of absolute priority, we will demolish those socialist flats at the entrance. Flats erected by a socialist, architect-prime minister. A man steeped in knowledge but poor in wisdom.

Presently, we enter our capital hugging a corner, scurrying like socialist mice. We will clear the rubbish and replace this cold entrance with the former austere, awesome four arches. A narrow, dark entrance with enfilade slots on both sides. We will then be blinded by the Mediterranean sun as we cross *Piazza Europa* with the rebuilt Barry Theatre greeting us. On both sides, two huge, imposing bastions stand guard over the City Gate, protecting our people. An Architectural Aristocratic message. Aristocracy as a way of life — Aristocracy of Character, of Spirit.

NEW ETHOS

We will give a new *Relevance to Architecture*. A new *Relation to High Politics*. We will win this cultural battle ensuring that *Architecture will reflect a New Ethos*: where modest democracy, fragmentation, atomisation of the person and of society — the non-hierarchical chaotic architectural compositions, will no longer apply.

Malta, that paradise to the Egyptians, the Aryans before them.

Malta, this gem, this jewel. Malta, this Paradise turned into a *Miżbla* (rubbish dump)!

A PARADISE LOST AND FOUND!

Our Architecture will reveal the Sacredness of *Melitae*. We of *Imperium Europa* intend to return our homeland to its Pristine Beauty. To make it the Spiritual Focal Point: the missing Pyramidical Stone: that Pyramidical Peak! the Apex! of the coming, inevitable, unstoppable *Imperium Europa*.

Our priorities are indeed Archaeology and Architecture. We will excavate our past. We will leave no stone unturned, no sea-bed unexplored in our quest for our past. A relentless quest that will re-forge that missing link between our Past and Future.

An Architecture befitting a National Futurism. A Regionalism, an *Identity of Regions* as against the artificial Nation States. An Architecture giving us Europids, all Europeans, those Biological Aristocrats that gave humanity everything: worthy buildings in consonance to our Race Mind.

We will use new mediums, new materials, colours. We will erect buildings with titanium durability. We will train creative, young Architects who will give us buildings that will disprove Ouspensky — buildings that are both *Beautiful and Useful!*

Imperium

0504

XXXIII

CRESCENDO
TO
IMPERIUM

W HEN I WRITE ABOUT THE coming, inevitable, unstoppable *IMPERI-UM EUROPA* many question the tempo of events. These include intellectuals who have known me for years and understand my views, even though they may not wholeheartedly agree with them. How is it possible, they ask, for an *IMPERIUM EUROPA* to be in place by 2012 when it took fifty years of wrangling to reach the present EU state of confusion? A stage where the EU is still undecided, even as to where it is heading. An ambivalence as to what kind of Europe we should have. Indecision also, as to which countries should be admitted within the club.

Good questions which have a very simple answer. Simple that is, for those of us not brainwashed by the controlled media, that fountain of misinformation that warps our vision of events as they unfold. When the founding fathers of the EU, mostly Christian Democrats and Socialists, set about building the club, they started off from a fundamental error, which still impinges on all political thought within the old continent. They set the horse before the cart. They inverted their priorities. They put economics, and not politics, at the head of the agenda.

Any person who is not imbued by the fallacies of Christian Democracy or Socialism, ostensible adversaries but, in effect, both squalid collectivists embracing egalitarian dogma, knows that economics should be placed at the very bottom of priorities in the struggle for survival of any State or Nation. England, a tiny island with a small population, held an Empire stretching around the globe, subjugating billions. Prussia, a sandy seashore with no mineral resources whatsoever, dominated Europe. So did Austria, a mountainous little country bereft of any material riches. Clearly, it takes something other than economics to enable a Nation or State to survive and thrive. In fact, today the EU is nothing but the expression of decadent economism and rampant materialism.

Above economics come politics. Not the petty politics of parliamentary politicians, parroting platitudes, pandering to the lowest common denominator and squabbling amongst themselves, always with an eye on the next elections. Not that kind of politics, but High Politics that take into account, first and foremost, the long-term true benefits and survival of the Nation. High Politics that keep an unerring compass for the ship-of-state, pointed towards a future of ever increasing virility, strength and will-to-power, for both Nation and State.

Above High Politics stands culture — High Culture. Not the perverse, low culture of Negro music and dance. Or that of Jerry Springer parading multi-racial couples and deviants of the lowest calibre. Not the slime poured every day through the controlled media by that tribe of international mischief-makers. For what is American TV today? As Kramer of Dallas fame himself said 'It's easy creating a Dallas series and such like — we just combine Jewish brains with gentile faces'. No, not this low alien, diabolical culture, contaminating the Europid, but authentic Culture, High Culture harking back through a continuous, thin thread to our past. Hayden, Nietzsche, Schopenhauer, the Greek classics, Wagner, Mozart, Sibelius, right down to present, healthy, White music.

Above High Culture there dominates the imperative of Race! The *sine qua non* for the survival of any Nation. No matter how low the economy of a country, no matter how poor the population may be financially, how dispersed and far-flung, no matter what calamity or defeat may have been suffered: if the race is maintained intact, then the people, the *Volk*, is strong. Within itself, within their genes lies the possibility, the certainty of resurgence. Once the genes are polluted through miscegenation with a different, incompatible race, then all possibility of progress, even the maintenance of the existing civilisation, is doomed.

The history of mankind is littered with the debris of civilisations that have disappeared. Recently we have witnessed the collapse of colonial Africa. South Africa, one of the strongest countries in the world up to a few years ago, was impoverished, ravished within just four years of Black rule. Elsewhere in Africa, the sad story is the same. Let the White Man retreat, let the Black take over, and within an incredibly short span of time there is total collapse. Huge countries like Nigeria, the Congo and Tanzania, countries endowed with all the mineral resources one can mention, vast agricultural lands and an ideal climate, languish in poverty and squalor. Why? Simple… the Blacks just lack the right genes to create a civilisation, any type of civilisation. — And no whining Liberal can alter that fact!

Likewise, the USA is doomed. America as we know it will not last through this decade. It is inevitable, unavoidable. The freeing of millions of black slaves was a shock: cultural, political and economic, from which that once great country cannot ever recover. More than that, it was a racial disaster. Today, the pernicious, controlled TV portrays the Blacks as role-models, heroes and the good guys in any TV film. Year in, year out, daily, this obvious fallacy is pushed down the throat of White children in their formative years. American girls since the sixties have been increasingly cohabiting with Blacks — something unheard of before the presidency of Kennedy. The inevitable result is the polluting of the genes of a once great and proud people.

America is no longer a nation but a polyglot of people all squabbling among themselves for a few bucks. History has shown that no multiracial country can survive for long. That fences make good neighbours. That without the separation of different, incompatible races, dissolution and disaster inevitably follow. Spengler, Pareto, Lukas and Polin, to mention just a few, amply and emphatically demonstrate this with numerous historical examples.

Within a short time, there will be an implosion in America. The Whites will be cornered and constrained to regroup and fight a second civil war, where the colour of the skin will be the uniform. A short, sharp cruel war with no Geneva rules, no quarter given or asked. Europids will have to resolutely expel all aliens from their territories, confining them to the cesspool cities like New York, Philadelphia, San Francisco and Los Angeles. Whites will defend and maintain the farmlands of central USA, starving out all the rest. Within six months America can be cleaned up and regained for the European. Our enemies will be surprised to what lengths we are ready to go to recover our nations.

And above Race, there comes the splendour of *Spirituality*. Not the whining Christian message of pity and equality — two thousand Christmases have brought us to the brink of extinction as a subspecies. Christianity, an abject religion fit for children and slaves. An anti-life religion, preaching disdain for Mother Earth and a lifelong pipe-dream of a pie-in-the-sky. Christianity; the aberration of all healthy instincts — a *Chandala* religion. A new belief harking back to that primordial, pre-Christian, pagan purity, potentiating our forefathers. Where each of us will realise, in our own way, will feel attuned to the *Cosmic Force*. Where the *person* will experience a mystical ecstasy, a *Spiritual* transformation uniting him as one with the Cosmos — and which is the exact opposite of any Judeo-Christian, synthetic ritual.

SPHERICAL VIEW

Unlike all the rest, we of the Radical-Racial-Right-Revolutionary-Reactionaries (RRRRR), have a Spherical view of history, as against a linear one. As a ball on a billiard table can move suddenly in any direction, so is the historical march of the human races.

The decadence of Western Man peaked with the French and then the Bolshevik revolutions — both satanic cataclysms. We are now at point

ZERO — an interregnum, a *Spiritual* wasteland. Where a progressive disappearance of diversity is taking us, hoodwinked, towards a world civilisation: that hellish creation of the international-manipulators, those eternal mischief-makers. A world where the White Man, that biological aristocrat, would be submerged in the teeming billions of the Third World.

However, as the dark moon passes, so is a new era dawning. The *Umslag* — *la svolta* — the great turnabout may happen at any moment, suddenly, cataclysmically, as September 11th has so vividly shown us! Europa — *Quo Vadis!*

The future belongs to us! We, the precious few: that Elite paving the way for the Superman, brooking no opposition or restraint in our fight for the survival of our Race. Knights in shining armour, this time not in the service of that most abject of all depraved symbols — that of a man hanging from the cross — but defenders of the Race: *Kshatrija*, Spartan hoplites, Roman legionaries, Templars, Teutonic Knights, Waffen-SS — High Culture Bearers: the best of the best, guiding the White Man on a galactic quest.

The pace quickens. More and more young people are waking up from the stupor, the soft-suicide, the materialism of Liberalism-Collectivism-Capitalism. Instead, a soft *leitmotiv* swells towards a Crescendo to *IMPERIUM EUROPA!* Soon, the Imperium will *live*: by the year *2012: Anno Zero!*

IMPERIUM

0107

XXXIV

EU to NE to IE

The EU is not IE:
But it is heading that way!
Even the blind can perceive this.
The European Constitution
Is good news to us of *Imperium Europa*.
It gives the EU the power to empower itself!
The EU is like a child:
Sweet, stumbling, silly.
But it is a growing child.
Who is to shape the child?
That is the fundamental question!
We of the RRRRR can do it!
We can take over legitimately:
And then do what we want!
Because of the power to empower oneself!
European Union to *Nova Europa*:
To *Imperium Europa*:
Uniting the Whole White World.
We of IE in Malta must ensure:
Our presence in the EU parliament.
Must lead the European RRRRR.
The RRRRR is crying out for leadership.
Only the Sacred Island of *Melitae*
Can give the necessary Spiritual impetus.
The group only needs nineteen MEPs
From five different countries.

It can be done quite easily.
We will lead the group.
We will be the clarion call.
We will be the spark.
A spark that will set Europa ablaze.
An *IDEA* whose time has come.
Imperium Europa!

In order to form a recognised group, like the PEP or the Socialists, one needs nineteen MEPs. But they must come from at least five countries (i.e. you may not have nineteen all French MEPs and form a group).

Now, the RRRRR can be formed with us (IE) leading it. It will include the Vlaams Belang, Alessandra Mussolini, Polish Farmers, Front National and others. The RRRRR is crying out for a Voice, a Leader!

The important thing is to form the first group of RRRRR with the first nineteen.

Any convergences will do. Differences will be ironed out in time, but the important thing is to have a voice as a group. As it is, the MEPs nearest to the RRRRR vision are loosely grouped under 'Independents'.

The *Lega* is in a tactical association with the EuroSceptics of Bonde! Can you imagine! However, it makes sense. As I said at Verve, the extremities of the bow, under tension, will almost touch.

We are living at a very important time for our continent and the White Race. A period of great tension, danger from without and within — a political phase brimming with possibilities, laden with opportunities. Anything can happen! Anything.

The situation can precipitate at any moment before 2012. Therefore, it is imperative that the RRRRR will have a voice, as a recognised group, in the EU. Even more important, the RRRRR must have a leader — a leadership that will galvanise it. A fearless leadership, immune and inured to the threats of international Jewry. That Leadership can only be *Imperium Europa*.

XXXV
THE ROLE OF WOMEN IN THE
IMPERIUM

Very often I am accosted by women who are genuinely interested in our Movement and Ideas. They tell me that they are in full accord with us on the immigration issue, our stand on the environment, the Imperium *IDEA* and so on. Then comes the inevitable question: 'But what is your position with regard to women?' My usual reply: 'I'm normally on top!'

Our stand on women during the last MEP elections must have cost us some votes. However, we could not do otherwise. We had to be ourselves. We had to be consistent and coherent and, most of all, truthful to our listeners — and primarily to ourselves.

We do not envisage a society with our women frivolously spending their days at beauty parlours and cafés, sipping cocktails and indulging in continuous tittle-tattle. A life of idle gossip — while their men adequately provide for them and their children.

We do not believe that our women are merely receptive 'fountains of pleasure' — 'ladies in waiting' for warriors who may take them when, where and how they please. We do not think this at all. We, the men folk of the Europid race, come from a long tradition of respect, awe even, of our women.

A FEW EXAMPLES

In Malta, at Tarxien, lies the original world centre of the Female Goddess. The Cult of the Great Mother, the progenitors of whom are the two virgins, both from Ephesus: Diana and Mary. The huge, Mother Goddess statue, representing the central role of the all-powerful Mother — of Mother Earth — *Yin*.

The Berserkers, those fierce Norsemen who fought naked in a delirium, a frenzy, struck terror in the hearts of the Roman legions. When surrounded and beaten, the Romans were amazed when their formidable enemies let them rest, dusted them down and then returned their swords so that they could carry on fighting! The Berserkers loved the fight and never wanted it to end. During these battles it was noted that, when the Norsemen seemed on the verge of defeat, their women appeared on the crest of the hill, naked, carrying their babies and holding the hands of their young ones. This sight alone and its implications redoubled the frenzied fighting spirit of the men and normally was enough to save the day.

The Romans were amazed at the loyalty of the Germanic and Norse women. When captured, they would grasp the moment and fall on the Roman sword, rather than submit to the enemy. Of course, eventually Roman strategy, tactics and teamwork won the day.

In Sparta, it was the women who wielded the real power. In can even be said that Sparta was a matriarchal society. Renaissance Italy had as many woman artists as men — and just as brilliant. In France, Napoleon, the most powerful man in Europe, found time to write twenty-six letters to his beloved Josephine during the battle of Waterloo.

It was only the Catholic Church that stigmatised women, debating even whether they had souls! The Catholic Church, embracing a non-Europid religion, an abject religion worshipping a jealous, wrathful god — an anti-nature religion that sprang from that pesthole of the Middle East, treated women as animals. During the Inquisition, two Dominicans,

Kramer and Springer, burned over sixty thousand of the most beautiful women in Europe, accusing them of bewitching men.

This then is our Europid tradition: a tradition of respect and protection for our women. A reverence even, a knowledge that in them lies the future of our race and somehow, a sublime female intuition that can never be grasped by man.

OTHER RACES

But how does the rest of humanity treat their women? Worse, much, much worse than we would ever dare dream. The Arab treatment of their women is well known, especially to those of us who have travelled throughout the Maghreb. I was once in Libya, lunching in a sprawling villa some twenty miles outside Tripoli, guest of a leading government high functionary. After a huge meal of lamb and delicious vegetables, I asked to meet the cook and compliment him. The minister called his wife and she peered through the crack of the door! She would not be allowed in.

The Chinese have practised female infanticide since time immemorial. During the Sung period, women were indeed 'receptive of fountains of pleasure and sexual experimentation' by the Taoists. In India it is much the same: the *Kama Sutra* revealing a wooden approach to sex, as if the woman is a plastic doll.

Japanese society is masculine, severely masculine. Throughout its Shogun history the Japanese rendered their women as servile, abject whores. Modern Japanese companies compensate their successful executives, not by salary increases or office perks, but by sexual orgies where foreplay is inexistent, and the sex act explicitly ugly, brutal and short.

The Kaffrid in Africa has no concept of marriage or fidelity. Anyone who has been to Southern Africa, knows fully well what the idea of love is to the Black man. Girls normally get pregnant at thirteen or less and the father usually walks away. The girl then raises a brood of children through chance encounters with gardeners, cooks, taxi-drivers, whatever, whenever — just like our stray dogs and cats.

Negroes in the USA call their women 'bitches'! The girls not only do not mind but also take pride in this. In the world of the Black, it is an accolade, a compliment, our equivalent of 'darling' or 'sweetheart'!

The Orthodox Jews are the oddest of the lot. Anyone who has not read *The Hole in the Sheet* would not otherwise believe what religious fanaticism can do to warp a man's mind. I leave the readers to find out for themselves!

This then is the picture: the comparison of that noble race that is the White Race with the rest of them, in their treatment of women. But what would be the role of our women in our future Imperium?

Our world would be divided into two: Dominium and Imperium. In a recent article of mine I wrote:

> In my view, there is no other way except for Western Man to unite within a new Empire — on a planetary basis. Such an Empire will be divided broadly into two main parts: Dominium and Imperium.
>
> Dominium is the female side of politics, and refers to all that pertains to the Individual: his freedom of choice, religion, language. His preference and pertaining to an ethnic group, with common imageries, common memories, frustrations, fears, modes of recreation. In short, all that which is anarchist, all that falls within the framework of private life: be it addiction to drugs, alcohol, preference to music, literature etc.: the Individual is free! *The Dominium is Diogenes.*

Within the Dominium women will be encouraged to pursue their education to its highest reaches. No post will be barred from them. Let us remember that in the so-called masculine society of National Socialism, the mass rallies and the Olympic games were directed and filmed by pioneering film-maker Leni Riefenstahl.

However, women will be urged to rediscover their original sacred role, that of bearers of the Race. Within them, within their sacred bodies, lies the very future of our Race. Let us remember that Mother Goddess is the divinity of fertility. That the *Tao* refers repeatedly to the 'Valley Spirit', which is feminine, and that the very word '*Tao*' is female. In Chinese the *Tao* paragraph, 'The *Tao* is forever undefined. It has no beginning and no end', is throughout in the female sense. Thus by implication, the very Universe is female.

Within the Dominium sphere, women will be free to be equal and to overtake men in all fields. This includes the Spirituality of our Race. Immediately, Madame Blavatsky comes to mind.

BLAVATSKY

I had the pleasure of reading her *Secret Doctrines* and *Myth and Magic Amongst the Shamans of Tibet* when in my early twenties, at about the same time I discovered Nietzsche. Blavatsky was a unique woman. A truly emancipated woman, a century ahead of her time and a towering figure when compared to the silly bra-burners of today.

Almost always alone, she travelled round the world, twice, sojourning in countries at the time forbidden to foreigners, let alone women. She spent years in Tibet, acquiring esoteric knowledge about the root-race, our Hyperborean and Lemurian forefathers. She is possibly the only Westerner to have read extracts from the oldest book known to man: the *Dhyzan*—pre-Atlantean, possibly early Hyperborean. A truly formidable woman and a precursor to National Socialism.

Blavatsky may also be considered as the Western founder of our *Cosmotheism*. Many of our present *Cosmotheist* beliefs, expounded by Dr. William Pierce, founder of the National Alliance, are in fact akin to hers. Ancient Wisdom knew—and continues to—deep and vast knowledge about ourselves, our purpose in life, nature, the universe, the highest divine principles, and man's long pre-history on this Earth.

Some of her Theosophic principles are really our *Cosmotheism*:

> Everything in the universe originates from one boundless, eternal, unknowable source. After a period of manifested existence the universe returns to that source.

> The universe itself is an organic whole, alive, intelligent, conscious, and divine.

> The laws of nature are the result of intelligent forces.

We are the cause of every joy and pain in our own life.

Evolution applies on a grand scale to all of life.

This evolution achieves experience, self-awareness, and ever increasing perfection. Evolution occurs on the physical, mental, and spiritual planes.

The origin of the species is due to intelligent design.

Humanity experienced significant evolution over long periods on the continents of Atlantis and Lemuria.

At the moment of death we have a review of our life just past, as we cast off this physical frame.

Often during this life, our spiritual nature is obscured in our self-centred daily lives, as we cater to our immediate needs and desires. But the spiritual self is always there to guide us if we seek it with strong, earnest desire.

The religions of the world are branches on the tree whose trunk is the one ancient — once universal — wisdom religion. The religions are the tributaries of one great river. They borrow from each other, complicating issues and causing strife.

Mythology often transmits some of this Ancient Wisdom in symbolic form.

Periodically, great teachers come amongst us to help us in this evolutionary path. They may create another branch on the tree. They are 'the giants that enable us to travel on their shoulders' as Newton used to say.

THE REAL BLAVATSKY

All this modern nonsense of trying to portray Blavatsky as some multi-racialist is pure humbug! Actually, it is the usual tribe of perverters who have polluted Blavatsky's doctrines, just as they destroy anything else they touch.

As I said, she toured the world twice, except for sub-Saharan Africa, which she never visited. She was a racialist and believed in the original, superior race, the root-race that once inhabited the planet. A race that had contaminated itself, bred itself down, by committing the crime of bestiality: that of mixing with sub-humans.

So even here, in the realm of Spirituality it was our world, the world of 'the Radical Racialist Right' that gave women the impetus to delve into the deepest secrets of the Universe. This Universe, in itself *Yin* and *Yang*, copulating with itself, creating new stars, millions of them, galaxies anew, ever expanding, ever increasing, ever dying and being reborn. We now know there are hundreds of thousands of galaxies, each equivalent to our own Milky Way, each in themselves have hundreds of thousands of stars and planets. It is only a matter of time until our people reach them.

YIN AND YANG

Male and Female: neutron and atom, ears, nostrils, hands, testicles, clitoris and vulva, all the organs of the body relate to one or the other. The Moon, female, reflecting the power of the male Sun. The mighty river, water, rushing into, being absorbed by the female sea. The Valley Spirit, abundant, rich, fruitful and female as against the rugged Mountains, male.

And so in the world of politics:

There is no future *political* role for women in the Imperium. For by its very nature, the Imperium is Male.

As I wrote in my book *CREDO*:

The highest authority in a Nation is the State. This is Male, imbued with a Sacred High Dominance quite apart, distinct, and distanced from the Nation. Perfect examples of it are the Holy Roman Empire and the Prussian State where, at the apex, a Sacred Elite, the Teutonic Order, stood as guardian of the Eternal Values:

Authority in the State must be absolute or it is no authority at all. It is unconditional, not subject to any other power or right. It is not subject to the law but above it — *Princeps legibus solutus est*. The State is not and should never be a representation of society — it is above it. For the political sphere is separate and above the social, purely economic and social aspect of the Nation. The State is form — Nation is matter. And it is a false notion of today's degenerate world that the family is portrayed as the basis of the nation. This is a Female concept in tune with democracy.

And elsewhere:

> On the other hand the Imperium is male, dynamic, dominant, powerful, and merciless. It sets itself no limits. It grasps every opportunity for expansion, penetration and domination. Its prerogatives are mainly Race, Territory and High Politics.
>
> - Race will be protected from miscegenation.
> - Territory will never be ceded.
> - High Politics will be the realm of the Elite.
>
> This Elite body of men, two million strong, will be the Guardians of the Imperium.

In my writings I described them briefly:

> We must breed a new religious caste. The members of this Elite will be experts in cosmology, the Arcane Tradition, genetics, genetic engineering, anthropology, eugenics and medicine.
>
> They will forge a new *Science of the Spirit*.
>
> They will research and study the distant origin of our race and the insoluble bind between the White Man and the Cosmos, which is the fundamental basis of our existence and evolution. They will help the White Man rediscover himself. These future priests will underpin the goals of the Europid and urge him onwards to both racial and individual self-realisation. *Race and Individual* — an indissoluble bond.
>
> A race-mind; a race-consciousness gripping the *Volk*; the Europeans linking them to a distant past and an ever present, all-encompassing Aryan identity and future.
>
> A truly individual mystical experience; a mystical ecstasy. A momentous attunement with the cosmic-force; the *Vril* — the Divine.
>
> A religious Elite forging an esoteric, healthy, nature-oriented new belief that befits the White Race. A primordial, sub-stratum, pre-Christian, pagan wisdom for that Elite attuned to it — conscious, through personal experience, of the Eternal Truths that express the essence of the universe. A strong, indomitable caste of veritable Supermen on Earth — living Zarathustras.
>
> A credible Elite to replace that democratic minority; those posturing poltroons, perennial political puppets, picayunes, pathetically pandering to their pathogenic masters; the international-manipulators.

One has to target the best: artists, writers, soldiers; *Bisogna scavare nei più provondi abbissi, per trovare dei fondamenti, per ereggere nuovi edifici, alti e belli.*

Such intrepid individuals can be found in all classes. From 'errant' nobility, to the most humble folk. An inherent, anarchic, savage, nomadic instinct sublimated into an organised, coagulated, liberating action against the whole, rotten structure.

A new race of ascetics, breathing Inequality, Hierarchy, Class, Competition, Distinction, Discrimination, Distance. For there can be no liberty within equality — it is self-evident! True Liberty can only be within a system based on Inequality.

A minority of less than a quarter of a million, spread over the White World, representing the best of this biological aristocracy which is the Europid race. A minority of High Culture Bearers.

A minority of Supermen who are the prime target of the international-manipulators. These last are always on the look-out for these Absolute Individualists, ready to vilify them through the controlled press. Ready to go to all lengths to crucify them — if need be, to exterminate them.

The Inhuman, sublimated into the Absolute Individualist in the Nietzschean sense, disciplined, inured to solitude, formed into the Philosopher-Soldier, the Statesman, The Elite; The Superman of the Future. A new Heroic Aristocracy; an Aristocracy of the Spirit, of Character, of a Total View of Life — an innate, unerring *Weltanschauung.*

A Periclean Age — an age that rediscovers those Aryan, Eternal Values and Spiritual ideals which come to us from time immemorial — pre-dating the Romans — from the 'Battle-Axe-Race', arch-Achaean-Doric, founders of both Rome and Sparta.

An Elite Order, at the top of which stands a Rex, beholder of an *IDEA* embodying that mysterious, indefinable, charismatic, Spiritual authority bestowed 'from above'.

In the Imperium sphere, we believe that government should be in the hands of qualified persons. In fact, the most qualified: the Elite. Bred to lead, trained to endure hardship and stress, above all mundane vicissitudes, this group of Supermen will ideologically, disdainfully discard the socialist, equalitarian dogma of death.

Both Race and Territory are safeguarded by High Politics. This is the realm of High Culture Bearers: the Elite — not millions of minions casting their useless votes every five years. The masses, those masticating bison, can carry on living their lives of miserable ease! They can continue enjoying their 'freedom'. Their only scope for existence will be as a genetic source-pool, from whom the Elite of the future can be drawn.

And where is the Individual in such an Elite body, one might well ask? Well, any group of persons, whatever their number and reciprocal similarity, whichever the degree of their firmness in assessing their opinion and their convergence of ideas — that group ends with breaking into smaller groups, adhering to different variants of the same opinion. Within these subgroups in turn, there emerge other, smaller under-subgroups, and further on, down to the last limit of such division — that of the single Individual!

And who elects the Elite? They elect themselves! For history is nothing but the eternal struggle amongst competing Elite, with their concern with the secrets of nature, as they seek to positively impact and alter the entire culture, structure and direction of society. The Imperium is the exclusive domain of the Elite.

Only an *IMPERIUM EUROPA* will have the intrinsic Spiritual power, translated into a Racial bond uniting the four Europid cousins: the Anglo-Saxons, the Teutons, the Slavs and the Latins. A bond manifested through High Politics under the iron leadership of The Elite. Only the Imperium could save the White Race in the coming, planetary struggle. A Lower House would comprise within it all the economic categories. It would run on a qualified vote system and restrict itself to economics, never above, but subject to politics. This would be the domain of the Higher House composed of a much smaller Elite, including the military caste. It would retain the prerogatives of High Politics and Race.

Only in extreme situations would the Higher House intervene in economic affairs, when these imperil the Higher, Eternal Values. It would have power to overrule the Lower House. Above the Higher House, assisted by a Sacred Elite, stands the Sacred Sovereign, embodying the Organic State.

It is within such *Union of Men* that the Organic State must be based. A leadership above the Nation. The *auctoritas*, the IMPERIUM. The Apex, the Soul, the *IDEA* of Eternal Values is safeguarded by this Elite: *Union of Men*. A divine mystery of High Dominance — a Divine Right of Kings.

An Elite scorning money. A Spartan Elite: austere, diamond-hard. Where the family or intimate affections are not the highest priorities. An Elite beyond parliaments, parties, politicians, prostitutes and pernicious priests. A powerful Elite, not an Elite based on raw power. An Elite of the best, bravest, brainiest, most beautiful and belligerent. A Racial Elite, ushering in a new Aryan Millennium: *Anno Zero!*

A mystical union between high dominance and the authority of an Elite, with the mysterious obedience of a healthy *Volk*. That loyalty and dedication to duty which petrified and immortalised the Roman soldier at Pompeii. An Elite Order as was the Teutonic and the Templar.

An Order composed of the best elements of patrician families, nobility, dynasties. An Elite Order, directing the Absolute Individualists in their battle against democratic liberalism and subversion in every White country. An Elite Order out of which will be chosen the Sovereign.

This Elite has within itself that natural dominance, distance, leadership quality, vision, calm influence, authority, prestige, that the masses can only vaguely aspire to — and will willingly and loyally sacrifice themselves for.

History abounds with instances of men who have died willingly, sacrificing all, obeying a command. Stalingrad, Salò and Berlin in 1943–1945 are this century's most glorious examples. No tyrant could have induced, by force or terror, such a sacrifice.

New Knights in shining armour; Templars — this time not in the service of that most abject of all depraved symbols, that of a man hanging from a cross, but Leaders of the White Race in a new millennium of a mystical fusion of *Science and Spirit*, a Divine combination. For God does not exist — only the Divine!

Templars; a Sacred Elite, initiated into the ancient, Aryan Sacred Rites; Sacred Blood, *Sangue Real*, the true meaning of the Holy Grail. A Sacred Elite Order, Sacred Sovereignty and the Sacred, Eternal Values of Race.

An Imperium founded on the discerned laws of Nature. A permanent struggle and selection of what is fit and strong. Creating harmony out of chaos-order. A totality in outlook; cosmic philosophy extending to all parts of life in a coherent structure: economic, political, Racial. For Race will have a primary role in human affairs, ensuring a permanent ascent of the White Man.

An Imperium based on that of the Holy Roman Empire, with a central authority, embodying both the Political and the Spiritual. A centre, to which all the White World will refer and relate to. A hub, whereby all parts of the Empire would feel organically whole, while retaining the specific peculiarity of each region. Retaining initiative, diversity, interaction, castes, classes, character, personality, hierarchy, all converging to a superior *IDEA*. — A common language will bind us all: Latin.

An Imperium which recognises the paramount creative and civilising potential of the Aryan, as against the inherent, obstructive and destructive capacity of the Hidden Enemy. Aryan order versus instigated chaos.

A Spiritual outlook on politics, government, Imperium, life — a mysticism, a new religion: Divine Guidance for the White Race. For we are an expression of Cosmic Forces. The Earth has a skin, and its antenna, its sensory organ, is Man. The White Man, the Europid, as the Earth's attunement to the Cosmos.

A Creed in conformity to Nature. Man viewed as a functioning aspect of the Cosmos in its great, eternal rotational process of growth and decay. A continuous change of death and birth.

A transformation, whereby the decomposition of one life-form, results in the composition of new forms of life and the beginning of a new cycle. Man, originating from the soil and its atmosphere which is part of him — and to whom he returns in a never-ending cycle of life.

A Cosmic conception of Man. His struggle for ever higher forms of being, of identity. His courage against adversity, his self-overcoming and a higher form of happiness and fulfilment.

A Creed propounding an Organic State with a Racial outlook of the body, mind and spirit. *The Sacred Gene Pool* — the kernel of our *CREDO*.

We, the precious few, we the Elite, we who know and understand the fundamental issue, the nature of the struggle: this war of civilisations, 'questa battaglia di civiltà'—this spiritual struggle between Aryan order and chaos.

We, the bearers of the IDEA of IMPERIUM EUROPA, we who are spread across the entire White World, know that victory will be ours, by 2012. It is inevitable. We know, with messianic certainty, why. It is written in the ancient Hindu texts. The Dark Age of Kaliyuga has just ended. The New Golden Dawn is with us: the age of Kritayuga. The White Man will soon rule the universe for more than a million years!

We, the Elite, the precursors of The Order, High Culture Bearers of the IDEA of IMPERIUM EUROPA, will see this fight through! We will lead, usher the White Man into a new era, a million years of peace, progress and Aryan order. This, by the year 2012, Anno Zero!

On our Sacred Island of Melitae one huge university, drawing students from all over the Imperium, would serve as an intellectual magnet for the Elite, High Culture Bearers, specialising solely in the Spiritual origins of the Europids. They would study the scores of temples, buried under tons of concrete, that forty years of 'progress' have dumped on our tremendous past. Special submarines would serve as moving observatories of the other, numerous temples, submerged offshore around our beaches and cliffs. Indeed, Malta would become the focal point, the Spiritual Apex of the coming IMPERIUM EUROPA.

Melitae—The future centre for an authentic, nature-oriented belief for the Europid. The fundamental importance of a high White birth-rate of healthy, intelligent Europids: explorers, astronauts, adventurers.

Malta will be to the Imperium what the Easter Islands were to the pre-Colombians: a Sacred Space, a spot, an island beyond the horizon to where the Europid would do pilgrimage and discover his Spiritual roots. Where each of us will discover that primordial, pre-Christian, pagan purity, potentiating our forefathers. A purity profaned and polluted through two thousand Christmases.

The cult of the Great Mother Goddess, a thaumaturgic figure, has monopolised the attention of archaeological studies in Malta. Our world-famous Hypogeum, recently restored with meticulous care, draws serious scholars and students. The importance of this site is so great that a similar site in Siberia discovered in 1928 was named 'The Malta Settlement'.

A top priority will be an *Ordensburg*, a center of studies for The Elite. A vessel, adequate to sustain the Spiritual capacity, the impulse necessary for the radical reformation of present society. Situated hundreds of miles from anywhere, preferably at Omsk, at the centre of the Eurasian landmass, or 'World-Island', this Spiritual-intellectual university is of the utmost importance. For world history is nothing else but the struggle for power of competing Elite, with their concern with the secrets of nature, as they seek to positively impact and alter the entire culture, structure and direction of society. Always ahead, in anticipation of the next advancement necessary, in the evolution of the race — the Elite, with its aura of prestige and pride, infuses, implants that Spiritual impulse into the masses. These, in complete freedom of choice, may continue to live their ordinary lives, so long as the imperative of Race is safeguarded.

A continuous planting of the best seed for the future of the Race, the Elite improves itself over time. As with the apex of a pyramid, just a slight turn, a shift in emphasis by the Elite as it evolves, greatly affects the whole base, the people. Principled stimuli often have far reaching results. Hence the importance for the highest standards, moulding these veritable Supermen on Earth — living Zarathustras.

Life at the Elite Ordensburg will have definite organisational characteristics: a principle-centred existence that is applied to day-to-day affairs. An increasingly esoteric, hierarchical Elite seeking that mystical knowledge of the Race, wherever it may be found: the Egyptian Temple system, the Essenes, Cathars, the Grail quest, the Templars. A synthesis linking the White Man to his mythical, pre-Christian, unadulterated past and propelling him to his future. A galactic quest in the fulfilment of his destiny.

For our next step, our next adventure, will be the terraforming of Mars and the other planets, within the solar system. The Europid will colonise these planets for himself. Then onwards, towards the furthest reaches of the universe, till we come face to face with Godhood — and finally, fully realise ourselves!

Imperium

0501

ADDENDUM

In 2003 I had written to David Lane of The Brotherhood, a scholar of Sacred Numerology, asking him to enlighten me on the Hierarchy of the Elite. At the time he was serving 190 years in solitary confinement in a maximum security prison in the USA. I had managed, through friends of his, to get his prison number. My letter was returned by the prison authorities stamped 'Not known at the address'!

In 2005 I gave a speech at The New Right conference in London and, on my return to Malta, found a letter waiting for me signed by David Lane himself. I never got to know how he had got to read my original letter and how, two years later, he had managed to answer me in writing.

David Lane gave me this numerical Pyramid for The Elite:

12

144

1,444

14,444

144,444

1,444,444

1.   A Council of 12, or CORE group including a GrandMaster who has the casting vote.

2.   Meritocracy, not hereditary (as Evola suggests). Hereditary power is lost within three generations as degeneracy sets in.

3.   Some elements of Freemasonry may be borrowed. The Oath of Adherence, for instance, must be blood curdling and executed whenever necessary.

4. Polygamy for The Elite.

5. Eligibility: square in body and mind and spirit. In short, the very best of the four Europid sub-races: the Anglo Saxons, the Teutons, the Slavs, the Latins.

6. Spirituality based on *Cosmotheism*. Christianity can never, ever be the spiritual basis of The Elite. Christianity is Female, the Elite are all Male.

The numerical pyramid structure of The Elite is based on Sacred Numerology. It shows the various stages of hierarchy within the sacred numbers. The base (1,444,444) consist of the Elite Army, who are above the Imperium Regional police forces and who may be rushed, to any part of the Imperium, to safeguard any of the five prerogatives of The Order.

Koenigsburg could well be the seat for the Top Twelve Elite or CORE. To the East, between Omsk and Tomsk, protected by the rivers Irtysh and Ob will be a vast, 'Forbidden Zone' — and an exclusive area reserved for the Elite Army.

There, young men will be trained for war, turned into warriors, inured to pain. *Ordensburgen* for The Elite will girdle the Imperium — each specialising in a particular subject: the Arcane Tradition, Cosmotheism, Race, Genetic Engineering, High Politics, Archaeology

A string of Sacred Spots will adorn the Imperium, like pearls. Stonehenge, Grotte du Lazaret and Sarlat, Val Camonica, Malta, Koenigsburg, Moldova/Ukraine, Buret/Siberia and others. — A diary of the White Race.

Imperium: Masculinity, Absoluteness, Aristotle.

Dominium: Femininity, Freedom, Diogenes.

IMPERIUM

0711

CHAPTER XXXVI
A ONCE GREAT BRITAIN

JUST BACK FROM A FORTNIGHT trip to a once Great Britain.

Back to Yorkshire and Lancs. Countryside all round, with green pastures over the Pennines. Sheep grazing peacefully while cows languidly look in wonder at us humans, driving along the roads in the frantic race against time.

The awesome Yorkshire moors, desolate, covered in heather and elephant grass. It takes a brave hiker fifteen days to trek across — an unforgettable experience as one feasts the eyes on lakes, unspoilt skylines, grouse, hares and woods in the distance.

To Manchester, an elegant city that once saw better days. Today, ghettoes for the various ethnicities have formed and solidified. Blacks in the Moss side where murder and drug wars are now frequent and ferocious. Chinatown, where the authorities have lost their count of births and deaths. Council houses reserved exclusively for Pakistanis, who complain that toilets are facing Mecca and have them ripped out. A multiracial mess — initiated, organised and pushed by the Hidden Enemy. The same Tribe that was behind immigration in every country in Europe, including and most especially, Britain.

Huddersfield even worse — Iraqis, Iranians, Somalis all drawing on the social handouts. Council estates in destitution as Blacks turn them into Bronx-like skeletons within eight years. New ones are hurriedly built for them of course, by the accommodating, acquiescing local councils.

Riots at the drop of a handkerchief, with 'racism' as the convenient excuse. The newcomers get away with murder because of that one word: racism. That word instilled, inserted into our laws by the hidden enemy. The police are intimidated, cowed into non-action. They frequently look the other way when Whites report foreign yobs attacking their homes, their children on their way to school.

3rd Sept: the anniversary of the declaration of World War II. A day-long orgy of Jewish lies on every TV station. Jewish suffering shown as the central theme of that gigantic struggle, that fratricide amongst Europid cousins. Every TV station, all Jewish controlled, carried the nauseating stories. Jewish bodies turned into lampshades and poor-quality soap — and the rest of all their lies!

War documentaries showing the British, still sound as a Nation, queuing quietly for their daily ration. No jumping of queues, no riots — a quiet determination to get on with it notwithstanding the daily, heavy bombing. The admittance that rationing actually increased in 1946 and '47, revealing the absurdity of that war, the futility — and that Britain had actually lost.

That old fool, Churchill puffing happily at his cigar as he threw away an Empire. That old fool who fought the wrong war, at the wrong time, against the wrong enemy — with America and the Soviet Union, like vultures sharing the spoils over the broken bodies of two dead youths: Germany and Britain, cousins — led into a bloodbath, a fratricide by those eternal mischief-makers.

Smithfield market, Manchester: a zoological experience! Blacks that look more simian than humans ambling about. At times holding hands with beautiful, long haired, slim blonds — a dysgenic disaster.

Chadors and Burkhas by the dozen, with eyes covered by fine mesh. While Boobus Bush pompously proclaimed his intention of saving Afghanistan, of liberating Afghan women from the burkha, such clad women stroll around Manchester and London as if in Kabul. The treason of our leaders. The incredible takeover of a once noble people.

With the Brits at last! Just the native British at *Highgate Greyhounds*, Doncaster. The greyhounds, lean and mean, bred for speed, pounding past the goalpost — the power! All in silence, not a sound by the crowd watching — the race is over in seconds. Not a foreigner to be seen, no Blacks, no Chinks, no Pakis — just solid Anglo-Saxons. Talking to them, the native people, and one gets the standard reply: 'It's gone — this country is gone and nothing can be done about it.' — The resignation, the despondency, the defeatism.

And yet they all watch Geography TV, where programme after programme show the inexorable cruelty of Nature, the struggle for survival of the various species. I watched one of such series where, thankfully, the British otter is making a comeback, since hunting it has been prohibited for the last few years. Meanwhile however, the American mink, imported for its fur, has infested the river banks and is killing the local river-vole. This endemic, mole-like little creature is now facing imminent extinction. Short-sighted Greens and animal lovers had freed some minks from captivity, and now they are destroying everything in their path. They are ferocious creatures. Luckily, the otter has come to the rescue! It is the only species capable of affronting and beating the merciless invader. Otters are killing minks wherever and whenever they encounter them.

Every thinking Brit I talked to realises that the war in Iraq is now lost. It cannot be won. It is irretrievably lost — whatever the lying Jews and their media say. Afghanistan will be lost as well, in a year or so. Brits die every single day in Afghanistan and Iraq — they die senselessly, just as they did during WWII. And just as they did in 1940–45, Brits die on behalf of the Jews and Israel.

Most Brits realise that war on Iran would be another folly, costlier, far costlier than either Afghanistan or Iraq. A major strategic blunder, again in the service of the hidden enemy. That enemy that relentlessly pushes for war, for a first strike against Iran, peripheral Europids, who are proud of their heritage and distinguish themselves from Arabs.

Meanwhile, Blair and Brown bash and batter each other. The undignified struggle for power, sheer power and nothing else. Blair and Brown, two small men, minions, the product of modern democracy on TV every day, stabbing each other in the back. Brown has already given us his recipe: more troops in Iraq, more in Afghanistan, stronger measures 'in the war against terror', greater support for Israel etc. More of the same.

Slowly more Brits are becoming aware of and talk openly about the real menace. Many ruefully regret the Second World War and praise Hitler openly. 'It was those Jews who made us give that stupid guarantee to Poland, since they had so much investment in that country' is what I heard a young man say on TV.

Brits realise that they stopped the Germans from invading and now they have been invaded by a far more dangerous enemy — invaded not by cousin Teutons but by African savages of all sorts, by millions of Muslims and Chinese and what not — all represented in the House of Commons, blackmailing the government at every turn.

Leaving Manchester airport back to Malta. The security arrangements: boots off, no belts, no liquids, infra-screening, armed police everywhere. It must be costing Britain millions — all through those scheming rodents who set us up against the Muslim world.

The airport crawling, infested with non-Eurpids. Muslim women refusing to take off their Burkhas to be identified. Whites in a minority. As I look back from the escalator at the departure terminal, more Islamabad than Manchester, I feel sorry for the British — a people betrayed by their leaders, puppets to that alien race of culture destroyers.

The unfolding tragedy of a once Great Britain.

XXXVII

FABULAE
MELITAE

A New Mythology for the Sacred Islands of Melita

We are indeed a speck in the universe. Our beloved planet Earth, *la nostra Gaia*, is but one of the nine planets circling our sun, forming our solar-system. The sun, though central and most important in our system, is but one of billions of other stars, many dwarfing ours in size. These billions of stars, with trillions of planets around them, form our galaxy — our Milky Way.

We now know that there are over 120,000 galaxies — and more are forming. Trillions upon trillions of stars and planets. Our universe, as we have seen in my *Our Destiny*, is indeed the Conscious Whole.

Nature abhors equality. There is not one meteor, one planet, star, sun, galaxy similar to another. They are all different — all have their different material composition and their aura, their metaphysical nature.

THALASSOCRACY & TELLUROCRACY

Our Mother Earth consists of Air, Land and Sea. The last two form the

basis, the battleground for geopolitics: the arena for the struggle for survival.

Land and Sea are Soft-Hard: *Yin* and *Yang*. Land is stability, gravity,
fixity, space as such. Water is mobility, softness, dynamics, time. The two
natures, Male and Female, permeate our earth, our very being (bones and
blood). They also determine planetary politics.

Throughout the ages and right up to present times, political and military
power has been either Thalassocratic or Tellurocratic. A nation, state or empire projects its power through its preference, its propensity for either. It is not
so much the actual geography that determines the political projection, but the
consciousness of the people: its being a race of sea-farers or landed people.

A few examples:

The USA, though a huge landmass, is an obvious Thalassocracy. Just
nine aircraft-carriers dominate the oceans and project power, at whatever
hot-spot, wherever and whenever the USA so wishes. In Malta we had the
perfect demonstration of this difference between the USA and Russia, the
latter being a Telluric power.

When President Bush Snr. met Gorbachev on the island, they were
both stranded on their respective ships — just 200 yards away from each
other! They couldn't meet due to inclement weather and a ferocious sea,
with waves crashing over our high bastions. Now, while Gorbachev remained on his ship, with most of his entourage sea-sick and depressed,
Bush grabbed a small, police high-speed launch and boldly took a ride
around the harbour. Had not a panicking White House sent a blistering
message for him to stop the nonsense, he would have sped out of the relative safety of the harbour. Back on his ship, Bush exclaimed, 'Unlike us,
the Russians have no love of the sea!' It said it all.

Britain too is an obvious Thalassocracy. A small island with no great
resources or raw materials, it lorded over an empire stretching around the
globe. Occupying a few choke points: Gibraltar, Malta, Aden and Singapore, a thin red line of men held the empire together. It was sea-power
that enabled them to do so — the power to replenish, reinforce or recap-
ture lost garrisons in a short time, through the display and use of naval

power. Even today, with the empire gone, the Falklands war was a splendid demonstration of Thalassocratic power.

On the other hand Japan, a similar small island, is a Telluric nation-state. The Japanese feel themselves as a Telluric people and not as sea-farers. One remembers how, after the first attack on Pearl Harbour, they beat it for home, missing a second air-strike that could have turned the outcome of the Pacific War. Quasi-invincible and displaying incredible courage on land, they had no stomach for sea battles.

Germany and Russia are the quintessential Telluric states. They form the bulk of the Eurasian landmass. Their geopolitics have always been Telluric, often with disastrous consequences for both.

In 1905 the Russian fleet was destroyed by the waiting Japanese, after it had set sail from Murmansk all the way round the globe to Port Arthur, in Manchuria. This defeat of the White Race by the Yellows had ominous implications. It gave the Asians the confidence they lacked. It cleared that ingrained inferiority complex towards the White Man, in that it showed that we can be beaten, after all. This defeat was a precursor to Korea, Vietnam and all the sorry lot that followed.

Germany too, showed a short-sighted Telluric mentality. In WWII the Germans goose-stepped across one country to another, leaving guerrilla forces behind them, as in the Balkans and all over the Russian steppes. Italian Supermarina, or Navy High Command, correctly lamented to their German counterparts that the war could have easily been won — and with a fraction of the forces deployed on the Russian front. All that was needed was to take Malta first, then replenish Rommel and choke off the Suez canal. The empire would have withered like a sawn vine. Britain would have sued for peace and then, Germany would have been free to settle accounts with the Bolshevists.

Extreme forms of Sea and Land powers would be, on one side, the Phoenicians, Corinth, Venice and Genoa: all sea-powers that depended on open sea lanes and free trade. The battles these sea-powers fought were not for more land, but for the continued ability to trade with far-away buyers and suppliers.

On the other hand, the extreme side to a Telluric power was Genghis Khan — completely terrestrial, nomadic, as was also the Arabian khalifat born out of desert nomadism.

Since the beginning of sea migrations, waves of peoples from the West left their centres located on the Atlantic, taking their cultures with them. Thus began the eastward movement. Tibetan shamanic tradition holds that the Tibetans came from the West. The Mediterranean civilisation also moved from Gibraltar to the Near East, rather than the other way. We shall discuss this later in the sub-section: The Mediterranean.

On the contrary, excavations in Siberia prove that exactly here were the most ancient centres of civilisation — that is, the central lands of the continent were the cradle of the Euro-Asian mankind. Prehistoric sites in Siberia, Russia are identical to those found in Malta, here in the centre of the Mediterranean. One such prehistoric site in Siberia is actually called the Malta Settlement.

Historically, Thalassocracy is linked to the West and the Atlantic Ocean, while Tellurocracy to the East (China/Japan and the Eurasian landmass).

AURA and CHARACTER

Every Land and Sea has its own particular characteristics and these affect the people and their politics. The sea civilisation of the Black Sea or the Mediterranean Sea are qualitatively different from the civilisation of the oceans, those insular powers and peoples (Indians in North America) dwelling on the shores of the open ocean.

One world-renowned yachtsman who sailed round the globe stated in his autobiography that the worst storm he ever encountered was in the Mediterranean, off the Algerian coast. It was worse than those huge waves in the South Atlantic. These rolling monsters are predictable, having a regular timing, a rhythm. The waves of the Mediterranean he said, are erratic and cruel.

Tellurocracy too, has its particular forms and identities. So, it is possible to distinguish a civilisation of the Steppe and a civilisation of the

Forest — of the Mountains and of the Plains — of the Desert and of Ice. The varieties of aura and character of the landscape have symbolical complexities affecting state, religion and ethics.

Of all the Himalayan range, there is not one mountain that has the character, gives the specific aura that Monte Rosa does. Mountaineers who have climbed it testify to this. Likewise, the desert of the Sahara is different to the Gobi, the Chilean or the Nevada. I know of a particular Italian lady, captivated by the aura and mystical atmosphere of the Algerian south-Sahara, who visits the place religiously once yearly. She seduces one of the men in the safari group and makes love in open desert, at sundown and sunset.

Islands are different too — and not just weather-wise. Crete can hardly be compared to Madagascar, while the Sacred Island of Melita would stand out, apart from all the thousands of islands of Macronesia, Melanesia and Polynesia. The character is different — the aura is different — and so are the people.

GEOGRAPHY and GEOPOLITICS

Geography affects peoples and politics. Mountains for example are redoubts, refuge centres for people fleeing the expansion of others. Swaziland is a case in point: a tribe of relatively short Negrids, fleeing the Zulu waves. Albania is another. No civilisation has ever been born around mountain-tops. However, there is a sacredness surrounding these peaks. Hermits and men of the spirit seek them in order to find themselves — and be at one with Godhood.

It is the hills that are the symbol of political power. A king or a great leader always chooses a hill, overlooking the plains and valleys where his people toil. The seven hills of Rome became the centre of the world. The seven hills of Prague were prophesied to be the place where a fair city would bloom, whose fame would rise above the stars (Capitol to the Holy Roman Empire and court of great astronomer Tycho Braha among others). Some modern leaders, like the communist Ceauşescu, even went to the trouble of building an artificial hill on which he built his palace, overlooking Bucharest.

Forests are peripheral and of no political consequence. Likewise the Tundra and the Deserts, and of course, the Ice-Caps. Though of great shamanic and religious importance, it is not in these places that the geopolitical struggle is won or lost.

EAST AND WEST

Traditionally the East has been known as 'The Land of Spirit'. 'East is the mansion of the gods' states the sacred text of the ancient Aegyptians. The word 'east' or 'neter' in Aegyptian also meant 'god'. East is the place where the sun ascends; *'vos-tekeat'* in Russian: Light of the World—symbol of Divinity and Spirit.

The West has the opposite symbolical meaning: the 'Green Country' as the Aegyptians described it. Here, a completeness turns to an inexhaustible need. Eastern Spirituality and interiority becomes exteriority, outgoing, materialist. This perception of East and West is still valid today, notwithstanding the great industrial progress of both China and Japan with their tiger economies. According to Chinese tradition, the East is *Yang*: the male, bright, solar principle—West is *Yin*: the female, dark, lunar side.

The West is liberal-democratic, individualistic. Priority is given to economics, to trade and technical modernisation. Progress, evolution, progressive development are the catchwords—anathema to the traditional Eastern world—as also to those periods of Western history, when a rigorous Sacred Tradition existed: as in the Middle Ages, a period of great metaphysical tension.

In the West the Law of Money replaced the Rule of Law and the Rule of Idea. An Anglo-Saxon mercantile view of the world, as against the socialism and authoritarianism of the East. Moreover, as we have discussed in previous articles, this mercantile, productive view of man has given way to the speculation of Finance Capitalism. This in turn deadens, brutalises man into a productive tool or commodity.

NORTH AND SOUTH — 'RICH' AND 'POOR'

This idea, this perception of the North: 'Nordism' has, since the most ancient times, affirmed the primacy of the North over the South. The symbolism of the North relates to a Spiritual Source, to an original northern paradise, from where all human knowledge originated.

Ancient Iranic and Zoroastrian texts speak about the northern country of 'Aryiana Vaeijao' and its capital 'Vara', which the ancient Aryans were forced to abandon due to glaciation. The ancient Veda also refers to a Northern country, the ancestral home of the Hindu: Sveta-dipa or the 'White Land in the far North'.

The ancient Greeks spoke about Hyperborea, the northern island with its capital Thule. This land was considered as the motherland of the bright god Apollo. Thus, North is the land of the sun. A land where the sun never sets even at night — a Sacred Space, a beacon, a sacred spot of eternal light.

The North is the idea of the Centre, the Immobile Pole, the Point of Eternity around which the cycle turns — the cycle of space and time. The point where contrasts converge and parallels point, drawn by a powerful, Cosmic Magnetic Force. The place that is not subject to the laws of cosmic entropy. This Centre is symbolised by the Swastika. It stresses both immobility and constancy of the Centre, with the revolving action of the periphery. It symbolises a Nordic Spiritual polar-paradise: light, purity, unity, completeness, eternity.

A polar, full semi-annual Day and one full semi-annual Night. The Day and Night of the Gods and Heroes. A sacral, Spiritual, supernatural Cardinal North: the dwelling place of 'spirits' and 'forces from beyond'.

The South symbolises something directly opposite: matter, darkness, viscosity, plurality.

In the South the original symbolism of Hyperborea is lost and becomes 'culture and legend'. The Purely Spiritual acquires material, visible outlines. The South is the reign of substance, life, biology that corrupts the northern purity of spirit, yet preserves some traces in materialised features, fethishes and feasts. The South degrades the Nordic Spirit into a coarsened, material embodiment.

The North 'Spiritualises' the South. Since primordial times Nordic messengers gave their Spiritual view of Life to all the rest — the foundation of all civilisations.

When the South fails to recognise the primacy of the North, a 'War of Continents' begins. The antediluvian great war between North and South: Hyperborea and Gondvana, the ancient paleo-continent of the South, is the cardinal lesson. Whenever this occurs, it is the South that is responsible, by breaking the sacred rules. This could again happen, should the coming Arab-Unitary-State come to rebel against our IMPERIUM EUROPA.

The Sacred North defines a special human type: the Spiritual Man, a biological, racial embodiment, but also with the capacity to raise every object of the physical, material world to its archetype, to its Idea (Plato's 'chair-ness').

The Man of the North is not simply White, 'Aryan' or Indo-European because of his blood, language and culture — but he is rather a particular kind of human being, possessing a direct intuition to the Sacred. To him the cosmos is a texture of sacred symbols. He is the 'Solar Man': *Sonnenmensch*: creative, pouring out light, force and wisdom from the Spiritual essence of creation.

True, the pure Nordic Civilisation disappeared with the ancient Hyperboreans. However, the Nordic messengers had laid the bases of all present civilisations, religions, traditions, cultures, of all continents and colours of skin. Traces of Hyperborean cults can be found among the Indians of Northern America, the ancient Slavs, the founders of the Chinese civilisation — and even among the natives of the Pacific.

A true Spirituality, a supra-rational Mind, divine Logos — capacity to see through the world to its secret Soul: these are the defining qualities of the Man of the North.

On the other hand, the Man of the South, the Gondvanic type, is directly opposed to the Nordic type. The Man of the South lives in a circle of effects, of secondary manifestations — he dwells in the cosmos that he venerates, but does not understand. He worships exteriority, but not interiority. He is not able to proceed from mere symbols to the symbolised. He lives by passions and puts the psychic above the Spiritual, which he does not understand, since he has never come to know it.

The cult of the Great Mother — of matter generating out of a variety of forms: from the 'scarab-beetle pushing dung' to the 'sow suckling piglets' is typical of the Man of the South. He is a man of the Moon, receiving, not giving, light — the female valley. The Man of the South is a *Mondmensch*. Thus the civilisation of the South is a receptive civilisation: the Moon receiving light from the Sun of the North.

At the very beginning, the people of the North and South opposed one another. Later Northern Man penetrated into southern lands, founding some bright expressions of the 'Nordic' civilisation: ancient Iran, India. Also, the Southern Man sometimes went far northward: Finns, Eskimos, Chuckchi etc. Gradually the original clearness of the sacred-geographical panorama became muddy. However, the typological dualism was preserved in all times and epochs. Today, it has become an internal conflict within the same civilisation: Western civilisation.

The paleo-continent of the Nordid Hyperborea physically disappeared millennia ago. Yet it remains a Spiritual reality. A beacon for the precursors of the Elite of the future: embodiment of the ancient 'White Teachers' — We, the Elite, with our *IDEA* of IMPERIUM EUROPA.

The ancient, original North-Tradition may be regarded today as a meta-historical, meta-geographical reality. The same can be said also about the 'Hyperborean Race' — a 'race' not in the biological, but in a pure Spiritual, metaphysical sense, as explained so well by the great Julius Evola.

The North is perceived today as 'rich', as 'the advanced North'. This connotates the development of the material, economic side of life. 'Rich North' is rich not for being cleverer, or more intellectual, or more Spiritual than the 'South', but because it maximises material wealth.

Geopolitically, 'rich North' actually means those countries where the forces directly opposite to Tradition and Spirituality have won. Those forces of quantity, materialism, atheism, Spiritual degradation and emotional degeneration. In other words the 'new world order' — that pseudo-paradise of those whom Nietzsche called 'the last men'.

Today the Spiritual North exists only in Russia and the Slavic peoples. The Northern Eurasian landmass is the only territory on earth not completely mastered and corrupted by the 'rich North'. To the modern world it is a *terra incognita*, inhabited by Traditional peoples.

This is the last redoubt, the last outpost of the Traditional or Spiritual Way of Life. However, it is inertial, passive and defensive. It is not pro-active. This geopolitical initiative, this Spiritual renewal can only come from the Spiritual North: the truly 'Rich North'.

We have to go back to a Spiritual Europe — a Europe of Regions and Peoples, of boroughs, cantons, and traditions — instead of the marketplace of Maastricht.

We, of the Radical-Racialist-Right-Revolutionary-Reactionaries, have to lead the struggle against the materialism of the present North. We must ally ourselves with the Traditional forces of Russia, the Spiritual residue of the original North in order to end this dark era. For according to the Arcane Tradition, we are now in the very latest period of the 'dark cycle', 'the age of quantity': that of *Khali-Yuga*. The age-old Vedic cycles of the *Yugas* or four ages: Gold, Silver, Copper and Lead.

An intellectual, planetary revolt by the Slavs and the Latins against the 'rich North' in order to convert, to revert to the genuine Sacred North, the Nordic Source. For we have a common enemy: the degenerated, anti-sacred White populations ensnared by this 'Modern World'. The creation of an IMPERIUM EUROPA founded on the original, Traditional, Spiritual values of the North — the Hyperborean Spirit.

We must lay the groundwork that ensures the Final Victory of the coming, sacred Avatar. We will give those worthy ones, a Spiritual abundance. We will again raise the Hyperborean meta-continent from the glacial abyss. We will re-discover and restore The Sacred North.

MALTA: LUNAR AND SOLAR

Since primordial times the Maltese archipelago occupied a most strategic position in the Mediterranean: geographic, cultural, religious, Spiritual.

Our neolithic temples are the legacy of a culture unparalleled in the Mediterranean. They represent a continuation of the unique and important phase in the evolution of the Aryan.

The cult of the Great Mother Goddess, a thaumaturgic figure, has monopolised the attention of archaeological studies in Malta. Our world famous Hypogeum, recently restored with meticulous care, draws serious scholars and students. The importance of this site is so great that a similar site in Siberia discovered in 1928 was named 'the Malta Settlement'.

Palaeolithic artefacts produced by the same people, both in Malta proper and Malta, Siberia, were found also all across the Caucasus, Crimea, Russian steppes, Siberia, the Altai and near the River Dnestr. These are characteristic stone implements 500,000 to 350,000 years old!

Female figurines from the Malta-Siberia dwellings are worthy of particular attention. There are exceptionally rare, early Palaeolith figurines wearing some form of garments. Found also are plates made from a mammoth tusk, depicting a mammoth and snakes, as well as figurines of stylised flying birds. Arrow tips are in also in the form of stylised birds, signifying the oneness of shooter and target.

The artefacts at Kostenky I have more geometrical patterns, while a Female Figurine dating 23,000–21,000 BC is very similar to the Maltese Goddess.

The latest Maltese prehistoric inhabitants came from Stentinello in Southeast Sicily around 5,000 BC. They were peaceful agricultural settlers and highly skilled builders and engineers, constructing a string of megalithic temples and burial sites across the islands. These have no parallel in the Mediterranean. The Hypogeum site alone, was the burial place of over 7,000 people.

This whole era is *Mondmensch*. The Female predominates: she is everywhere venerated. The temples themselves, like the splendid Mnaj-dra, are shaped like a Female displaying her vulva towards the rising sun at the winter solstice: the beginning of every Life cycle, the 'Gates of the Gods' according to Hinduism: the oldest religion, the original belief of the Aryan!

ARYANS — HIGHER CASTE

I am reproducing *in toto* an interesting article that appeared in *HERA* magazine, Rome, Italy by Vittorio Di Cesare and Adriano Forgione.

I leave the reader to evaluate for himself:

In the megalithic temple of Hal Saflieni, in Malta, men with extraordinary cranial volume were buried, these skulls bearing peculiar abnormalities and/ or pathologies. Sometimes inexistent cranial knitting lines, abnormally devel-oped temporal partitions, drilled and swollen occiputs as following recovery from traumas. But above all, a strange, lengthened skull, bigger and more peculiar than the others, lacking of the median knitting. It seems to belong to a strange human stock and if properly analyzed, could create an ideal link between the ancient Mesopotamian and Egyptian cultures with a race of sac-erdotal men identified with the snake.

The skulls were all found in the Hal Saflieni Hypogeum, where a sacred well was dedicated to the Mother Goddess and where also the small statue of a sleeping goddess was found, associated to a relic with a snake inscription on it. A very pronounced dolichocephalous, in other words, a lengthened pos-terior part of the skullcap, besides the lack of median knitting, technically named 'sagitta'. This last detail has been considered 'impossible' by medics and anatomists to whom we turned, not having (as far as known) analogous pathological cases in international medical literature. It is a characteristic that emphasises the anomaly of this finding with the result of producing a natural lengthening of the cranium in the occipital area (not due to bandaging or boards as used in pre-Colombian civilizations). We believe that the discovery of this skull and the like at Hal Saflieni isn't accidental.

Malta and Gozo were very important centers since pre-historic times, places where 'medical cures' were conducted, oracles and ritual encounters with the priests of the goddess. There, on both the islands, existed many sanctuaries and thaumaturgic centers, where priests surrounded the healing goddess, direct expression of her divinity. It is well known that, in antiquity, the serpent was associated to the goddess and to healing capacities. The snake also belongs to the subterranean world. Therefore, a Hypogeum dedicated to the goddess and the water cult was the right place for a sacerdotal group that was defined, in all the most ancient cultures, as the 'Serpent Priests'. The long head and drawn features must have given a serpent-like appearance, stretching the eyes and skin.

The presence of these skulls might be that of the last exponents of the most ancient sacerdotal caste that built the megalithic temples and, never having blended with the local populations, had continued reproducing through the millenniums within familiar unions (as was the usual practice among the elite) and consequently impoverished its genetic patrimony until inevitable pathologies manifested, finally disappearing.

The Phoenicians will also erect temples to the Mother Goddess in Malta, calling her Astarte, the snake-faced Goddess. Again we find the representation of a Goddess who is associated with the snake and healing powers, almost as if the Phoenicians wanted to continue an interrupted tradition. But it's the date of 2500 BC that presents a fundamental key of interpretation for understanding who these long-headed individuals were, and to use it, we must move from Malta to nearby Egypt.

Professor Walter B. Emery (1903–1971), the famous Egyptologist, author of *Archaic Egypt*, who excavated at Saqquara in the 30s, indeed discovered the remains of individuals who lived in pre-dynastic epoch. These presented a dolichocephalous skull, larger than that of the local ethnic group, fair hair and a taller, heavier build. Emery declared that this stock wasn't indigenous to Egypt but had performed an important sacerdotal and governmental role in this country. This race kept its distance from the common people, blending only with the aristocratic classes, and the scholar associated them with the *Shemsu Hor*, the 'disciples of Horus'. The *Shemsu Hor* are recognised as the dominant sacerdotal caste in pre-dynastic Egypt (until approximately 3000 BC), being mentioned in the Turin papyrus and the list of the kings of Abydos. It's interesting to note that Emery writes: 'Towards the end of the IV millennium BC the people known as the Disciples of Horus appear as a highly dominant aristocracy that governed entire Egypt. The theory of the existence of this race is supported by the discovery in the pre-dynastic tombs, in the northern part of Higher Egypt, of the anatomical remains of individuals with bigger skulls and builds than the native population, with so much difference to exclude any hypothetical common racial strain. The fusion of the two races must have come about in ages that concurred, more or less, with the unification of the two Egyptian Kingdoms'. Therefore, what occurred in Malta is also reflected in Egypt. It's noticeable that in Lower Egypt, the pharaoh's symbol is a bee named 'Bit'. It isn't coincidental that Malta's ancient name is 'Melita', which derives from the Latin word for honey. Malta's symbol was also a bee and its hexagonal cells. Melita has its origin in '*Mel*' or '*Mer*', which in Ancient Egypt was the name attributed to the pyramids. Besides, the English term, 'honey' is strictly related to the original name of Helliopolis, which is 'ON'. It is an interesting correlation that in Egypt, the *Shemsu Hor* guaranteed the respect of a Solar religion and even today in Malta the sun is called '*Shem-shi*'. '*Shem*' is a word of 'Accadic' origin, not Egyptian, deriving from the Babylonian term for the sun, that is '*Shamash*'. This proves that the *Shemsu Hor* came from the fertile half-moon area. An umpteenth correlation is the fact that this sacerdotal long-skulled caste disappeared in Egypt, as in Malta in the same period, which is between 3000 and 2500 BC. Who writes is convinced, although, that a third nucleus was present in the Euphrates zone, becoming part of the Aryan stock known as Mithans, who the Egyptians called '*Naharin*', 'Those of the Snake' (from *Nahash*, snake). The Mithans, who occupied a part of the Kurdistan area, were Abraham's people (*HERA* 15, page 26), whose description is analogous to that of the *Shemsu Hor* made by Emery (fair hair and robust build). The 'Serpent Priest' tradition (*HERA* 13 and 14) originates in the Middle East, with its foremost center right in Kurdistan, where at about 5000 BC. the matriarchal culture of Jarmo represented the mother goddesses as divinities with faces of vipers and lengthened heads. These divinities will successively be associated to the 'fallen angels' or Nephelims, that are most explicitly cited in the 'Testament of Amran' in the Qumran scrolls (*HERA* 6, page 52) in which is written: 'One of them was of terrifying aspect, like a snake and his mantle was multicolored', and also 'his face was that of a viper and he wore all his eyes'. It concerns, in our opinion, not divinities in the strict sense, but individuals in sacerdotal or shaman expression, belonging to a highly developed and profoundly wise culture that had relationships with lesser-organized societies of the period. Its members were considered as 'half-gods' for the knowledge they possessed, just like in Egypt with the *Shemsu Hor*. Analogous viper-faced statues of mother goddesses are found in the land of the Nile, dating back exactly from the archaic period of the *Shemsu Hor*. It can be therefore concluded that these Serpent-Priests were the most ancient race that first occupied the fertile half-moon area (particularly Anatolia and Kurdistan) and Egypt (following migrations dating back 6000–4000 BC.; *HERA*, p. 10) until reaching Malta to disappear around 2500 BC. But this culture survived in the Middle East and probably included one of the most famous and yet mysterious pharaohs of Egypt. It concerns the Mithans and the pharaoh Akhenaton. The reason why Akhenaton was linked to the Mithans will be the subject of a following article but the way he was portrayed in his statues and bas-reliefs (and with him, the whole royal family) is indeed that of an individual of lengthened head and human face but with serpent-likeness, characteristics found in the pre-dynastic Egyptian stock mentioned by Emery, besides being the exact representation of the features of the Nephelims and probably the long-skulled individuals of Malta. The craniums of the Amarnian dynasty statues and the Malta craniums result as being practically identical, a not so fortuitous fact, also proved by the X-rays of Tuthankamon's skull, Akhenaton's son, which showed a dolichocephalous cranium. Substantially, the Maltese craniums are the relics, archeologically still not understood; of a sacerdotal race that, in Egypt and Malta, from archaic ages, survived till 2500 BC. It's the group that created the religious and Spiritual sub-strata that characterized the greatest civilizations of the Old World, from long ago (600 BC or even earlier). This group continued in the Middle East and somehow returned in Egypt around 1351 BC giving birth, through the heretic pharaoh Akhenaton, to a religious reform that aimed to restore the ancient order. And if the hypothesis that this pharaoh was linked someway to the figure of Moses is accepted, then the rest is history.

ATLANTIS IN MALTA

Malta is a platform, an elevation of the sea floor that demonstrates it has immersed itself into the sea more than once. Thirty-five pre-historic temples distributed on the two major islands, Malta and Gozo, and many others actually submerged by the sea, make one think of a catastrophe that must have happened here around 3000–2500 BC, something that left its sign. Steep reefs falling vertically to the sea, contrarily to the more sloping northern shore, form the southern coast of Malta, the Dingli Cliffs. It's as if the island's major axis rotated around itself, submerging most of the coast that faces Sicily. Some local archeologists, including the already mentioned Dr. Anton Mifsud and Dr. Charles Savona Ventura, consider this cataclysm to be the real cause of the Atlantis legend's birth, the history of which would re-emerge from a number of relics of the island's mysterious megalithic past. The population that created extraordinary structures of giant stones, at a certain point of the island's history, just disappeared.

Two hundred and fifty years of darkness actually characterize the story of these people until the arrival of the new populations that successively occupied Malta. What had determined such an immense catastrophe? Perhaps an earthquake or the subsiding of the calcareous platform on which Malta stands. However, we know from the Leningrad Papyrus (a hieratic scroll dated 1115 BC, conserved at the Hermitage Museum), an Egyptian document composed around 2000 BC, dating back to the XII dynasty, that a serpent populace was destroyed by a 'star falling from the heavens'. Only one survived on an island 'destined to be completely submerged'. What is this strange fable? Was it the record of a catastrophe that destroyed a particular Mediterranean region? The myth also connected the serpents to the figures of Mother Goddesses such as Tanit, Innanna, Isis and Eve. They are feminine divinities that carry the baton of a culture to which the snake brings wisdom, medical, scientific and esoteric knowledge. But a doubt arises: couldn't these serpents rather be human beings of strange physical form, perhaps even a handicap? Mythology is full of weird beings that often seem more likely clinical cases than true divinities. For example, Cecrops, the mythical founder and first king of Athens, according to tradition, was born from the soil and his appearance was half human and half serpent. According to others, he came to Attica from Egypt and built the Acropolis, diffusing the cult of Zeus and Athena. Pythia (or Python) was a priestess of Delphi, taken by Apollo, who pronounced oracles. She took her name from Python the snake, killed by Apollo and believed to be buried under her temple. The woman enunciated the verdicts sitting on a sacred tripod set on the mouth of a natural gorge, from which vapours exhaled and communicated them to an assistant priest (said prophet), whom in turn transmitted them to the postulant (*HERA*, 17).

But let's go back to Malta. Even Saint Paul shipwrecked in the Maltese bay that still bears his name, dealing with a snake that bit his foot. In reality, in the days of Saint Paul, the first century AD, these animals didn't exist in Malta. So it's strange that such a reptile bit indeed this Holy man. This legend may well be interpreted in a different, simpler manner. The serpent was the last priest of the Great Goddess left on the island, whose thaumaturgic power was threatened by that of Paul, obliged to dismantle what was left of the last pagan bastion of the great Healing Goddess.

End of HERA article.

There were giants in the earth in those days; and also after that, when the sons of God came in unto the daughters of men, and they bare children to them, the same became mighty men which were of old, men of renown.

GENESIS 6:4, NEW KING JAMES VERSION

Now it came to pass, when men began to multiply on the face of the earth, and daughters were born to them, that the sons of God saw the daughters of men, that they were beautiful; and they took wives for themselves of all whom they chose... There were giants on the earth in those days and also afterward, when the sons of God came in to the daughters of men and they bore children to them. Those were the mighty men who were of old, men of renown.

GENESIS 6:1–4, NEW INTERNATIONAL VERSION

When men began to increase in numbers on the earth and daughters were born to them, the sons of God saw that the daughters of men were beautiful, and they married any of them they chose... The Nephilim were on the earth in those days — and also afterwards — when the sons of God went to the daughters of men and had childred by them. They were the heroes of old, men of renown.

GENESIS 6:1–4, HOLMAN CHRISTIAN STANARD BIBLE

MUNDUS SUBTERRANEUS

Serious and reliable persons have told me that, on numerous occasions, many visitors to the Hypogeum, including German and British tourists, have fled the chambers screaming in terror. Now, these were not impressionable, uneducated people, but qualified professionals. Highly educated, sensitive persons, who became aware and attuned to a force, evil or otherwise, emanating from within the bowels of the Hypogeum.

The Phoenician gods Baal and Moloch were not Sun gods, but related to the Lunar side — the Dark side: Middle-Eastern origin. Phoenicians were probably a people originally of Greek origin who created our modern alphabet. Through their genius for seafaring trade, they established themselves as a powerful Thalassocracy in the Mediterranean. The Phoenicians founded the city of Carthage, present day Tunis, just opposite the bottom of the Italian peninsula. Carthage was to become one of the Roman Empire's greatest foes until it was finally crushed during the Punic Wars.

Since the time of the Carthagians, Malta has had many rulers: Romans, Arabs, Normans, Argonese, Castillians, the Hospitalers or the Order of St. John of Jerusalem, later known as the Knights of Rhodes, and still later as the Knights of Malta, who remain there to this day, having dual headquarters in Rome. A few miles south of the town of Valletta, Malta, is the small village of Casal Paula. In the year 1902, workmen who were digging a well literally fell into the earth. What they discovered (or rather re-discovered) was a series of ancient caves, mostly excavated out of solid rock, which descended into the earth and into three lower levels below. These multi-level catacombs became known as the 'Hypogeum of Hal Saflieni', named after the street beneath which they were discovered. A *hypogeum* is the Latin name for an underground structure.

Near the floor of the last chamber, within the 3rd and last (officially recognised) sub-level of these ancient catacombs, there are a few so-called 'burial chambers'. These are only a few feet square and situated right next to the floor, and one must get on his knees just to look into them. These 'burial chambers' are just large enough for one to crawl through.

There have for years been rumours that one of these 'burial chambers' does not end, but continues into deeper and unexplored caverns beyond.

This, according to certain sources, was the subterranean passage and chamber which was referred to years ago in an article which appeared in the August, 1940 issue of the *National Geographic Magazine*. The article stated the following concerning several people who disappeared in these catacombs without a trace. Many subterranean passageways, including ancient catacombs, now are a part of the island's fortifications and defense system. Supplies are kept in many tunnels; others are bomb shelters. Beneath Valletta some of the underground areas served as homes for the poor. Prehistoric men built temples and chambers in these vaults. In a pit beside one sacrificial altar lie thousands of human skeletons. Years ago one could walk underground from one end of Malta to the other. The Government closed the entrances to these tunnels after school children and their teachers became lost in the labyrinth while on a study tour and never returned.

According to researcher Riley Crabb, Director of Borderland Sciences Research Associates, and as detailed in his printed 1960s lecture 'The Reality of the Underground', the remains of the builders were of normal human type and stature. This did not explain the many tiny tunnels, carved from solid rock, which led away from the main, 'upper' yet still subterranean chambers, and down and away into darkness. These tunnels are only a few feet in height, and would have been utilised by beings of extremely small stature. Yet there are rumours of and evidence for other types of beings lurking beneath Hal Salfini, and perhaps the entire island of Malta. In addition to the small tunnels, others of larger size, long-since covered or blocked off, once led away into subterranean catacombs and caverns.

TROGLODYTES

During the Knights of St John rule of Malta, there lived a troglodyte community at a large cave near Dingli. Nearby are the so called 'Clapham Junction' cart ruts. This community predates the Order by hundreds, possibly thousands of years.

Jesuit Athanasius Kircher (1601–1680) was a universal authority, a man of encyclopaedic knowledge and founder of the Musea Kirceriano in Rome. He stayed in Malta for seven months (June 1637 – February 1638) accompanying the Landgrave of Hesse and as a mathematics teacher for the novices of the Order at the Jesuit College.

Kircher was a guest of the Grand Master Lascaris at Verdala Palace, close by to the cave. He visited the troglodyte community and published his findings in his Mundus Subterraneus in two volumes in 1664 and 1885.

He describes the cave-dwellers as living in an orderly, organised way with a great attachment to their way of life. After a rare errand to the capital city Mdina, not far away, they would hurry back to the cave 'lest they spend even one night away'.

The troglodytes were strict vegeterians by choice since they sold their cows, sheep and chickens, never eating any. The grand master himself once tested them by inviting the community to lunch. He laid out two tables, one with sumptuous food, meat and delicacies, the other with cheese, onions, garlic, cauliflower and macaroni. To a man the troglodytes all went to the second.

The troglodyte community was dispersed by the British in the 19th century for health reasons. However, the troglodytes kept coming back to their cave and so it was finally broken up to discourage their return.

MALTA — SOLAR

It is becoming increasingly evident that in Malta there was also a Solar veneration. Recent important discoveries by Prof. Michael Vella at Xemxija ('*Shem-shi*' — sunny) clearly reveal this. This archaeological find is of the utmost importance as it places Malta within the fold of the Solar veneration, higher type of Nordic, Hyperborean, genealogy of Spirituality.

Prof. Walter Rodel of Mainz University observed the rising sun penetrating the eastern or lesser temple at the Ggantija (Giant) temple at the Malta sister island of Gozo, at the summer solstice.

A similar occurrence was observed at the western temple in Malta at both the winter and summer solstices and at the March and September equinoxes at Mnajdra.

In 2000 at Xemxija Prof. Vella also discovered, hewn into the smooth hard rock, a huge gigantic snake-like creature with webbed feet. To me it looks quite similar to the flying bird at the Siberian, Malta Settlement. As an artist, I can discern the gradual metamorphosis of a stylised, slim, bird into a snake (actually, the same happened in reverse during natural evolution!) — a gradual change spanning the years 21,000 BC–10,000/6,000 BC. The same Aryan people, originally Hyperborean — a Solar veneration degenerating into a Lunar one.

Similarly, petroglyphs discovered at the Xemxija site show a bird with outstretched wings, possibly a vulture. It parallels the Egyptian goddess Nikhbet, the Lunar Aegyptian goddess of death and funerary cults.

Other links between the Maltese islands and ancient Egypt abound. For example, the world-famous Maltese Hound *tal fenek* was considered a Maltese dog by the Aegyptians themselves. It probably inspired the birth of the god Anubis. Even the very word Malta, in ancient Aegyptian Mlita, has the pre-Phoenician meaning 'Place of Large Stones'.

The Aegyptian concept of heaven, their Elysian Fields or Abydos are described in the very oldest of Aegyptian texts as an abode of 'that group of islands, situated below the western horizon, enjoying a perpetual spring and many Temples of the Gods'.

Thus, Malta as a Spiritual focal point, similar to the Easter Islands for the pre-Columbians, predated and later coincided and overlapped briefly with the flowering of the Ancient Aegyptian civilisation. Even the Osiris myth speaks of the 'Lord of the Afterlife abiding in a group of islands to the west of Egypt'.

At the National Museum in Valletta, there are numerous amulets of the gods Horus and Anubis, that were found in various localities in Malta. This proves a much earlier Aegyptian connection, predating the Lunar influence of the Phoenicians.

Malta was indeed a Sacred Island. Spirituality enshrouded it. Religion permeated every facet of life. Indeed, it can be said that Malta, inhabited by the surviving Aryan-Atlanteans, gave Ancient Egypt the creative impulse to build their pharaonic civilisation. All this circa 10,000 BC, after the glacial era, culminating into the Solar veneration of Akhenaton — and then degenerating into Phoenician Lunar cults.

The demise of the 'Island of the Gods' was sudden and mysterious. It was probably due to Thassalocratic pressure by the Phoenicians. The Egyptians, clearly Tellurocratic, could not effectively oppose such a penetration so far away from their shores. — The islands were reluctantly abandoned.

This then is Malta: the Sacred Island of Melita. This magnificent, mysterious, mystical stone in the midst of the blue Mediterranean. The Apex: the Pyramidical Peak: the missing last stone of the Pyramid!

Malta's temples remain the earliest free-standing monuments of stone in the world. They probably date around 12,000–10,000 BC, possibly much earlier, as with the Siberian Malta Settlement. At around 3500–2500 BC their Solar orientation was gradually replaced by a Lunar concept of Life. With this change came burial, instead of cremation.

These super-monuments must have taken years to build. Their corbelling walls technique was to be copied a thousand years later in the tholoi in Mycenae. They were added on and improved, becoming more elaborate, over thousands of years. Most are within visual range of each other, always on a slope facing South East. A structural architectural achievement unrivalled anywhere in the world at the time (10,000 BC).

A gradual transformation, degeneration from Solar to Lunar. From the Aryan simplicity of a shining disc, denoting Oneness, completeness — to more complicated and degenerate Phoenician Mother Goddess cults.

Facing South East on a slope, never a hilltop but always in the vicinity of a spring and caves, where these unusually healthy Aryan people presumably lived. These were the Cantabrian Cro-Magnon, Battle-Axe warriors occupying Greece, Italy and Sicily. These Traditional-Spiritual people gave more importance to their temples than to their own dwellings.

All these treasures: remains, caves, temples, stelae, amulets and especially pottery, whose perfection is comparable to that of Classical Greece — buried quite recently under the frenzied impetus of a materialistic 'rich North' — will again be excavated in our coming IMPERIUM EUROPA.

Yes! We will find all our lost temples and bring them back to light! We will let the Mediterranean sun caress them again! We will relentlessly raze all buildings postdating 1800 to the ground. We will revert modern Malta, this rubbish-dump in the Mediterranean, back to its former, glorious Spiritual self — The Sacred Island of Melita.

THE MEDITERRANEAN

With the total disappearance of the Ice Age, certain biological changes did start to creep into the proto-Nordic race. In Southern and Central Europe, a process of an increasing head breadth began to develop, which eventually resulted in the Alpine race (Maltese).

The Mediterranean race also appeared at about this time — also originally of Nordic extraction. It appears as if Mediterraneanids developed their own physical characteristics due to long periods of isolation around the Mediterranean basin.

The 'Mediterraneans' of today are in fact different to the original, Nordic Mediterraneans. They are somewhat darker to various degrees than the original Mediterraneans.

The most well-preserved example of this Mediterranean age comes from caves in Southern France, called the Azilian culture, after the caves at Mes d'Azil. Here stones were found with what appears to be writing on them dating from this period — but they have never been deciphered, and what they exactly mean remains speculation.

The people who lived in the Middle East at the time we are talking about were a mixture of proto-Nordics, Alpines and Mediterraneans, with the latter being in the majority. Although they do not predate the Upper Palaeolithic settlements in Europe, they can most certainly be said to have provided much of the impetus for early White civilisation.

The Neolithic (farming) revolution slowly spread through Europe, first along the Grecian peninsula, Italy, up the Danube River and reaching Northern Europe about 7000 years ago. These civilisations are what is known as the 'Old European Civilisation'. They included such places as Crete. The palace at that island's capital city, Knossos, had the first running water toilets — this about 4,500 years ago!

THE SWASTIKA

The most powerful sign in the universe is the Swastika. It has been with us since Palaeolithic times, evolving from spiral geometrical figures into the symbol we know, and instantly recognise, today. It is found wherever the Aryans travelled, from Greece to Tibet, except for Australia.

The Swastika is a Fundamental Symbol — The Universal Language of Sacred Science — The Science of the Spirit.

From time immemorial it has been recognised as a cosmic emblem, an etiological sign. The word Swastika derives from the Aryans of ancient India. In their Sanskrit language *su* meant 'well' and *asti* 'being' — to which the substantive suffix *-ka* was added. It is thus a sign of well-being and prosperity, of integrity and fertility. Its four arms, the four Ls, represent Light, Life, Love and Luck.

In the natural world the Swastika appears both in the micro: DNA molecule, crystals, fractals — and in the macro: hurricanes, spiral galaxies.

With its singular, symmetric configuration, the Swastika also connotes perfect order and balance, as well as eternal dynamism. It can take two forms: destroverse and sinistroverse. Many confound the issue here. It is the revolving action that determines the form. The Hero specifically chose the one with arms pointing towards the left, because the revolving movement is destroverse.

The Swastika is the primordial emblem of a Higher Power. A Sacred Symbol of that ultimate Cosmic Force behind all Creation. The Will of the Universe — a Divine Conciousness — the Divine Essence!

It is a good sign.

It is the sign of Godhood.

It is the sign of Aryan destiny: Cosmotheism — Our Divinity!

IN HOC SIGNO VINCES!

It is to be noted that the eight-pointed Maltese Cross is actually formed by two, touching Swastikas: one destroverse and one sinistroverse. The Hero was fascinated by the Maltese Cross.

See illustration 10 http://www.imperium-europa.org/thebook
Hypogeum
The Sacred Island of Melita

See illustration 11 http://www.imperium-europa.org/thebook
MOTHER GODDESS
Ħaġar Qim — Malta 3000 BC

See illustration 12 http://www.imperium-europa.org/thebook
VENUS OF MALTA
Ħaġar Qim — Malta 3000 BC

See illustration 13 http://www.imperium-europa.org/thebook
SIBERIA PALEOLOGICAL STONE
Siberian Malta Settlement
Spiral theme — Swastika Concept
Circa 21,000 BC

See illustration 14 http://www.imperium-europa.org/thebook
MALTA NEOLITHIC STONE
Four symmetrical spirals — proto Swastika
Circa 10,000-5000 BC

See illustration 15 http://www.imperium-europa.org/thebook
BOWL WITH SWASTIKA - ATHENS
Swastika adorned bowl — Athens
Circa 800 BC (destrous Swastika)

See illustration 16 http://www.imperium-europa.org/thebook
ROMAN SWASTIKA - MALTA
Mosaic floors — Roman Baths 1st century BC

See illustration 17 http://www.imperium-europa.org/thebook
ROMAN VILLA — MALTA
Swastika Mosaic floor with optical illusion 1st century BC

See illustration 18 http://www.imperium-europa.org/thebook

THE MALTESE CROSS
(Composed of two Swastikas)

See illustration 18 http://www.imperium-europa.org/thebook

SWASTIKA

(sinistroverse) & (destroverse)

DELTA 32

Thanks to the bubonic plague, Europeans have developed a gene-mutation called Delta 32. This renders them fairly immune to such diseases as AIDs and other infections. This gene is fairly well distributed throughout the European peoples. Practically every European inherits it from either of the parents.

Here in Malta, due to the limited space of the island and the inter-breeding of the relatively small population, the plague lasted a long time. Notwithstanding rigid measures of quarantine, it returned several times mainly through contagious ships visiting our harbours.

For exactly the same reasons — small population in a small island — the Maltese inherit this Delta 32 gene-mutation from both parents, something quite rare in Europe. This renders the Maltese the hardiest race in the world as regards immunity to infectious diseases. We are fairly immune to practically everything, so much so that AIDs in Malta is quasi -inexistent, notwithstanding the over one million tourists visiting the island every year — some of them intentionally making it a sex holiday!

We Maltese, custodians of the Sacred Island of Melita — Tenants on this very special Spiritual Sacred Spot — must rediscover our Spiritual Delta 32. We have to become immune, hardened to the 'rich North'. Those influences that have infected the rest of Europe, contaminating all Western Europeans except, for the time being: the Slavs.

MELITA — HYPERBOREAN CENTRE

As we have discussed earlier on, the Northern Hyperborean Spiritual Tradition has transformed itself into the 'rich North', or more accurately, the 'wealthy North'. The Atlantic Northerners (UK/USA) have lost their Spiritual bearings and have become wealthy, solely in the vulgar, mercantile, industrial sense of the word, especially so since the Industrial Revolution and the two World Wars.

Today, the Spiritual richness of the North is preserved solely amongst the Slavs, particularly the Russians. That is why the Atlantians, the Thalassocratic forces, are launching a massive, destructive attack on the Slavs in order to corrupt, defile them with their mercantile view of the world. This is the most crucial battle going on in the world today: the battle between the wealthy North (Atlanteans) and the Rich North (Slavs).

And this is where the unique, Spiritual significance of The Sacred Island of Melita comes to the fore. For Malta stands symbolically at the very centre of the planet — between the wealthy West and 'Poor' East — and also between the wealthy North and 'Rich North'.

Malta, the Sacred Island of Melita, geographically but more importantly, metaphysically, will soon become the Polar Centre, the Unmovable Centre, the Point of Eternity, in this final struggle for the soul of the Europid. Malta: that tiny Island in the Mediterranean. Malta: that land of honey. Melita: the Sacred Island.

We Maltese must become hardened, inured to the Judaic influence of profit, pleasures and perdition. This is the only way of return to the primordial perfection that was lost by the Aryan in his Garden of Eden, when allured by that serpent-race. Yes, hardened to the materialistic frenzy of feminine fads, fetishes and fashions intoxicating the White Man.

Malta's very duality, spanning thousands of years, the duality of Solar and Lunar veneration, the duality of North and South, could make of Melita the meeting point — not that absurd meeting point pontificated by our pompous politicians, parroting platitudes, painting Malta as a bridge between Africa and Europe! — But a *Pontifex Maximus*, a converging focal point of both the 'rich North' and the 'poor North' — both of the same Europid race. In other words: the Thallasocracies and the Tellurocracies.

Melita will be the new Hyperborean, Nordic, Polar, Immovable Centre around which the whole Imperium would revolve. The Spiritual North, The Centre, The Immobile Pole, The Point of Eternity, The Apex, The Pyramidical Peak around and to which everything revolves and relates. The point where contrasts converge and parallels point, drawn by a powerful, Cosmic Magnetic Force. That Sacred Spot beyond cosmic entropy. The immovable centre of the Swastika our Maltese Cross, with its spinning arms creating universal order out of chaos.

Malta: The Sacred Island of Melita: The Spiritual Centre of the coming, inevitable IMPERIUM EUROPA!

KALIYUGA — KRITAYUGA

Why is the Imperium inevitable? Why are we, of the Radical-Racialist-Right-Revolutionary-Reactionaries, so convinced that we are winning — that we will win?

Our origins are in the ancient antiquity, our primordial past, our Hindu past. For when the Aryan first appeared, Hindu was already there! It had, and Hinduism still does have, a directness that results from its having been revealed to man in a remote age. A pure age when there was not yet a need to make a distinction between esoterism and exoterism. When the truth did not have to be veiled. A Golden Age.

An age where the Swastika was omnipresent, testifying to the good fortune prevailing on the Aryan Race. In Hindu, it is a symbol associated with Ganesa, the pathfinder — Prometheus!

All the trees bearing the fruits of knowledge in the Garden of Eden where there, free for the Aryan! — free for the Aryan to pick and choose, inquire and learn, instaure and improve, build and belong, behold and BE himself! — All the trees of knowledge except for that one, single root of poisonous fruit, offered by that serpent race!

The Mayas had the best, most accurate calendar on the planet. It stops at the year 2012. They called it 'the end of the universe'.

In Hindu there is also a calendar, or more accurately, cycles of time — cycles within cycles, circles within circles — eternal recurrence.

The four major Hindu cycles (*Yugas*) are:

The Age of *Kritayuga* — the Golden Age

An age of justice and duty, where men are contented, healthy and virtuous and where their God is WHITE. An age lasting 1,728,000 years.

The Age of *Tretayuga* — the Silver Age

Where virtue falls short by a quarter. Where men act not out of pure goodness, but for ulterior motives. Where men become quarrelsome.

An age lasting 1,296,000 years.

The Age of *Dwaparayuga* — the Copper Age

Lying abounds. An age lasting 864,000 years.

The Age of *Kaliyuga* — the Lead Age.

Our age. The age of quantity not quality. Where the majority are Sudras, or slaves. They are wicked, quarrelsome, beggar-like. They value the degraded and live in cities full of thieves. The men are dominated by their womanfolk who are shallow, garrulous and lascivious, bearing too many inferior children. There are famines, numerous wars.

This last age, our age, can only end with the coming of Kalki, the destroyer!

To the Hindus the end of the last age, the age of *Kaliyuga* will also end in 2012.

To the Aryan, unlike that for the Maya, the year 2012 will not be the end of the universe: as it will certainly be for the Maya descendants, the Mexicans and the rest. For the Hindu, the Aryan WHITE MAN, it will be but the beginning of a New Dawn: a new Golden Age — a new Golden Dawn — a new cycle: the Age of *Kritayuga!*

The Kalki is coming! He is already here! Perceive Him!

He will bring to an end the present, pervading rot. The decadence of kings and politicians who, in their short term of office, think only of their own gain. All their wealth will be of no avail to them when the hour of reckoning comes.

He will destroy the decadent, false priests who only go through the motions of their rites: mere washing rather than purification.

He will expunge those sitting in office not through merit, but through their outward robes. He will confer the right to govern to real leaders.

Kalki, riding a White horse, galloping through the world like a comet, his arm aloft bearing a drawn sword. The destroyer will purify the world of its wickedness and usher the Golden Dawn for the Aryan Race!

IMPERIUM
WRITTEN THIS YEAR: 2012: ANNO ZERO!

XXXVIII

THE

IDEA!

THE *IDEA* OF IMPERIUM UNITING the Whole Wide, White World, nurtured slowly within me since my travels to Southern Africa.

This *IDEA* explained in my book *CREDO: A Book for the Very Few* — published in January 2000.

I became convinced that Malta would be the spark to set Europe ablaze and instil, install the Imperium *IDEA*.

On Saturday, the 15th June 2002 at 4.15pm, I had a transcendental experience.

I was in Siggiew, a small village, at a hamlet in a farmhouse with adjoining fields, guest of friends.

After lunch, I strode alone, away from the group and laid on the dry moss, under a plum tree, taking shade from the blistering sun.

I was struck by a sudden force, an energy that gave me immense serenity, happiness and an unshakeablecertainty that I am untouchable.

That I am destined to launch this *IDEA* of Imperium.

That I would be instrumental in uniting all Europids under one coming, inevitable, unstoppable Imperium.

From that day, I never hesitated or looked back.

I dedicated my life, my whole being to this *IDEA* that will take shape in 2012.

An *IDEA* that will change the world.

Imperium

0707

XXXIX

VERSI PERVERSI!

GAZE!
He gazes at her. Long, penetrating gazes.
She mesmerises him.
Her femininity overwhelms him.
She gives him sidelong glances full of desire.
Gaze!

DOPPELGANGER!
Frenetic, frantic, fantastic!
Hours of love, passion, tender feelings.
He is everywhere!
She responds, attuned to his masculinity.
Doppelganger!

WHALE OF LOVE!
Bludgeon in hand.
He carries her to his den.
She cowers, afraid yet ambivalent.
She succumbs to his coarseness, crudeness, cunnillingus.
A whale of love!

PEARLS!
So pure, pendulous, perfect.
Enticing: a perfect avenue.
She flaunts them, moves them, alluringly.
His gaze plunges in-between.
Those pearls!

LIVING!
We the living!
Us as against them!
We, the majestic Free Spirited.
We: alive, beautiful, creative.
Living!

ANGELIC DIVE!
Cooing, cuddles, caresses.
Breathing, sighing, groaning.
Quivering, clasping, adhering.
She spreads herself to him.
Angelic dive!

RIPPLES!
Nipples floating on the calm, blue Mediterranean.
Ripples gently surrounding.
Pickles, peccadilles, *pensieri perversi.*
Swimming alongside her.
Ripples!

BREAST-STROKE!
Swimming alongside her.
His massive manhood: a periscope!
She feigns indifference.
He lunges upwards: finds her.
Swimming together — breast-stroke!

STUCK!
Soft, sweet kiss: tantalising lips:
Pecking, nibbling, teasing.
Never loosing contact, ever, whatever.
Up and down, an unending rhythm.
Suck, fuck, stuck!

TWO TO ONE
Not One to Two: But Two to One.
Permutations, never ending: *mènage à trois.*
A delicate balance: a triangular bond.
Trust, friendship, eternal memories.
'So nice!' — Two to One!

SPAWN!
The next generation.
We must ensure ourselves.
We must live again.
Eternity must be ours!
Spawn!

SURFING!
Wind, waves, waving!
Surging sea, balance, dexterity.
Muscles taut, tendons aching.
She admires from the safety of the golden sand.
He waves back — surfing!

BOUDOIR!
Thick carpets, curtains, candles.
Crimson everywhere; negligée, lips, wine.
Celtic music, sensuous, inviting.
Intimacy, attunement, atonement: *tradimento!*
She understands and forgives — Boudoir!

COUPLE!
Lotus position, eyes meeting.
Interminable moments, space of time, eternity.
Minds open, cosmic consciousness.
Ever slight movements, feelings, ecstasy.
Caring, courting, copulating: Couple!

MADAME!
Analytical: a budding flower.
So tight, so exquisitely clasping.
That extra, special gift to her worthy lover!
Never allowed to the husband.
Sex Post Fuckto! Madame!

RAGING BULL!
Furious, full of foaming froth.
He charges blindly; clumsily, impatiently.
Her tantalising, twittering taunts, goads and guides his weapon.
He finally pierces — a piercing cry!
Raging Bull!

OVERFLOW!
West side of the island of Melita.
Glorious Glow, glowing, glorifying!
Surfeited, full, she cannot take more!
She waddles home: contented.
Overflow!

MODEL!
Elongated, elegant, exquisite.
Minimalist body form: sculptured.
Rib cage perfectly exposed, enumerated.
Concerned, caged, she walks the catwalk — cocaine!
She yearns for her liberator — Model!

TANTRA!
Cosmic view of *Yin* and *Yang*.
Two couples copulating.
Slant eyes, almond eyes, long and longing eyes.
Mantric intonations; orange, red and black.
Mantra — Tantra!

AFFAIRS!
Obstructed love.
Compelling, constrained, complicated.
Love-making under the eyes of the *bourgeoisie*.
Breaking rules, regulations, restraints!
Ardour, autonomy, audacious Affairs!

CRUSTACEON!
Breaking the silence, the ice, her shell.
Tentatively at first: timorous, tenderly tip-toeing.
Growing confidence.
Locomotive train charging, thundering ahead!
That g-spot! — crumbling Crustacean!

AQUARIAN EYE!
Aquarius.
Atlas, Atlantis, Atlas Mountains.
Atlantians: our beautiful forefathers.
Pre-diluvium, pre-vulgarity: blue and gold.
Aquarian Eye!

CLONING!
Genetic patrimony.
Affinity, consciousness, race-mind.
Physique, intellect and culture-spirit.
Arrow shot through the architectural-arch.
Towards a distant future: Cloning!

SNAILS!
Hermaphrodites.
Getting the best of both worlds!
Oozing spermatozoa.
Till the last dreg, dropping egg!
Snails!

TOFFEE!
Elastic, mucous, viscous, sticky.
Wild dreams, berserkers!
We want to get off the train! Away from modernity.
Masticating-mass, majority-mediocrity, moroseness, morbidity.
We want our Toffee!

GOURMET!
Candlelight dinner: *tête-à-tête.*
He speaks eloquently, forcefully, convincingly.
She responds: placing her exquisite pearls on the soft table-fabric.
The compensating factor!
Gourmet!

MELODY!
Melody of feelings.
Melody of words.
Melody of emotions.
Melody of love.
Melody of time, of secret, sensuous spaces: Melody!

NEPTUNE!
Awakening — Stirring — Emerging.
Male, manipulator, masculine.
Embracing, expanding, extending, penetrating!
Dominating: The Magnificent Dark Lord of the Ocean.
Neptune!

MAGIC FINGERS!
Playing the violin, the violincello and the cello.
Piano pianissimo, adagio ma non troppo.
Andante, Allegro con garbo.
Vivace, Allegro con brio! Fortissimo!
Virtuoso! Bravo! Bravissimo! — Magic Fingers!

CELTIC QUEEN!
Brave, bold and belligerent.
Bared, beautiful breasts — behold!
Shakti: Smiles, sex, scythes.
Dominatrix: whiplash in hand, blowing a soft kiss.
Boadicea — Celtic Queen!

NEFERTITI!
Petite, platinum blond — Perfect figure and face.
Articulate, clever and creative.
A Queen, tied up in knots, kneels and kisses.
Submissively she performs: everything!
That her King and master commands — Nefertiti!

AVE EVA!
Mother of the living!
Eva: bewitched by the male serpent.
Eva: fornication, fecundity, felicity.
Eva: Unlike Adam; unrepentant!

APPENDIX

Since the first edition of this book, there have been numerous developments in Europe and the world, which have likewise influenced the evolution of the Imperium Europa *IDEA*. The reader is invited to visit the following links for further information:

www.imperium-europa.org
www.vivamalta.net
www.imperat.org

OTHER BOOKS PUBLISHED BY ARKTOS

SRI DHARMA PRAVARTAKA ACHARYA	*The Dharma Manifesto*
JOAKIM ANDERSEN	*Rising from the Ruins*
WINSTON C. BANKS	*Excessive Immigration*
MATT BATTAGLIOLI	*The Consequences of Equality*
ALAIN DE BENOIST	*Beyond Human Rights*
	Carl Schmitt Today
	The Indo-Europeans
	Manifesto for a European Renaissance
	On the Brink of the Abyss
	The Problem of Democracy
	Runes and the Origins of Writing
	View from the Right (vol. 1–3)
ARTHUR MOELLER VAN DEN BRUCK	*Germany's Third Empire*
KERRY BOLTON	*Revolution from Above*
	Yockey: A Fascist Odyssey
ISAC BOMAN	*Money Power*
RICARDO DUCHESNE	*Faustian Man in a Multicultural Age*
ALEXANDER DUGIN	*Ethnos and Society*
	Eurasian Mission
	The Fourth Political Theory
	Last War of the World-Island
	Putin vs Putin
	The Rise of the Fourth Political Theory
MARK DYAL	*Hated and Proud*
KOENRAAD ELST	*Return of the Swastika*
JULIUS EVOLA	*The Bow and the Club*
	Fascism Viewed from the Right
	A Handbook for Right-Wing Youth
	The Mask and Face of Contemporary Spiritualism
	Metaphysics of War
	The Myth of the Blood
	Notes on the Third Reich
	The Path of Cinnabar
	Recognitions
	A Traditionalist Confronts Fascism

OTHER BOOKS PUBLISHED BY ARKTOS

GUILLAUME FAYE
Archeofuturism
Archeofuturism 2.0
The Colonisation of Europe
Convergence of Catastrophes
A Global Coup
Sex and Deviance
Understanding Islam
Why We Fight

DANIEL S. FORREST
Suprahumanism

ANDREW FRASER
Dissident Dispatches
The WASP Question

GÉNÉRATION IDENTITAIRE
We are Generation Identity

A. J. ILLINGWORTH
Political Justice

PAUL GOTTFRIED
War and Democracy

PORUS HOMI HAVEWALA
The Saga of the Aryan Race

LARS HOLGER HOLM
Hiding in Broad Daylight
Homo Maximus
Incidents of Travel in Latin America
The Owls of Afrasiab

ALEXANDER JACOB
De Naturae Natura

JASON REZA JORJANI
Prometheus and Atlas
World State of Emergency

RODERICK KAINE
Smart and SeXy

PETER KING
Here and Now
Keeping Things Close

LUDWIG KLAGES
The Biocentric Worldview
Cosmogonic Reflections

PIERRE KREBS
Fighting for the Essence

STEPHEN PAX LEONARD
The Ideology of Failure

PENTTI LINKOLA
Can Life Prevail?

H. P. LOVECRAFT
The Conservative

OTHER BOOKS PUBLISHED BY ARKTOS

OTHER BOOKS PUBLISHED BY ARKTOS

Printed in Great Britain
by Amazon